D E A T H
BY
INSTALLMENTS

The Ordeal of Willie Francis

Arthur S. Miller
and
Jeffrey H. Bowman

Contributions in Legal Studies, Number 44

GREENWOOD PRESS

New York · Westport, Connecticut · London

Library of Congress Cataloging-in-Publication Data

Miller, Arthur Selwyn, 1917-1988
  Death by installments : the ordeal of Willie Francis / Arthur S.
Miller and Jeffrey H. Bowman.
     p.   cm. — (Contributions in legal studies, ISSN 0147-1074 ;
no. 44)
  Bibliography: p.
  Includes index.
  ISBN 0-313-26009-5 (lib. bdg. : alk. paper)
  1. Francis, Willie—Trials, litigation, etc.   2. Trials (Murder)—
Louisiana—Saint Martinville.   3. Capital punishment—United
States.   4. Judicial review—United States.   5. United States.
Supreme Court.   I. Bowman, Jeffrey H.   II. Title.   III. Series.
KF224.F69M55 1988
345.73′0773—dc 19
[347.305773]   88-3124

British Library Cataloguing in Publication Data is available.

Library of Congress Catalog Card Number: 88-3124
ISBN: 0-313-26009-5
ISSN: 0147-1074

First published in 1988

Greenwood Press, Inc.
88 Post Road West, Westport, Connecticut 06881

Printed in the United States of America

∞™

The paper used in this book complies with the
Permanent Paper Standard issued by the National
Information Standards Organization (Z39.48-1984).

10 9 8 7 6 5 4 3 2 1

DEATH
BY
INSTALLMENTS

Recent Titles in
Contributions in Legal Studies
Series Editor: Paul L. Murphy

This book is dedicated to the
memory of Arthur Selwyn Miller

Contents

Preface

This book is a case study of one of the more celebrated Supreme Court decisions of this century: *Louisiana ex rel. Francis* v. *Resweber*. It concentrates on two themes. First, there is the question as to what happened to a young black teenager who was convicted of murdering a white man in southern Louisiana. The state bungled his scheduled execution; he did not die. Eventually, the question of whether Louisiana would have a second chance reached the Supreme Court of the United States where the Justices divided 4–1–4 in answering the question. The volume adds to the growing literature on capital punishment and poses this fundamental issue: Do the methods of execution present a constitutional question, one as yet unanswered by the Supreme Court? Second, the book covers what occurred within the Supreme Court when the *Francis* case reached it. The discussion here is a detached study of decisionmaking within the High Bench. By concentrating on one case, the volume shows the often highly subjective manner in which some justices make decisions. The necessary inference here is that, in such decisions as *Francis* and doubtless elsewhere, law as a set of interdictory, external rules has little to do with the results reached. The details of the internal dynamics of the Court as the *Francis* case was decided present a rare inside look at the Court.

The authors gratefully acknowledge the immensely helpful research assistance of Bonnie J. Brownell in the preparation of the manuscript, and also the generous aid of Professor Ronald Labbé of the University of Southwestern Louisiana. We owe a large debt to Professor and Mrs. Paul Nolan for their assistance and hospitality during our research trips in Louisiana. We are also grateful to Scott E. Thomas and Charles N. Steele for their patience and encouragement during this project.

Finally, we wish to thank the men and women who consented to be interviewed concerning Willie Francis. Thanks are also due to the literary executors of Justices Black and Jackson for permission to quote from some of their unpublished papers. We also wish to thank Professor Harry S. Martin III, and Professor Paul A. Freund for permission to quote from the Felix Frankfurter Papers at the Harvard Law School Library. Likewise, we thank the Michigan Historical Collections for permission to quote from the Frank Murphy Papers at the Bentley Historical Library, University of Michigan. We also wish to thank the DePaul Law Review, which published our earlier work on the *Francis* case.

DEATH
BY
INSTALLMENTS

I

The Botched Execution

The time was 1946. The place: a jail cell in rural Louisiana. A slim, black teenager named Willie Francis was nervous. Understandably so. The State of Louisiana was going to kill him in less than six hours.

It was dawn and Willie was alone. The day's first light began to filter into his jail cell window overlooking the town of New Iberia. For the last eight months he had met each morning with a growing fear that this day would come. Stretched out on his jail cell cot, Willie wondered where his body would lie and his soul would rest at day's end. For one thing was certain: no one cheated the electric man.

It had been a month since Willie had been told that he would die in the electric chair on the third of May. The time had passed quickly. He remembered seeing the signed death warrant from the governor of Louisiana. Willie smiled. He thought it was funny that the warrant was so carefully written in long, drawn-out lawyer's language. It seemed as if the State of Louisiana was afraid he might raise a fuss and say, "You can't kill me because you have a word wrong here."[1]

The smile disappeared as Willie's thoughts drifted to the previous day—his last full day of life. Early that morning, he had been frightened about what was going to happen. But an afternoon visit from Father Charles Hannegan of New Iberia helped to calm him. Father Hannegan had visited Willie often during the previous eight months.

On this last visit it was clear to the priest that Willie was afraid. The boy's fears exaggerated his already bad stutter. Father Hannegan tried to reassure the youth by telling him he was lucky—lucky that he knew when he was going to die. Using himself as an example, Father Hannegan explained that he might accidentally fall down the jailhouse steps

1

and break his neck. Or he could die in his rectory that night. Unlike most people, Willie had a chance to prepare himself for that moment.

This idea struck Willie as strange and difficult to grasp. His thoughts on death had been limited to the fact that he wouldn't be alive anymore. He was more concerned about the way he would die and about whether the chair would be painful. He couldn't figure out how or why he should want to prepare to die.

Father Hannegan continued. Willie had a new life to start when he got up from that electric chair. He should prepare to go bravely into that new world—not crying like a baby. Even though he was only sixteen, he had this one chance to prove he was able to die like a man. One of the hardest things in life, the Father continued, was to make yourself learn how to die. Besides, Willie had nothing to fear. The electric chair would not hurt him; it would only tickle at first and then it would all be over. Willie was fortunate, Father Hannegan assured him, that he was not being hanged. Now, that would be a terrible way to die.

Willie felt a sense of purpose after Father Hannegan's visit. If he had to die, he would be ready. Nobody wants to die if he can help it, he thought, but since he couldn't do anything to stop it, there was no point in crying or worrying.

Around suppertime Sheriff Gilbert Ozenne, the sheriff of New Iberia Parish, came by Willie's cell and said that Willie could have anything he wanted to eat for his last supper. Willie said he thought that he would like some ice cream. The sheriff chuckled and asked if that was all he wanted. Willie stammered that he would like something else if it was all right—a steak. Within an hour, the sheriff returned with a large steak, which he proclaimed the best in town, and more ice cream than Willie could eat.

Willie liked Sheriff Ozenne and got along well with both him and his deputies. Unlike other police officers, they had always been nice to him. They never talked roughly or cursed him. When they asked him to do something, he always did it. And when he asked for something, they usually gave it to him.

After supper, when it was dark and he was alone, Willie again began thinking of the next day. If Father Hannegan was right and the electric chair only tickled, Willie wondered, why was it called the "hot seat"? If it was hot, it must burn. And if it burned, how could it just tickle? Willie decided that it didn't make any difference, for he would try to behave like a man and not a child. He would not cry.

Willie's thoughts turned from the physical to the spiritual. He had been baptized a Roman Catholic and regularly attended church with his family, but he did not consider himself to be particularly religious. It was hot when he wore his Sunday best, and he would much rather have been outside church playing on the grassy banks of the bayou. The imposition of the death sentence, however, had forcefully concentrated his mind on religious matters. Soon after he was placed in a death cell, his father brought him a Bible from Willie's mother. This Bible became Willie's constant companion. Over the last eight months the Book had become well worn as a result of frequent consultation and slow, painstaking reading.

Willie got down on his knees and said his prayers for the last time. He prayed, "God, tonight is the last night I will sleep in a bed, because tomorrow I will have to sit in that chair and die. Please help me to die." It was very late before Willie finished his prayers for himself and his family. Finally, he fell into a fitful sleep.

The next morning the quiet of the cell block was interrupted by familiar footsteps and the rattling of keys in the iron lock of a nearby cell. A moment later, Sheriff Ozenne and a fellow black prisoner whom Willie recognized from across the corridor appeared at his cell door.

The prisoner stepped into the cell and apologetically told Willie that he would have to shave his head. Willie knew that that was where they were going to make the electricity pass through his body. The prisoner had a towel and shaving equipment in his hands and stood awkwardly as if he had to do something he didn't want do do. Still, preparations had to be made for the execution. It was true that in order to allow for the free flow of the electrical current, the crown of Willie's head and one thigh would have to be shaved. There was also an aesthetic concern. Any hair not shaved and touching the electrode would smolder from the twin jolts of 2,500 volts of electricity and leave a sickening odor in the execution room. A fellow prisoner had been chosen to perform this unpleasant task.

Slowly, the prisoner began his work of preparing Willie for the electric chair. Willie sat down, and the prisoner began clipping his hair with scissors. The hair had to be first cut down to a stubble before the head itself could be shaved with a razor. Both the prisoner and Willie felt ill at ease. The prisoner tried to make small talk while he went about his work, but Willie did not feel like answering back.

When he had finished, the prisoner took a step backward and paused briefly, almost as if to admire his handiwork. He smiled and said, "Well, Willie, I guess that's one haircut you won't have to pay for." Anybody else might have punched or cursed the prisoner for such a remark. Willie thought, however, that the prisoner was just trying to take his mind off the electric chair. Willie started to laugh, and so did Sheriff Ozenne and then a deputy waiting outside the cell. Soon, the foursome were trading jokes. Everybody was being so nice to him, Willie thought, that for a while dying didn't seem like such a bad thing.

About eleven o'clock, Sheriff Ozenne returned to Willie's cell and asked him if he was ready to make the ten-mile ride from New Iberia to

St. Martinville, Louisiana, and the electric chair. Willie had spent all of his sixteen years in St. Martinville, a small, quiet town where everyone knew or knew of everyone else. Like most southern towns and cities at that time, there were two sections—one for whites and one for blacks. Racial harmony existed as long as whites tended to their business and blacks to theirs.[2]

Willie told Ozenne that he was ready. The sheriff cuffed and shackled him and then stepped aside to allow him to walk out of the cell. Willie took several steps and paused in the doorway to take a final look around his home of the last eight months. As he looked, he got a funny feeling in his stomach.

Willie took a deep breath and walked out of his cell toward the elevator. The New Iberia jail was located on the third floor of the parish courthouse. The usually friendly sheriff and his deputy were now serious and unsmiling. After seeing their grave countenances and realizing that only ten miles and little over an hour separated him from the electric chair, Willie's heart began pounding hard. As he walked, Willie could see the other prisoners staring at him. Not a word was said, but there was a look of sympathy in their eyes. There was an especially sorrowful look in the face of the prisoner who had shaved Willie's head. As Willie waited outside the elevator, the prisoner stuck his arm through the cell bars and curiously waved his little finger at Willie in farewell.

Standing next to the deputy and the sheriff in the small elevator, Willie was thinking so hard about how scared he was that he wondered if the deputy and sheriff could hear him. By now, he felt dizzy and the motion of the elevator ride almost made him sick.

On the ground floor, a deputy opened the elevator door. With the sheriff and a deputy on either side, Willie was escorted through the courthouse lobby to the bright sunlight outside. The sun hurt Willie's eyes as he walked past the huge aluminum front doors onto the concrete veranda outside of the courthouse. Raising his handcuffed hands above his brow as a visor, he could see a black sedan waiting at the curb with its back right door swung open. Carefully negotiating the eleven courthouse steps with his shackled feet, Willie tried to walk bravely as Father Hannegan had encouraged him.

When they reached the curb, the deputy got into the back seat of the car first and slid over to the left door. Before he got in, Willie turned to look up at his cell window a final time and then followed the deputy into the car. After Willie, Sheriff Ozenne stepped into the back seat and sat next to the right rear door. In the interest of maximum security, it was normal procedure for a prisoner to sit between two police officers during a transfer. Sheriff Ozenne liked Willie and would have liked to have allowed him a clear window view on this last ride. But he didn't want to put any ideas of escape into Willie's head by even allowing him to sit next to a locked door.

Willie's mind was not on escape as the sedan pulled away from the New Iberia Parish Jail. Rather, it remained on the electric chair and on Father Hannegan's urgings to be brave. Willie, however, had no desire to mention these fears. Indeed, even if he had wanted to speak it would have been difficult, for his tongue was stuck to the roof of his mouth and his ears were now ringing from his nervousness. Similarly, the sheriff and his deputy were not speaking to Willie. Their outward friendliness was gone, and there was none of the joking that occurred in his cell earlier that morning.

As the car drew nearer to St. Martinville, Willie's heart began to beat harder and his knees began to shake almost uncontrollably. Willie looked out the window at the road and scenery he knew so well. As the car crossed the bridge over the Bayou Teche, he recalled the times he had spent with his friends swimming and fishing. He also remembered playing baseball whenever he and his friends could find a baseball. It was hard to believe that he wasn't going to see or be a part of these scenes again.

Whether deliberately or not, the driver of the car had chosen a route that led through the heart of the black section of St. Martinville. Realizing this, Willie sat up straight in the back seat and leaned over Sheriff Ozenne's lap for a better look. The road they were on ran past the front of Willie's home.

As they approached his house, it seemed that the car slowed down. Craning his neck Willie could see the house on Randolph Street, but he couldn't see anybody in or around it. The car was still traveling too fast. Willie had hoped to catch a glimpse of his mother, but he wasn't disappointed. It was nice to see the house again, he thought, but in a way it was good he didn't see anybody he knew or a member of his family. Dying would have been only that much harder.

All too soon, the black car pulled up through the courthouse square and met a crowd that had been waiting for him since early that morning. The St. Martinville courthouse, built by slave labor in 1859,[3] was located near the center of town and, like so many other southern courthouses of the time, was whitewashed and pillared. This was the same courthouse where, eight months before, Willie had been convicted and sentenced to death for the murder of a white man—Andrew Thomas, the popular owner of the town drugstore. The murder of Thomas had roused St. Martinville from its slumber. Emotions raised by the crime were such that after Willie's arrest, an unruly crowd had gathered outside the St. Martinville jail. Fearing a lynching, Willie had to be held for "safekeeping" both before the trial and after sentencing in the nearby New Iberia Parish Jail.[4] Now, finally, Willie had returned home, if only to die.

As the crowd caught its first glimpse of Willie, their memories of the last eighteen months became very near and real. Whites recalled their murdered neighbor, Andrew Thomas, and blacks remembered the stories and the rumors of a frame-up—with Willie the unwitting victim. The crowd became hushed. Amid the anger, there was a strong sense of sadness in the air. Everyone knew that their feelings would not die along with Willie Francis.

Chained and shackled, Willie was helped out of the car by Sheriff Ozenne. Suddenly, the crowd surged forward for a final look. Walking slowly through a press of familiar faces, Willie was led to the back of the courthouse. There, awkwardly appended to the courthouse, was the red-brick, two-story St. Martin Parish Jail. It was a difficult walk for Willie, not only physically but emotionally. For as soon as he had left the car, he knew that the electric chair had arrived and was waiting for him. The noise from its revving electrical generator was both deafening and unmistakable.[5]

Unlike most states, at that time Louisiana had no central place for executions. Instead, the state had a portable electric chair. When the heavy, oversized wooden chair was not in use, it was stored at the Louisiana State Penitentiary in Angola. When the chair was needed, however, it was loaded along with various electrical apparatuses in the back of a pickup truck and driven to the appropriate parish jail. Accompanying prison officials from the state penitentiary would then unload and install the electric chair.

That day two men from Angola were responsible for the proper operation of the electric chair in St. Martinville: Captain E. Foster, a prison guard, and Vincent Vinezia, an inmate from the penitentiary.[6] Foster was not an electrician,[7] but Vinezia was an assistant to the chief electrician at the Louisiana State Penitentiary, U. J. Esnault. As usual, Esnault did not accompany the electric chair to St. Martinville. He had, however, tested the chair on May 1, two days before the execution date, and had pronounced it to be in good working condition.[8]

Noticeably absent from the trip was Warden Dennis J. Bazer. Ordinarily, Warden Bazer accompanied the electric chair on its periodic visits to the various parish jails in Louisiana. On this particular day, however, he was hosting a reception at his home in Angola for Louisiana Governor Jimmie Davis. A study done by the United States Department of Justice Bureau of Prisons had recently exposed barbarous conditions in the state penitentiary at Angola. The study concluded that Louisiana's penal system "[fell] far short of desirable standards . . . in practically all respects."[9] The study had found that Louisiana's handling of prisoners was outmoded, that its administrative organization required change, that the sanitary and medical facilities were "deplorable," and that the state penitentiary buildings in Angola were "depreciated and dilapidated almost beyond repair." Davis was in Angola to minimize any political damage caused by the report and to propose a "modernization program" for the aging penitentiary. With Bazer thus preoccupied, Foster and Vinezia were on their own.

Early on the morning of the execution, the two men began the difficult and cumbersome process of installing the electric chair. A hot Louisiana sun made the entire operation much more difficult. First, they unloaded an electrical switchboard and the chair itself, which weighed approximately three hundred pounds, from the truck and hauled them up to the second floor of the jail. Then, wires had to be run from the pickup truck containing the generator outside the jail up a wall and through a window to a switchboard connected with the electric chair. Finally, dozens of feet of exposed wiring had to be checked for breaks and the electrical connections secured.

According to a witness, the installation did not go smoothly. After setting up the chair once, a testing of the electrical current indicated that something was wrong. So Foster and Vinezia tore down the wiring and began again.[10] After another test, the two men quit their work, apparently satisfied that the chair was ready. About 11:30, the men returned to their work and started up the noisy electrical generator. Court affidavits later alleged that a flask was passed between the men working on the installation of the chair.[11] The court affidavits further alleged that that same morning, "the executioner and other persons with him visited several saloons in New Iberia, and while drinking therein extended open invitations to various individuals to go with them to attend the electrocution."[12]

Outside the parish prison where his doomed son was being held, Frederick Francis paced crazily back and forth and then in circles. He had just missed Willie's arrival from New Iberia and was left waiting outside with the hearse and coffin he had brought to carry Willie's body away from the prison. Exhausted, Francis had spent the previous night placing a small tombstone over the plot of land where his son's body would soon rest. These final acts, combined with the strain of the previous eight months, had finally taken a high emotional toll. A proud, hard-working man, Francis was bereft with grief over the state-planned killing of the youngest of his thirteen children.

Upon reaching the St. Martinville jail, Willie was led upstairs to the execution chamber. As he entered the L-shaped room, Willie noticed the northern wall. There sat a heavy-looking chair with leather straps dangling from its arms and legs. The overcrowded room was quiet, and all eyes were on Willie. Uncertain as to what he was supposed to do, Willie shuffled in his shackles over to the chair and started to sit down in it. Before he did, however, Sheriff Leonard Resweber seized his arm and led him out of the chamber to a cell across the hall.

Waiting on a cell cot was Father Maurice Rousseve, Willie's priest from

St. Martinville. Father Rousseve told Willie that he shouldn't be frightened because he would soon be in heaven. The Father assured Willie that he would take good care of his family and help them through the sad days ahead. Little else needed to be said: Willie was fully resigned to his fate. He stood up. Sheriff Resweber, waiting outside, opened the cell door. Resweber was a large man who, as Sheriff of St. Martin Parish, still patrolled the Parish on horseback. Willie looked at the sheriff who said nothing but instead gave him a slight nod. Not fully understanding what to do, Willie left the cell, walked across the hallway, back into the execution room, and sat down in the chair. This time no one stopped him.

Once seated, the sheriff's deputies removed Willie's handcuffs and shackles and began strapping him into the chair. Dressed in the drab gray shirt and trousers issued to him at the New Iberia jail, Willie looked small in the chair. His shirt was soon opened to the waist and the left leg of the trousers was slit open up to the knee. The deputies securely wrapped straps around Willie's arms and legs and then around his waist. Next, wires and metal electrodes were attached to his head and left leg.

Willie became dizzy watching Captain Foster and the deputies. They walked up to and around him, attached an electrode, and then moved away. He began to feel cold, and his hands were wet. His ears were beginning to ring from the roar of the electrical generator outside the jail. Turning his eyes to the witnesses, he felt strange in the way a person feels when he is being stared at—here, not just by one other person, but by a small crowd of official state witnesses.

After several minutes, Willie heard Captain Foster say "OK" to Sheriff Resweber. The sheriff walked over to Willie's side and asked if there was anything he would like to say before they pulled the switch. Willie shook his head no. Numb with fear, he couldn't speak. Father Rousseve then came forward and pressed a cross to Willie's lips. Both the sheriff and the priest then retreated to the other end of the room. Willie tried to be brave as Father Hannegan had told him.

Willie heard a sudden movement behind him and felt a wet hood being placed over the top of his head. The hood was black and covered the upper part of his face, except for a small slit to enable him to breathe. The State of Louisiana was being careful not to suffocate Willie before they executed him. The hood itself had been dampened in order to promote the free movement of electricity to Willie's head. Startled by the blinding hood, Willie could see nothing now, and his sense of fear was heightened. Now, around him he could only hear mumbling, some movement by the witnesses, and the deafening noise of the electrical generator.

On the other side of the room, Captain Foster crouched over the electrical switchboard lying on the floor. A half-smoked, unlit cigar stuck out of the side of his mouth. The needle of the meter on the switchboard had to indicate that the electrical generator outside was capable of producing 2,500 volts of electricity before he could pull the switch.[13] For the last forty-five minutes, the generator had been slowly building up to that fatal level. Now, it was nearly there.

Suddenly, Willie heard Captain Foster say in a loud, almost cruel voice, "Goodbye, Willie."[14] Willie wanted to answer and say "Goodbye," but petrified with fear, he could not respond. With a wide, sweeping gesture, Foster pulled the switch on the board below him. Willie clutched his hands tightly into fists as the first currents of electricity surged into his body. It felt as if he was being cut and pricked by hundreds, no thousands, of razor-sharp needles and pins. His left leg ached, then his arms. Willie's body tensed and his lips puffed out. Soon, his whole body began involuntarily jumping and straining at the straps. The heavy chair began to move from its original position in response to Willie's pain.[15]

For a moment the current stopped. It was quiet and Willie thought he must be dead. So did Dr. Sidney Yongue, the coroner of St. Martin's Parish. Yongue turned to his assistant, Dr. Bernard DeMahy, and said matter of factly, "Well, let's examine him now."

Pointing at Willie, DeMahy replied, "It's no use to examine him—he's breathing."[16] Indeed, Willie's chest began to heave forward as desperate gasps for air could be heard in the stilled room.

Overhearing Yongue and DeMahy, Foster mumbled, "Well, we'll give him another one." Foster threw the switch again, and a second current of electricity hit Willie. Feeling the terrible pain once more, Willie realized he was still alive. After what seemed like an eternity, Willie heard Captain Foster frantically shout, "Give me some more juice down there." A voice outside yelled back, "I'm giving you all I got now."[17]

Something was wrong. The electricity, though reaching Willie, was not fatal. Still, the torture continued. Willie could take no more. He hollered for the executioner to stop. "Take it off. Take it off. Let me breathe," he gasped.[18] "You're not supposed to breathe," Captain Foster shouted back. "I am not dying," Willie stuttered. All this time, electricity continued to flow into Willie.

A moment later, Foster threw the switch off and the current stopped. Willie's head was slumped forward, his chin resting on his chest. Everything was quiet, and Willie was sure he was really dead this time. He could feel hands all over him removing the leather straps that had bound his arms and legs. Willie thought it was strange that you could feel hands when you're dead the same way as when you're alive. He also thought it was peculiar that Resweber and his deputies were in such an awful hurry to get him out of the chair and buried.

When the hood was taken off, however, Willie opened his eyes, looked around the room and realized he was still alive. The witnesses looked very excited and began talking in loud voices. Willie wasn't sure what they were saying, but it really didn't matter. He was alive.

After the deputies had removed the electrodes and unfastened the leather straps, Sheriff Ozenne helped Willie out of the chair. Willie was feeling the effects of the electricity, but he could walk. Slowly, the sheriff led Willie past the witnesses and a stunned Captain Foster into his temporary cell across the hall. Willie laid down on a cot and rested until the coroner, Dr. Yongue, with a black leather bag in hand, entered the cell, together with Dr. DeMahy. Pulling out a stethoscope, the coroner listened to Willie's chest and conducted a brief examination. He concluded that, although Willie was stunned and had difficulty breathing, he would recover. There was no question, in DeMahy's opinion, that Willie "actually got a shock."[19] Hearing this, Sheriff Ozenne asked Willie if he wanted to go out for some air and have something to eat. Willie said no; he just wanted to rest.

Meanwhile, Louisiana state officials puzzled about what to do. In a panicked telephone call, Sheriff Resweber informed Governor Davis of the startling news. Should he attempt, the sheriff asked, a second execution that afternoon? Davis consulted Attorney General Fred LeBlanc for a legal opinion. Could the State of Louisiana, having failed the first time, try to execute Willie Francis a second time? LeBlanc responded that it was a very close question with "too many complications." There were two factors to consider: "On one side, Francis was sentenced to die on a specific date. However, on the other hand, he was sentenced to be subjected to electric shock until dead. We'll have to decide whether he can be again put in the chair under the original sentence."[20]

Governor Jimmie Davis was a curious figure on the Louisiana political scene. First elected governor in 1944 as a reform candidate over the opposition of the Long machine, Davis's primary achievements prior to his election were as a country-western singer and the writer of such songs as "You Are My Sunshine" and "When It's Roundup Time in Heaven." Unable to succeed himself as governor under Louisiana law, Davis wrote a number of gospel songs in the 1950s, including "Down By the Riverside." Davis successfully ran for governor in 1960, promising to "preserve the southern way of life" and attacking his opponent for "consorting" with the National Association for the Advancement of Colored People (NAACP).[21]

Within an hour, the final decision was made. All the state officials were of one mind. They should try again and do it right this time: Kill Willie Francis. It was decided, however, that it would appear unseemly to attempt a second execution that same afternoon. In the interest of justice, a brief executive reprieve was appropriate. Governor Davis suggested that a second execution attempt be made in seven days, on May 10. Warden Bazer objected.[22] The portable electric chair would be in Leesville, Louisiana, for an execution on that day.[23] Two executions in one day would be impossible. Indeed, it was clear that the state had its hands full with only one execution in a day. At last a date was agreed on. Governor Davis telephoned Sheriff Resweber with an order that a second execution be scheduled for May 9, 1946—six days away.[24]

Upon receiving the governor's decision, Sheriff Resweber visited Willie in the temporary cell and told him that he had until the ninth of May. Then, he would have to suffer through the whole ordeal again. Willie slumped forward for the second time that day. He was happy to be alive. It was, he thought, like sitting on top of a gravestone without having the gravestone sitting on top of you. Now, however, his worst fears were being realized. Willie asked the sheriff, how could they make him sit down in that chair and try to kill him again?

Willie's question was brushed aside. It was time, the sheriff said, for Willie to be taken back to New Iberia. Willie stood up and began to walk on unsteady legs. As he left the cell, his eyes met those of an angry Captain Foster. Foster had remained near the execution chamber, removing the electrical equipment. Shaking his fist, Foster cursed Willie and shouted: "I missed you this time, but I'll get you next week if I have to use a rock."[25]

Willie managed to smile. He knew that Foster would be held responsible for what had happened, or rather, what had not happened that day. Deep inside, however, Willie was more concerned about his return to the electric chair in less than one week.

Walking outside to the same black sedan that had brought him to St. Martinville, Willie paused a moment and looked at the awaiting throng. He had hated the way the crowd, both black and white, had stared at him as he entered the jail. Now, it was his turn to stare at them. He could see a look of disbelief on their faces. It was almost as if they had just seen a ghost. In a way they had. They had heard the deafening sound of the electrical generator and had expected to see Willie being carried out feet first. Instead, he was walking in their midst. The crowd was still as Willie stepped into the car for the drive back to New Iberia. Not until the sedan had pulled out of courthouse square did the crowd begin to buzz with curiosity over why Willie had survived.

Upon his return to New Iberia, Willie was happy to see the inside of his cell. When he had left that morning, he had never expected to see its bright pink walls again. From his cell window, he could see the rooftops of the simple one-story houses near the New Iberia courthouse. The cell had been home to Willie for the last eight months and had come to represent a measure of security. And so it would continue to be, if only for another six days.

Soon after his return to the parish jail that afternoon, Father Hannegan paid Willie a visit. While Father Hannegan had been told of the day's events, his face still betrayed a look of surprise when he saw Willie in his cell. Willie detected Father Hannegan's surprise but said nothing. Though still slightly dazed from the electrical shocks, he was too eager to tell the priest how brave he had been. After hearing Willie tell of his ordeal, Father Hannegan reassuringly told him, "Yes, you were brave, Willie."

It was only late afternoon, but it had already been a long day for all concerned. With the heat of the Louisiana sun at it peak, it was time to rest and to collect thoughts. But the story of Willie Francis was news now. Reporters soon began to descend on the New Iberia jail demanding an interview with Willie. A beleaguered Sheriff Ozenne eventually relented and led reporters to Willie's cell.

Resting after his visit with Father Hannegan, Willie had just begun to feel less dizzy from his ordeal when he heard the reporters get off the elevator. Almost immediately the excited, fast-talking reporters fired a barrage of questions in rapid succession.

"What was it like being in the electric chair?" Willie heard a reporter ask.

"They walked me into the room and I saw the chair. . . . I knowed it was a bad chair," Willie drawled. "All I could think was: 'Willie, you goin' out'n this world.'

"They begun to strap me in the chair, and everything begun to look dazey. . . . It was like the white folks watching was in a big swing, and they'd swing away and back and then right up close. When they put the black bag over my head, I was all locked up inside the bag with loud thinkin'.

"The electric man . . . could of been puttin' me on the bus for New Orleans the way he said 'goodbye,'" Willie remembered, "and I tried to say goodbye but my tongue got stuck . . . and I felt a burnin' in my head and my left leg and I jumped against the straps.

"When the straps kept cuttin' me I hoped I was alive, and I asked the electric man to let me breathe. . . . They took the bag off my head. . . . " It was "plumb m-m-m-mizable," Willie stuttered.

"What went wrong?" asked another reporter.

"God fool'd with the electric chair," Willie answered.[26]

"How's that? What do you mean?" followed up a different reporter.

"The Lord was with me," Willie responded.[27] Willie was convinced that he was the beneficiary of divine intervention.

"What was it like to taste death?" asked one reporter.

Willie answered literally. "It tasted like cold peanut butter" and looked like "little blue and pink and green speckles, like shines in a rooster's tail."[28]

And so it went until the reporters, armed with these and other quotes, together with a picture of Willie reading the Bible, were satisfied and left. Soon, the jail cell lights were out, and Willie was once again alone.

"Merci Dieu [Thank God]!," cried Willie's mother in Cajun French as she collapsed to the floor of her small, clapboard house upon hearing news of the failed execution. "Le Bon Dieu [the good Lord]," she gasped over and over again with folded hands raised heavenward.[29] Around her, Willie's brothers and sisters screamed, laughed, and cried with joy. Overwhelming relief swept through the Francis household. A day that was to be filled with mourning and sadness had abruptly turned into a day of celebration.

That night, Willie's father stood alone in the darkness of the blacks' cemetery in St. Martinville. Using a sledgehammer, Fred Francis smashed his son's unused gravemarker into bits and pieces. It was no longer needed. Willie had cheated the electric man.

II

The Arrest and Trial

The murder of Andrew Thomas had stunned the small town of St. Martinville. Surrounded by a forest of primeval oaks draped in Spanish moss, St. Martinville is located in the heart of "Cajun" country in the southwest portion of the state.[1] The town was settled in the last half of the eighteenth century by Acadians, the French-speaking natives of Nova Scotia driven out by the English in the winter of 1775. In one of the most sordid and tragic chapters of English colonial history, entire Acadian families were split up and herded south in cramped ships to hostile ports. Only half of the refugees survived the harsh winter's journey. On the outskirts of St. Martinville next to the winding Bayou Teche stands a large oak tree—immortalized by Henry Wadsworth Longfellow in his poem "Evangeline." It was under this tree that Evangeline waited for her Gabriel, after being cruelly separated by English injustice.

Named for a fourth-century French bishop, Martin, the village attained a prominent position in Louisiana society by the early 1800s. Steamboat travel transformed St. Martinville into a pleasant summer resort for much of New Orleans society. The summer quartering of the New Orleans French Opera Company gave the town its own opera season. Royalists who fled France during the French Revolution honored the gaiety of the small town by giving it the name Le Petit Paris. The Civil War, a yellow fever epidemic, hurricanes, and the lack of a railroad branch changed all of that, and St. Martinville quickly returned to its docile small-town status.[2]

In 1928 St. Martinville was the site of one of Huey Long's most famous speeches. With characteristic eloquence and melodrama, the Kingfish spoke to a Cajun audience assembled at the Evangeline Oak:

Where are the schools that you have waited for your children to have that have never come? Where are the roads and the highways that you spent your money to build. . . . ? Where are the institutions to care for the sick and disabled? Evangeline wept bitter tears in her disappointment, but it lasted through only one lifetime. . . . Your tears in this country, around this oak, have lasted for generations. Give me the chance to dry the tears of those who still weep here.[3]

In 1929 the town attracted a measure of attention when parts of the motion picture *Evangeline* starring Delores Del Rio were filmed at nearby Catahoula Lake. But these events did little to change the quiet pace of life in St. Martinville.

Andrew Thomas, the town druggist, was the successful owner of Thomas's Drug Store in downtown St. Martinville. In November 1944 Thomas was fifty-four years old and a prominent figure in the St. Martinville community—as was the Thomas family as a whole. Andrew's brother Claude was the chief of police for the town of St. Martinville, and his brother Robert (nicknamed "Zie") was the secretary-treasurer for the St. Martin Parish Police-Jury. (St. Martin's Parish is governed by a police jury, a Louisiana local governing body similar to a county commission.) Unmarried, Andrew lived alone on the outskirts of St. Martinville in a large house across the highway from the Evangeline State Park.

On the morning of November 8, 1944, Mrs. Robert Thomas received a telephone call from Lucien Bienvenu, a local businessman in St. Martinville. Bienvenu had noticed that Thomas's brother-in-law, Andrew, had not yet opened his store for the day's business, although it was already 8:45 AM. Bienvenu had tried calling Andrew at home, but there was no answer. Was everything all right with Andrew? Bienvenu asked. Unable to answer the question and befuddled by Andrew's unusual behavior, Mrs. Thomas assured Bienvenu that she would ask her husband if he knew anything of Andrew's whereabouts.

After taking her children to school, Mrs. Thomas stopped by the St. Martinville courthouse to tell her husband, Zie, of the telephone call from Bienvenu. The call worried Zie Thomas. His brother was an extremely punctual and well-organized businessman; such an unexplained, late absence was clearly out of character. The absence was all the more unusual because Andrew normally told Zie if he was sick or out of town, so that Zie could then open and mind the drugstore. Zie suggested to his wife that they drive out to Andrew's house in the country on the edge of St. Martinville.

As their car pulled into the driveway of Andrew's home, the pair noticed that Andrew's car was in the garage, located fifty feet from the house, and the garage door was closed. Mrs. Thomas gasped. She could see a body lying in the back of the house on the cement walk midway between the garage and the back porch. She and her husband got out of the car and ran over to the body. It was Andrew, and he had bullet holes in his chest and head. Zie dropped to his knees at Andrew's side. He checked in vain for his brother's pulse. The wrist was cold and lifeless.

Many mourned Andrew Thomas's death. The local newspaper, the St. Martinville *Weekly Messenger*, eulogized him: "Mr. Thomas was well-loved in this community by all who knew him and no one can think of an enemy whom he ever had." Moreover, the paper concluded,

Mr. Thomas' death was a shock to the whole community as he was well-known and loved by children and adults. His drug store was a hang-out for the younger people here. "Drew" as the kids affectionately call him, would greet them genially. He is sadly missed by all who knew him.[4]

The Weekly Messenger reported that Andrew Thomas was "brutally killed . . . by unknown assailants." The identity of these "assailants," however, remained unknown. Indeed, a coroner's jury convened after the murder could only offer this stark conclusion:

From the evidence presented to the jury we do hereby opine and come to the conclusion that Andrew I. Thomas met his death from five gun shot wounds fired from a gun of the pistol or rifle type of about .38 caliber bullet; one striking him in the right eye, two on the left side, two in the back. Anyone of these wounds were made from a gun in the hands of an unknown party or parties, and we do hereby render a verdict that he was shot by an unknown party or parties.[5]

The coroner's jury could do little more than restate the obvious—Andrew Thomas was dead and his killer was at large. It was now up to the chief of police, Claude Thomas, to find his brother's murderer or murderers.

St. Martinville was astir over Thomas's death. With no suspects in custody, rumors began to sweep through town that the murder was the result of some romantic entanglement he had become involved in. Andrew Thomas was a well-known ladies' man. Popular opinion held that he was done in by a jealous husband or by the boyfriend of one of his lady friends. Or, perhaps, the murderer was a jilted woman or a jealous lover. Attention was focused on the intrigue of revenge and romance.

This speculation was fueled by the release of testimony presented at the coroner's inquest by Mr. and Mrs. A. L. Van Brocklin, Andrew Thomas's closest neighbor on the highway leading into St. Martinville. The Van Brocklin house was approximately an eighth of a mile east of the Thomas house and thus, nearer to St. Martinville. Mrs. Van Brocklin testified that on the night of November 7, 1944, she and her husband had been awakened by shots between 11:30 and 12:00. The shots "came fast one after the other." Sitting up in bed, Mrs. Van Brocklin saw a car parked with its lights on in front of the Thomas house. Convinced by her husband that the shots must have come from a nearby military camp, she did not notify the police. Mrs. Van Brocklin further testified that the car in front of the Thomas house could not have later traveled back into St. Martinville on the main highway past the Van Brocklin house. Mrs. Van Brocklin insisted that no car had headed toward St. Martinville past "the front of my house because I would have seen the lights."[6]

Suspecting foul play, Dr. Yongue, the St. Martin Parish coroner, followed up the point with Mr. Van Brocklin. "We would like to have a little more information. You are still under oath. We heard a little rumor that somebody across the bayou might have had something to do with this. Do you know of any associations that he [Andrew Thomas] might have had with anybody across the bayou?"

Mr. Van Brocklin responded affirmatively: "I saw his car at a lady's house out there several times."[7]

The woman named by Mr. Van Brocklin lived "across the bayou" and was married. Mr. Van Brocklin went on to name another woman, also married, whom Andrew had visited across the bayou. He had, however, never seen these or any other women at Andrew's house.

For seven months Chief Thomas, with Parish Sheriff Resweber, investigated Andrew's murder. It was a difficult investigation, for they had little physical evidence to go on. There were, for example, no fingerprints, nor was a weapon recovered at the murder scene. The two police departments spent hundreds of man-hours following up on the many rumors which the murder spawned. Their efforts were apparently unproductive, however. By summer 1945, nine months later, no suspect was in custody, and virtually all leads had been exhausted.

In mid-July 1945 Claude W. Goldsmith, chief of police at Port Arthur, Texas, met with Resweber in St. Martinville on unrelated police business. While there, the frustrated Resweber gave the Port Arthur police chief an account of the Thomas murder case. In desperation, Resweber requested that the chief "try to apprehend any man" from St. Martinville found in Port Arthur "because so far they had been unable to get the right man."

Less than two weeks later, Goldsmith and a deputy were awaiting the evening arrival of a suspected dope dealer at the Port Arthur train station. Spotting a suspicious figure leaving the train with a suitcase they thought could have been filled with contraband, the sheriff and his deputy followed the man. The subject of the police trail soon discovered that he was being followed and began to flee. Running from the police, the suspect dropped his suitcase and soon disappeared into the darkness. As Sheriff Goldsmith reached the abandoned suitcase, he "saw a man crouched down under a tree."

The "man" under the tree was a sixteen-year-old youth—Willie Francis. Willie had been in Port Arthur visiting his older sister during the summer. Outside for a stroll that hot August night to get some air before dinner, he saw two white policemen running toward him chasing a man. Willie ducked behind a tree to avoid involvement in the chase. While only sixteen, Willie had already heard too many stories of white man's justice in both Texas and Louisiana. But he was too late.

Mistaken for an accomplice of the drug dealer, Willie was arrested by Goldsmith and brought into custody. At the station the police quickly realized their error and dropped the drug charges, but they detained Willie and later charged him with the assault and robbery of a Port Arthur resident. Three or four days before, an elderly white man had been assaulted in his apartment and had been robbed and left unconscious. The person who had committed the crime had not been apprehended. Whether Willie was guilty of these charges has never been determined.

Once in the police station, the police began to interrogate Willie. Willie was frightened. He could only nervously stammer in response to the questions. After a few minutes, the police found out that he was not from Port Arthur; after continued questioning, they determined that he lived in St. Martinville. Chief Goldsmith recalled his meeting with Sheriff Resweber several weeks before and Resweber's plea "to apprehend" any man from St. Martinville found in Port Arthur. Police emptied Willie's pockets and found a wallet containing an identification card belonging to Andrew Thomas.

Chief Goldsmith began to question Willie about the Andrew Thomas murder. According to Port Arthur police, "after questioning Willie Francis for two or three or five minutes, he came out with a statement that he was the man who had killed Andrew Thomas in St. Martinville."[8] The police then asked Willie if he knew how to read and write. Willie did. According to the police, they then asked him "if he had any objection to reducing the statement to writing." Willie made no objection.

Willie then wrote a confession which the police entitled a "Voluntary Statement While in Custody." The statement was prefaced with the routine legal language designed to absolve police of charges of coercion—language obviously not written by Willie:

I, Willie Francis, being in the custody of Claude W. Goldsmith, Chief of Police of the City of Port Arthur, Jefferson County, Texas and having been warned by E. L. Canada, Justice of the Peace, Jefferson County, Texas, the person to whom the hereinafter set out statement is made by me, that I do not have to make any statement at all, and that any statement made by me may be used in evidence against me on my trial for the offense concerning which this statement is made, do hereby make the following voluntary statement to the said E. L. Canada, to wit:

Scrawled in a childish hand, directly below these neatly typed words, was Willie's confession, consisting of some seventy-five words arranged in a rambling string of disjointed thoughts:

I Willie Francis now 16 years old I stole the gun from Mr. Ogise at St. Martinville La. and kill Andrew Thomas November 9, 1944 or about that time at St. Martinville La. it was a secret about me and him. I took a black purse with card 1280182 in it four dollars in it. I all so took a watch on him and sell it in new Iberia La. That all I am said I throw gun away .38 Pistol.

No one ever determined what the "secret" was.

In what might be called an example of "informal rendition," despite the State of Louisiana's failure to make a formal request that Texas release Willie to it, the Port Arthur police immediately transferred Francis to Louisiana authorities.

According to Willie's baptismal certificate, he was born on January 12, 1929, and was fifteen at the time of the Thomas murder. Willie was one of thirteen children of a farm laborer who had an income of $9 per week.

What education Willie had was gained in segregated, poor-quality schools in Louisiana. Indeed, as evidenced by the confession made in Texas, Willie's writing skills were, at best, minimal. In addition, Willie had suffered through life with a very bad stutter. Despite his youth and background, no counsel was present during either the questioning or confession in Texas or the "extradition" to Louisiana.

During the course of the two-and-one-half hour ride in the Louisiana police car to St. Martinville, Willie allegedly made another "voluntary and complete confession" of the Thomas slaying. In this confession, likewise scrawled in a childish hand, Willie wrote while seated between two white deputies from St. Martin's Parish:

Yes Willie Francis confess that he kill Andrew Thomas on November 8, 1944 i went to his house about 11:30 P.M. i hide backing his gorage about a half hour, When he came out the gorage i shot him five times, that all i remember a short story

Sinarely Willie Francis

Later, Willie was said to have shown police a culvert next to railroad tracks behind the Thomas house where he had thrown the pistol holster away, at which spot police recovered it.[9] Willie is also said to have told police where he had thrown the murder weapon after the shooting. The police stated that this spot coincided with the spot where a .38-caliber pistol had been found soon after the Thomas murder. Again, no counsel was present at any point through the course of these proceedings.

On the basis of these two confessions, Willie was arrested on August 8, 1945, for the slaying of Andrew Thomas. The arrest was, of course, major news in the town of St. Martinville. The case had gained widespread notoriety not only because of the murder victim's popularity, but also because of the apparent lack of clues or suspects. Now, however, the mystery had been finally solved.

Willie was tried and convicted by the local newspaper before he ever set foot in a courtroom. There was no presumption of innocence until proven guilty by a jury of peers. The St. Martinville *Weekly Messenger* announced the arrest in large, prejudicial headlines: "Andrew Thomas's Murderer Found."[10] This story was of more interest to many than the news that on August 6, 1945, an atomic bomb had been dropped on Hiroshima.

The community had mentally branded Willie Francis the killer of Andrew Thomas. The tone was set and the conclusion foregone. Only the bare formalities of a trial, sentencing, and execution remained.

Presiding over Willie Francis's trial was Judge James D. Simon. The judge was a popular man whose composure on the bench, according to courthouse lore, cracked only once, and this was during prohibition

> "yes Willie Francis confess
> that he kill andrew Thmos
> on November 8, 1944 I went
> to his house about 11:30 PM
> i hide backing his gorage
> about a half hour, When he
> come out the gorage i shot him
> five times. That all i remember a short story
>
> Sinarely Willie Francis

when a criminal case involving the sale of liquor came before Judge Simon. The district attorney was questioning a witness on the stand and asked, "Where was this that they sold the liquor?" The witness responded with a general description of the location. The district attorney, attempting to seek a more complete description, pressed the witness with additional questions. After several minutes of this, the exasperated witness pointing to Judge Simon blurted out, "Ask T. Jim [Simon's nickname], ask T. Jim, he knows where the place is. He comes there all the time."[11] The courtroom burst into laughter as an embarrassed Judge Simon repeatedly banged his gavel booming in a deep voice, "Order in the courtroom. Come to order."

In 1954 Simon was elected to the Louisiana Supreme Court but only six years later was forced to resign in disgrace. He had been arraigned in federal court for income tax evasion. Facing severe political pressure and overwhelming evidence, Simon left the state bench; all investigations into his financial affairs were subsequently dropped.[12] But this was still in the future. In 1945 Judge Simon was the law in St. Martin's Parish.

Justice was neatly and efficiently packaged and dispensed in the judicial assembly line known as the St. Martinville courthouse. The accused could be led through the whitewashed front of the courthouse to be tried and sentenced in the courtroom and then moved to the ugly red-brick jail attached to the rear of the courthouse to be incarcerated and, if such was the case, executed. The finished product of the legal system was eventually spat out a side entrance of the jail—usually in the form of a repentent prisoner who had served out his time. Occasionally, however, justice took the form of a corpse removed from Louisiana's portable electric chair.

On September 6, 1945, a grand jury formally indicted Willie Francis for the murder of Andrew Thomas. Despite the confessions, Willie pleaded "not guilty" to the charge of murder and asked for a trial by jury at his arraignment on September 6, 1945. It was at this arraignment, one month after his arrest and less than a week before the scheduled start of his trial, that Willie first received legal counsel and assistance from two court-appointed attorneys. Willie's father had been financially unable to retain a lawyer in St. Martinville to handle the case.

Willie's attorneys, Otto J. Mestayer and James R. Parkerson, were both white and members of local bars. Their defense of Willie was singularly inadequate. According to the court records, the first recorded action of Willie's counsel followed Willie's plea of not guilty at the September 6 arraignment. Incredibly, "Counsel for the accused requested the Court the right to withdraw its plea of 'not guilty.'"[13] Article 740-30 of the Louisiana Code of Criminal Law and Procedure defined the offense of murder and provided that anyone committing that crime "shall be punished by death."[14] To withdraw a plea of "not guilty" in order to enter a plea of "guilty" to a charge of murder under Louisiana's mandatory death penalty statute would be tantamount to suicide. Fortunately, counsel did not withdraw Willie's plea of "not guilty." Nevertheless, consistent with this early portent of a less than spirited defense, counsel for the defense would prove to be of little value to Willie.

The trial of Willie Francis began on September 12, 1945, at 10:00 AM in the Sixteenth Judicial Court, Parish of St. Martin, less than two miles from the murder site. Willie's counsel had had fewer than six days to prepare their client's defense. At this time, it is impossible to know what actually transpired during the trial. No stenographic record was taken; the Court's deputy clerk made only sketchy minutes. The first entry in the minutes of *State of Louisiana* v. *Willie Francis*, Case No. 2161, for September 12, was that the state through the district attorney and counsel for Willie Francis "announced their readiness for trial."[15] Apparently, six days was enough time to prepare Willie Francis's defense. From those minutes it appears that after all challenges for cause and peremptory challenges had been exercised by the prosecution and the defense, a jury of twelve white males and one alternate was then selected from a pool of area residents. No objections to the composition of the jury were entered by Willie's counsel, even though the selection process had rendered meaningless the notion of a trial by a jury of one's peers. Furthermore, no motion was made for a change of venue despite the prejudicial pretrial publicity.

The trial opened with District Attorney L. O. Pecot reading the indictment for murder and making an opening statement. Counsel for the defense then rose and "waived the right of their opening statement but reserved the privilege of making such statement at the conclusion of the State's case."[16] The prosecution proceeded to call its witnesses and offer evidence until Judge Simon adjourned the court at 10:15 that night. With the exception of several brief recesses, including lunch, the first day of the Willie Francis trial lasted over twelve hours from opening to closing gavel.

The prosecution resumed its case the next morning at 10:00 by calling its other witnesses. Like the previous day, the temperature was 98° in both St. Martinville and the courtroom. The district attorney's case rested almost exclusively on Willie's two confessions and on witnesses' testimony that the confessions were made voluntarily. Nobody saw the murder, and the murder weapon itself could not be produced because it, along with several bullets produced from the Thomas autopsy, had been "lost in transportation"[17] after having been allegedly sent to the FBI in Washington, D.C., for ballistic tests.

The results of ballistic tests would have been important since the coroner could only conclude that the fatal shots were "fired from a gun *or rifle type of about* a .38-caliber bullet." Whether the murder weapon was a pistol or a rifle of a .38-caliber or some other caliber, the coroner could not state with certainty. After Willie Francis was arrested, the police stated that he told them where he had thrown the murder weapon. At that location, the police further stated that a .38-caliber pistol had been found several months earlier. Only ballistic tests would have shown whether the bullets found in Andrew Thomas's body came from the .38-caliber pistol indirectly linked by police to Willie Francis.

Despite the heavy reliance by the prosecution on the two confessions, defense counsel made no attempt to cross-examine the police as to the voluntariness of Willie's confessions. The 1947 Report of the President's Committee on Civil Rights had found "widespread and varied forms of official misconduct. These include violent physical attacks by police officers on members of minority groups, the use of third degree methods to extort confessions and brutality against prisoners."[18] If the defense could show that the confessions were made involuntarily, the confessions could not be admitted into evidence. States may not base convictions on confessions obtained by coercion. Without the confessions, the prosecution's case against Willie Francis would dissolve.

Yet, the question of whether Willie's confessions were coerced was apparently not probed by defense counsel on cross-examination. No one asked why the "confessions" read as if someone was telling Willie what to write. No one asked why the second confession, given in the Louisiana police car during the trip from Port Arthur to St. Martinville, read "*he* kill" at one point and "*i* shot him" at another. No one asked how Willie remembered he shot five times—no more, no less—when he said "That all i remember." No one asked whether Willie would have even used the word "confess."

The minutes of the trial do not record a single instance where defense counsel cross-examined any of the dozen witnesses called by the prosecution. Presenting its case without interruption, the prosecution "announced that it rested its case subject to rebuttal" by noon the next day.

There was, however, to be no rebuttal. Consistent with their previous performance, counsel for the defense rose and "announced to the court that it had no evidence to offer on behalf of the accused and rested its case."[19] That was Willie's entire "defense." Willie's counsel did not inform the jury that the alleged murder weapon had been "lost" and that the police took no fingerprints. Nor was any mention made of the errors in Willie's two confessions. For example, even though Andrew Thomas was killed on November 7, 1944, Willie's Texas confession listed November 9 as the date and the Louisiana confession listed November 8. No one has ever explained this discrepancy.

Most importantly, the defense failed to mention the most telling flaw in the State's case. To convict in Louisiana, the prosecution must disprove every reasonable hypothesis of innocence. Mrs. Van Brocklin had testified at the coroner's inquest that on the night of the murder, she had been awakened by shots and saw a car parked with its lights on in front of the Thomas house. This account was squarely inconsistent with the suggestion in Willie's confession that Andrew Thomas's car had already been parked inside the garage before any shots were fired ("i hide backing his gorage about a half hour *when he come out of the gorage* i shot him five times" [author's emphasis]) as well as later testimony from Sheriff Resweber ("when Mr. Thomas was closing the door of his garage he [Willie Francis] shot him"). Similarly, Andrew Thomas's sister-in-law testified at the coroner's inquest that the Thomas car was parked in the garage when she and her husband had discovered the body the next morning.

Coming from a poor family in 1944 Louisiana, fifteen-year-old Willie Francis did not own or use a car. And the car lights from Andrew Thomas's car were presumably out by the time he had parked his car and had come out of the garage in back of his house. If Andrew Thomas's car was parked in his garage and Willie did not own or use a car, whose car was seen in front of the Thomas house by Mrs. Van Brocklin after she heard the fatal shots fired? Was it possible that Andrew Thomas had been followed home that night? Where had Andrew Thomas been so late that Tuesday evening that he did not arrive home until midnight? Finally, if Willie shot Andrew Thomas five times in the head and chest as Thomas was closing the garage door—shots which, according to Mrs. Van Brocklin, "came fast one after the other"—why was Andrew Thomas's body found not near the garage door, but rather on the sidewalk between the house and the garage, some twenty-five feet from the garage?

The testimony of Mrs. Van Brocklin and the questions it raises may well have posed a reasonable hypothesis of innocence. This testimony, however, was never presented by the defense. Strangely, defense counsel chose, instead, to rest its defense without calling a single witness.

It came as little surprise when later that afternoon the jury found Willie Francis "Guilty as Charged" for the murder of Andrew Thomas.[20] The next day, September 14, 1945, trial Judge James D. Simon sentenced Willie "to suffer death in the manner provided by law" under the mandatory death penalty provision of Article 740-30 of the Criminal Code of Louisiana. Thirty years later, the United States Supreme Court would strike down a later version of Louisiana's mandatory death penalty statute because it did not permit consideration of mitigating circumstances surrounding the particular offense, including "Circumstances such as the youth of the offender."[21] In 1946, however, with the mandatory death penalty statute in effect, such circumstances as Willie's age (fifteen) at the time of the Thomas murder, his lack of education, and his poor economic background were of no concern in the sentencing procedure. Within eight days, Willie Francis had been tried, convicted, and sentenced to death for the killing of Andrew Thomas.

Other matters could still be considered, however, on an appeal to a Louisiana appellate court. The questionably "free and voluntary" confessions made in the absence of counsel were certainly the stuff of which successful appeals were made—even in the pre-*Miranda* days of 1946.[22] Only six years before, the United States Supreme Court had overturned the conviction of four black men in Florida for murder.[23] In that case, the most important elements in the prosecution were incriminating statements made by the defendants after five days of questioning by state authorities in the absence of any defense counsel. Looking at the totality of the circumstances, a unanimous Supreme Court concluded that psychological coercion, as well as physical torture, could produce involuntary confessions whose use violated due process.[24] If an appeal was taken, therefore, a strong argument could have been made that Willie's two confessions were not actually "free and voluntary." Rather, the confessions arguably were merely the expected, frightened responses of a sixteen-year-old black youth in the Deep South trying to protect himself from physical abuse while in the custody of white law enforcement officers. A victim first of fear and then of panic, Willie was certainly no match for the police in such an ordeal.

Strangely, Willie's attorneys did not file a motion for a new trial or present an appeal to any Louisiana appellate court asking the reversal of the conviction. Perhaps the two court-appointed attorneys thought that they had already done all they could for Willie, that he had received a fair trial, and that there were no grounds for an appeal. Or perhaps the two lawyers felt they could ill afford the expenditure of time demanded by an appeal. After all, they had already spent time on Willie's trial with little compensation, and there was no prospect for compensation from Willie's family on a prolonged appeal. Perhaps they feared that their professional lives in the white community would be jeopardized if they appealed Willie's conviction for the murder of a popular citizen.

Whatever the reason, Willie spent the fall and winter of 1945 waiting, without hope, for the announcement of an execution date. From the time that sentence of death was pronounced, Willie was without counsel. The time in which he could, under law, file an appeal passed slowly. While locked in his cell in New Iberia, Willie was completely unaware of his right to appeal. No lawyer advised him as to his rights. Since his sentence was the extreme allowed by law, he had everything to gain and nothing to lose by appealing. To say that Willie did not desire an appeal in these circumstances is to think that he was utterly mad. Willie, though poor and uneducated, was far from insane. Thus, Willie spent that critical period of time from the date of sentencing to the date of execution—a time usually filled with frantic legal maneuvering—alone doing nothing but waiting to die.

On March 29, 1946, Governor Jimmie Davis issued a death warrant setting May 3, 1946, for the execution. The warrant commanded Sheriff E. L. Resweber of St. Martin's Parish to carry out the execution by "causing to pass through the body of said Willie Francis a current of electricity of sufficient intensity to cause death, and the application and continuance of such current through the body of said Willie Francis until said Willie Francis is dead."[25]

III

The Appeal and Pardon Process

Following the botched execution attempt, Fred Francis left his small, wooden frame house to find his son a good lawyer. He would not again entrust his son's fate to court-appointed counsel. Of course, money was a problem in retaining better counsel. In season, Francis worked in the sugar cane fields that surrounded St. Martinville for $9 per week.[1] During the off-season, he did odd jobs for various businessmen around town. Among those he had worked for was Jerome Broussard, a local lawyer in St. Martinville. Francis decided to stop by Broussard's office first.[2]

Fred Francis liked Broussard and trusted him. He asked Broussard if he would be interested in taking his son's case. No description of Willie's dilemma was made, nor was one needed, for everyone in and around St. Martinville had heard of the failed electrocution. Broussard declined to take the case. He understood the father's anguish and believed that Willie should not be electrocuted a second time. Yet, Broussard specialized in oil cases and was not a criminal lawyer. He already had too much work for his two-man practice, and he recognized the large amount of work that needed to be done on Willie's behalf. There may have been an additional consideration—financial in nature. Broussard could ill afford to devote the large amount of time necessary to prepare for such a difficult case when prospects for payment were at best remote. Broussard therefore referred Francis to Bertrand DeBlanc, whose law office was next to his own.

A graduate of Louisiana State University Law School and a good friend of the victim Andrew Thomas, DeBlanc had just returned from World War II. DeBlanc's family roots were firmly settled in the Louisiana soil—his grandfather had signed the Louisiana Ordinance of Secession in 1861. When Fred Francis stopped by Broussard's office that Friday afternoon, DeBlanc had been struggling for several months to resume the law practice he had left behind when he joined the army in 1942. In fact, the back of the law office was home for DeBlanc, his wife and their three children. With a family to support, he did not find Willie's case to be financially attractive. Nevertheless, DeBlanc decided to take the case. In his heart, he believed that to electrocute Willie a second time would be cruel and unusual punishment. In his mind, he knew that the publicity that had already begun to surround Willie's case might give a boost to his struggling law practice.

Having taken the case, the fiery, sharp-tongued Cajun lawyer moved quickly. Governor Jimmie Davis had scheduled a second execution attempt for Thursday, May 9. In order to delay the execution, DeBlanc filed a petition for a writ of *habeas corpus* in Louisiana state district court on Tuesday, May 7.[3] A *habeas corpus* (Latin for "you have the body") petition is normally filed as a remedy for unjust imprisonment. The petition is usually addressed to the sheriff or warden in whose custody a prisoner is placed. The petition asserts that the individual is being held contrary to law. After the custodian produces the prisoner and states the reasons for the individual's detention, the matter is submitted to a judge for decision. If the prisoner's lawyer can show probable cause that a client has been imprisoned without good reason, the judge has authority to set the prisoner free.

The petition for *habeas corpus* filed by DeBlanc stated that Willie Francis "is now unlawfully and illegally detained against his will and consent in the . . . Parish Prison, and is in the illegal custody of E. L. Resweber, Sheriff of the Parish of St. Martin, who is without authority detaining [Willie Francis] and depriving him of his liberty."[4] DeBlanc asserted that Willie's imprisonment "is not authorized by any order, decree, judgment or sentence of any Court, or by any provision of law, and [Willie Francis] is desirous of regaining his liberty and to be released of his unauthorized and illegal imprisonment, and that a writ of Habeas Corpus is necessary." DeBlanc argued that Willie's "sentence has been carried out and through an Act of God your petitioner Willie Francis has lived through said execution." "Any further electrocution or threat thereof," DeBlanc continued, "constituted cruel and unusual punishment in violation of the Constitution of the State of Louisiana."

Several hours after DeBlanc filed the *habeas corpus* petition, Judge Simon, the same judge who presided over Willie's trial, denied the petition.[5] DeBlanc was neither surprised nor disappointed. He did not expect Judge Simon to set Willie free. DeBlanc had filed the petition only as a device to set in motion the slow wheels of the legal machinery. Anticipating Judge Simon's decision, DeBlanc filed papers he had already prepared with the Louisiana State Supreme Court several hours later, appealing Judge Simon's ruling.

In the appeal to the Louisiana Supreme Court, DeBlanc argued that a refusal to grant the writ of *habeas corpus* and to stay Willie's execution would constitute a denial of due process and equal protection of laws as guaranteed by the Fourteenth Amendment of the Constitution of the United States ("Nor shall any State deprive any person of life, liberty, or property, without due process of law"),[6] as well as Article I, Section 2 of the Constitution of the State of Louisiana. DeBlanc further contended that since Willie was electrocuted on May 3, 1946, and considering the ordeal to which he was subjected, any further electrocution would constitute "cruel and unusual punishment" in violation of both the Louisiana Constitution and the Eighth Amendment of the United States Constitution. Moreover, DeBlanc maintained, a second electrocution attempt would violate Article I, Section 9 of the Louisiana Constitution and the Fifth Amendment to the United States Constitution, both of which provide that no person shall be put in jeopardy of life or liberty twice for the same offense.

Time was now of the essence. As he awoke on the morning of May 8, Bertrand DeBlanc was worried for his client. Governor Davis had rescheduled Willie's second electrocution for noon on May 9.[7] And Sheriff Resweber had been quoted by the press as saying that the electric chair had been thoroughly checked out and that he stood ready to carry out the sentence on Thursday, May 9, "unless I am enjoined by the courts or other legal means."[8] DeBlanc wondered whether the Louisiana Supreme Court could consider Willie's case and issue a favorable decision in less than thirty-six hours.

Since DeBlanc's appeal to the Supreme Court was filed late Tuesday afternoon, it was not until Wednesday noon that the appeal finally wound its way through the clerk's office and into the justices' hands. Chief Justice Charles O'Neill of the state Supreme Court immediately recognized that it was impossible for the court to give proper consideration to the papers filed with it and render a decision before Thursday noon. Early Wednesday afternoon, O'Neill telephoned Lieutenant Governor J. Emile Veret (who was acting governor in the absence from the state of Governor Jimmie Davis) and asked that Veret grant Francis a reprieve not exceeding thirty days to allow the court an opportunity to study all of the questions presented in the case.[9] Veret immediately complied and granted Willie a thirty-day reprieve until 12:00 noon, Friday, June 7, 1946. Meanwhile, the court scheduled a hearing for the next day, Thursday, May 9, at 10:00 A.M.[10]

DeBlanc had succeeded in buying some time for Willie. Yet, the long-term problem facing him was difficult. How could he block a second execution attempt when there was no law on the subject and virtually no precedent? DeBlanc decided that Willie's best hope lay with the media and the influence of public opinion. An aroused public might induce the State of Louisiana to grant Willie clemency or, at the very least, prevent a second electrocution. There was also the chance that the elected justices of the Louisiana Supreme Court, sensitive to a public outcry, might bar a second attempt.

DeBlanc's strategy was founded on overwhelming public opposition to a second trip to the electric chair for Willie Francis. Willie's plight had quickly become front page news, not only in Louisiana but also across the country. On May 9, 1946, the day of the hearing before the Louisiana Supreme Court, the *New Orleans Times-Picayune* reported that, in the week following the first electrocution, the governor of Louisiana was "deluged with an unprecedented flood of mail. . . . Thousands of letters, telegrams and postcards poured in from all parts of the United States urging clemency for Willie Francis."[11] The newspaper report noted that: "Many of the telegrams and letters were from branches of the National Association for the Advancement of Colored People throughout the nation, while scores were signed by ministers of churches for themselves and their congregations. One such telegram carried the signatures of more than 200 persons."[12] Three days later, the *Times-Picayune* again reported that "Letters, telephone calls and telegrams from Maine to California continued today to flood into the office of Governor Jimmie Davis."[13]

The messages sent to Davis urged him to grant Willie executive clemency based on religious or humanitarian reasons. Boystown's Father Flanagan set the tone for the messages when he wired: "Deeply interested in saving life of Willie Francis now in death cell at New Iberia, La. Would you, dear Governor, use your power of authority to commute death sentence. May God direct you to do His holy will."[14] A telegram from a minister in Toledo, Ohio, read only: "But a greater power intervened."[15] One letter warned that another attempt to electrocute Willie would be ignoring the will of God and that "even gold and silver electrodes would corrode in the sight of the almighty," while another telegram simply asked, "How do you think Christ would handle this?"[16] Believing with Willie Francis that the failed electrocution was an example of divine intervention, one person wired, "God, not the electric current, was with him."

Other messages contended that a second execution attempt would be "uncivilized" and "barbarous."[17] Miss Jessie Binford, executive director of the Juvenile Protection Association of Chicago, agreed, emphasizing Willie's age: "It would be terribly brutal to make a mere boy go through that again."[18] Others argued that Willie had already suffered enough. "He carried out his part of the bargain," one letter stated, "it was the state that failed to complete the bargain." Another writer acidly warned the governor of possible political consequences: "Do you really mean to let the world know that Gov. Jimmie Davis is nothing but a sadistic moron?"[19] It was this public sentiment that DeBlanc hoped to capitalize on and eventually force the Louisiana Pardons Board to bar a second execution attempt.

Members of the legal profession also publicly argued that a second electrocution attempt would be inappropriate. Jerome Michael, professor of law at Columbia University, contended that a second execution attempt was unnecessary to fulfill the purposes of capital punishment. Michael noted that a person is sentenced to death to deter, through fear of the same consequences, other persons from committing similar crimes, and because the condemned person is a menace to society. "From those points of view," Michael said, "it is utterly irrelevant that the attempt to execute his sentence proved abortive."[20] Joseph Glesler, a well-known Los Angeles attorney, said, "The youth really died mentally, and in the name of humanity, the State should commute his sentence to life imprisonment. The mental death and physical confinement should be sufficient punishment."[21]

Not everyone, however, was sympathetic to Willie's case. There were those who believed that a black convicted of killing a white man should be executed no matter what. It was an important lesson, the thought went, which needed to be continually impressed on blacks. Bertrand DeBlanc was soon becoming a lightning rod of resentment from this element of the population. Recognizing that this sort of public sentiment would be injurious to Willie's case, DeBlanc attempted to blunt the criticisms with a letter to the editor in the St. Martinville *Weekly Messenger*:

> Although some criticism might be directed against me for having taken the case of Willie Francis, I have no apologies to make for taking the case. That is my profession—to defend people and see that they get all that the law allows them. I do not intend to be false to the oath I took as an attorney.
>
> Willie Francis' father came to see me and with tears in his eyes just as any good father would have for his own son no matter what crime he had committed, and he asked me to take the case but he had no money to pay me. I have not received one penny from anyone in this case. But I figure it this way—every man is entitled to his day in Court whether he is rich or poor, black or white. It's not what the Courts decide in this case that is of the greatest importance but the fact that a man is entitled to be heard. Otherwise, we might as well junk our system of law.
>
> I fully realize the tragedy of Andrew's death. I was in France at the time and I was shocked at the news of this brutal murder. I can say without fear of contradiction that I was one of Andrew's best

friends. I spent a lot of time going to the drug store just to talk to him. Being neighbors my three children spent most of their time around his store—and he liked them and they liked him.

Willie Francis was tried and convicted of murder of Andrew Thomas. He was brought to the Parish Jail to be electrocuted. But what happened—the State failed in its attempt to electrocute him. Now the whole thing has changed. A hundred legal questions present themselves as to the legality of another attempt to electrocute him. In a nutshell, the question is Can the State electrocute a man twice? My contention is that it cannot. It matters not whether the person involved be Willie Francis or anyone else—it might have been any of the 23 persons killed on that same chair. It is a legal matter and not a personal one. It involves our constitutional right of freedom from cruel and unusual punishment. It involves our constitutional right of due process of law and double jeopardy.

I have not urged and do not now urge that Willie Francis be set free—I merely seek to prevent his being electrocuted a second time and that course I will pursue to the end. If it means life imprisonment as the alternative then that is what I shall urge.

I have requested and urged the Lieutenant Governor of the State to give my client a stay of execution which he graciously did upon the recommendation of the Supreme Court. He was granted a 30 day stay of execution. Now he will have his day in Court. He will be heard.

I am not associated with any lawyer or firm of lawyers in this case. If any come here they come down on their own.

Therefore, I reiterate, I do not apologize for taking this case. But rather I am proud of having taken this case, because my critics will soon be dead and buried but the principles involved in this case of freedom from fear of cruel and unusual punishment and that of due process and double jeopardy will live as long as the American flag waves on this continent.

Sincerely yours,

Bertrand DeBlanc[22]

DeBlanc's letter and overall public sympathy for Willie Francis were of little value before the Louisiana Supreme Court. On May 15, 1946, the state court, only six days after oral argument, unanimously refused to grant Francis immunity from a second execution attempt.[23] The court decided that "the complaint made by the relator (Francis) is a matter over which the courts have no authority."[24] The Louisiana court reasoned that "[i]n as much as the proceedings had in the district court, up to and including the pronouncing of the sentence of death, were entirely regular, we have no authority to set aside the sentence and release the relator from the sheriff's custody. And the court certainly has no authority to pardon the relator or to commute his sentence."[25]

As he did after the failed execution attempt, Sheriff Ozenne again allowed reporters into the New Iberia cell block to interview Willie. Sitting in his jail cell, Willie calmly accepted the news of the Louisiana Supreme Court's decision. "Things look pretty bad, all right," Willie said. "But maybe the Lord will save me again. However, I'm not afraid to die. I've never been afraid to die. When I pray, I don't pray to be saved. I just pray for courage."[26]

With the state judiciary a clear dead-end, DeBlanc was left with two options—the state Pardons Board or the federal courts. DeBlanc decided first to seek to have the second electrocution attempt canceled by the Board of Reprieves and Pardons of the State of Louisiana. Under the Louisiana Constitution, only the governor had the power to grant reprieves, but he could not of his own authority grant pardons or commute sentences. For that he needed the consent of the Louisiana Pardons Board which consisted of the lieutenant governor, the attorney general, and the presiding judge of the trial court at which the conviction was had.[27] DeBlanc hoped that the Pardons Board would be more receptive to a fairness argument on Willie's behalf than the federal courts. Moreover, the pardons process was essentially a political process with two of its three members state officers. As such, DeBlanc hoped that the Pardons Board would be influenced by the public support for Willie.

The Pardons Board met to hear DeBlanc's plea at 10:00 AM on May 31, 1946, in the Louisiana State Supreme Court chamber in New Orleans. (Unlike most other states, the Supreme Court of Louisiana did not hold its sessions in the state capital, Baton Rouge.) Members of the Pardons Board were Lieutenant Governor J. Emile Veret, Attorney General Fred S. LeBlanc, and the trial judge James D. Simon. Once it convened, the Pardons Board called on the state, represented by L. O. Pecot, the same district attorney who prosecuted Willie at the trial level, to demonstrate why it maintained that a pardon should not be granted.[28]

The state presented as its first witnesses Dennis J. Bazer, warden of the Louisiana State Penitentiary, S. D. Yongue, coroner of St. Martin's Parish, and Vincent Vinezia, the inmate who assisted in the execution attempt. These witnesses were called to support the state's contention that everything possible was done to ensure that the portable electric chair was in proper working condition in St. Martinville. Moreover, the state argued that it was only as a result of an unusual electrical defect that no electricity whatever passed through the body of Willie Francis. Finally, the state wished to prove that no electricity reached Willie and caused him physical pain—essentially arguing that no harm was done by the failed electrocution. Because of its good faith effort and its contention that Willie was in no way harmed by the electrical defect, the state argued that the botched execution did not constitute cruel and unusual punishment and that a pardon was not warranted.

As the state's first witness, Warden Bazer recalled that the portable electric chair had been successfully tested before it was taken from the state penitentiary to St. Martinville. Bazer went on to say that "[u]sually I go along with the chair myself," but that "on this occasion I did not go." His absence, he said, "made no difference."

Mr. Esnault is our chief electrician and he keeps the chair up and whenever he takes the chair out to the one that is carrying it I sent the electrician along with him. I sent Vincent Vinezia, who is an inmate, with Captain Foster. The electrocutioner, who lives in Shreveport, has nothing to do with that—all he does is apply the switch and the chair is supposed to be checked out when it leaves the penitentiary in good shape and, of course, if something goes wrong with the wiring or anything on the way—of course—I am not enough electrician to explain that. Anyhow, that is how it is handled whether it is proper or improper, I don't know.

Warden Bazer then produced a letter he had received "this morning" from D. W. Stakes, general manager of the Texas prison system. Stakes wrote that a convict named John W. Vaughn was sentenced to be executed on April 22, 1938, in Texas. However, "for some reason the electrical appliances failed to function, and after several trials he called the governor." The governor granted Vaughn a seven-day stay of execution and reset the electrocution for April 29, 1938. On April 28, a county court judge issued a temporary restraining order to halt the state officials from carrying out the execution on April 29, whereupon the governor gave the prisoner an additional twenty-four-hour reprieve. Stakes stated, however, that a district court judge "dissolved" the restraining order the next day. "It was then the opinion of the prison officials that the matter was all clear, so Vaughn was duly executed in the early morning of April 30, 1938."

The state next called S. D. Yongue, the coroner of St. Martin's Parish, who recalled the electrocution scene:

As coroner I was watching the procedure of the execution. Willie Francis was strapped in the chair—the apparatus placed in position and a blindfold passed over his eyes with a slit in it whereby he could breathe through his nose. I watched him and I saw—it looked like a man throwing a switch over there—it sounded like it. Nothing special happened right away, then I saw the chair move around two or three times; something seemed to go wrong—there was no further movement of the chair. He threw the switch off and waited a minute and it seemed that he threw it back on again—nothing special happened right away. Directly, the chair swinged around a little bit and the blindfold slipped on his face and he says "take this off I cannot breathe" and I heard somebody say "you are not supposed to breathe" and he said "I am not dying" and after that he was removed from the chair—the switch was thrown off. Some officer had him by the arm and they walked into another room.

After the electrocution attempt, Coroner Yongue examined Willie for any lasting side-effects.

As Coroner of the Parish I supposed it was my duty to examine him afterwards, which I did and found nothing wrong with him except that his pulse was a bit fast—I took my stethoscope and examined his chest—I listened to his heart beat which was perfectly normal except a little bit accelerated, which could easily have been from apprehension or being excited but I found no serious impairment.

In response to questions from the Pardons Board, Yongue stated that he did not find any marks showing any burns. "I examined his forehead and his chest and I saw his legs. Neither did I smell any odor of burned flesh." Yongue further testified that he could not find any evidence of physical pain. Yongue did not know to what extent any mental anguish was inflicted.

Next, the state called Captain Foster and Vincent Vinezia, the penitentiary inmate. Both described how they had set up the portable electric chair for Francis's electrocution that morning and how the chair had worked perfectly when tested. Vinezia testified before the board that

We started about 8:30 to unload. We put it up in the courthouse where the electrocution come off and I hung it all up and go downstairs and stopped my engine and made my test and set the voltage at 2500 and test my ampmeter—A.C. and D.C.—and see that they all work perfectly. Then I run it for about five or ten minutes and see about my engine and generator and see if it is working good and turn it off. Left it until about ten minutes to twelve.

Both Foster, who was not an electrician, and Vinezia who was outside the jail at the time of the electrocution near the pickup truck-based generators, offered conclusions that no electrical shock reached Willie. Foster earthily explained: "We set the chair up and it worked perfect and when you throwed the main switch on there the needle went back to zero. There was a shortage—a little wire was loose and the current went back into the ground instead of going into the nigger." Similarly, Vinezia explained,

Captain Foster, after he threw the switch on the machine, signaled to me to give him more power on the engine so he could raise the voltage, to run it up to 2500 volts and I done so but he hollered to me and told me it would not work so I shut the engine down and go upstairs and checked over it and check it thoroughly and found one of the wires broke loose and I figured it just hit the ground. From the switchboard to the outside to the ground had broke loose and it all went back to the ground.

Lastly, the state called Sheriffs Resweber of St. Martin's Parish and Ozenne of New Iberia. Sheriff Resweber described the arrest and confession of Willie Francis, and according to Resweber, no force was used in getting the confession from Willie in the extradition from Texas to Louisiana. "Everything he told me was voluntary." Sheriff Resweber also recalled the sensation which the murder of Andrew Thomas created in St. Martinville. In response to District Attorney Pecot's question, "Is it not a fact that, after Andrew Thomas was murdered, the whole town was astir over this happening? Was not there a great many rumors flying fast and thick, day and night, which you were trying to run down—you and the State Police?" Resweber replied "Yes, sir. It kept us busy for eight months, night and day."

Sheriff Ozenne's testimony dealt primarily with Willie's condition after the electrocution attempt. Answering the board's question of whether Willie "appeared shocked," Ozenne said that Willie was "a little nervous and shaky." Later, when asked, "At the time of the electrocution did not the chair move around? Was it your opinion or not that he got a shock?", Ozenne evasively answered, "It was something that must have made him move." Ozenne also told the Pardons Board of a scrawl he had found written on the wall of Willie's jail cell which he claimed Willie wrote: "I kill Andrew Thomas and today he is lying in a grave and I am not a killer but I wonder where I am going to be lying and in what kind of grave I don't know."[29]

Having called its witnesses, District Attorney Pecot summarized the state's position. Willie Francis was properly convicted for the murder of Andrew Thomas. Judge Simon, Pecot maintained, "exercised every diligence and every possible care and caution in regard to this case." Similarly, Pecot insisted that Willie's court-appointed counsel "did everything they could possibly do" in Willie's defense. Pecot concluded,

Gentlemen, it seems to me this case is a question as to whether or not this Board is going to follow the judgment of the jury of twelve men who listened most carefully to the evidence before bringing in their verdict, or whether or not, because of an unfortunate happening due to no fault of anyone, but just a mechanical defect, this Board is going to say for that reason we are going to extend this man an extra portion of mercy—we are going to send him to the penitentiary for life instead of making him pay to society for the terrible crime he committed in the Parish of St. Martin.

For Pecot the answer was simple: the judgment of the jury must be followed, and Willie Francis must be electrocuted a second time.

To do otherwise, Pecot argued, would create serious problems down the road for the Louisiana judicial system. "How can we expect [juries] to convict men to pay their debts to society when, afterward, what they have done is undone by another authority of law having the power to do so." Pecot then closed the state's presentation to the Pardons Board with this warning: "There is another side to this case. I don't want to refer to an unpleasant question, but those are facts that happen. We have repeatedly known in the past, unfortunately, of lynchings going on after crimes are committed." Pecot's warning was real. From 1882 to 1946, Louisiana had witnessed 390 lynchings—giving Louisiana the fourth highest rate in the United States. Nearly all the victims were black.

Pecot continued. "The only way and safest way to keep that from happening is to bring justice and punish, according to each case, the guilty party. Society looks to us to do our duty, and I know that you gentlemen are not going to be carried away by sentiment in this case and that you are going to carry the law as far as it is possible to do so." In other words, Willie Francis must become an example to others.

Bertrand DeBlanc stood up and addressed the Pardons Board on Willie's behalf.[30] DeBlanc produced affidavits from six official witnesses to the first execution. One witness described how after "the switch was turned on, Willie Francis' lips puffed out and he groaned and jumped so that the chair rocked on the floor." Father Rousseve who also witnessed the electrocution recalled that "Willie Francis' lips puffed out and his body squirmed and tensed and he jumped so that the chair rocked on the floor." Another official witness likewise described Willie's body as "tensed and stretched" and concluded that "This boy really got a shock when they turned that machine on." DeBlanc argued that to execute Willie would plainly constitute double jeopardy for the same crime as Willie had already suffered the tortures of death: "Everything was done to electrocute this boy up to and including the pulling of the switch and the passing of electricity into his body. He died mentally, his body still exists but through no fault of his."

Observing that no boy fifteen years of age or less who had committed a homicide had been given the death penalty in the history of Louisiana, DeBlanc told the board:

The main point which I wish to stress, gentlemen, is that no man should go to the chair twice. No man should suffer impending death twice. The voice of humanity and justice cries out against such an outrage. You men who compose this honorable body are just and sincere and I know that you will be guided only by the hand of justice. I am not asking that this boy be set free. I am only asking that his sentence be commuted from death to life imprisonment in the state penitentiary. Is that too much to ask for a boy who has gone through the mental and physical torture that he has?

To reinforce his point, DeBlanc mentioned five instances in which an execution attempt had failed. Citing the examples of Daniel in the Lion's Den and the three men in the fiery furnace of King Nebuchadnezzar,

DeBlanc pointed out to the Pardons Board that failed executions often were regarded as instances of divine intervention.

DeBlanc then mentioned the 1889 case of an Englishman, John Lee. Lee had been placed on the hangman's scaffold three times only to have the trap fail each time. Subsequently, the home secretary granted Lee a reprieve. DeBlanc also noted the 1894 Mississippi case of Will Purvis. After the first execution attempt failed because the noose had slipped, allowing Purvis to fall to the ground uninjured, the sheriff immediately attempted to hang him a second time. The crowd witnessing the execution, however, so strongly opposed a second attempt that the sheriff returned Purvis to jail. On appeal, the Mississippi Supreme Court resentenced Purvis to death. Nevertheless, before the sentence could be carried out, a mob rescued Purvis, and he then lived for a time with a succession of friends and relatives. Eventually, the Mississippi governor pardoned Purvis. In 1920 another man confessed to the murder, and the state legislature voted to give Purvis $5,000 as compensation.

Finally, there was the strange case of Lonnie Eaton, a black, who had been sentenced to hang on February 4, 1921, in Monroe, Louisiana, for the murder of a white man. The parish sheriff wrote the governor of Louisiana sometime after February 4, that he had been "so rushed with work that he forgot to hang Eaton." Eventually, Eaton's sentence was reduced from death to life imprisonment. Surely, DeBlanc urged, "the case of Willie Francis, who sat in the electric chair, and had the current go through his body and lived through it is infinitely stronger than a case where the sheriff forgot to hang the condemned man."

DeBlanc had been speaking for nearly twenty minutes, yet, the Pardons Board seemed unmoved by Willie's plight. From his courtroom experience as a trial lawyer before the war, DeBlanc knew what signs to look for in determining whether his argument was making an impression. The hint of a sympathetic smile on a juror's face or a barely perceived nod of the head in approval from a judge were, of course encouraging signs. The Pardons Board members before him, however, sat absolutely still with expressionless faces and unsympathetic stares.

DeBlanc was prepared for such a reaction. Suddenly, he pulled out of his briefcase a picture of Willie strapped into the electric chair. Holding it high for the board to see, DeBlanc challenged the board.

I show you a picture of Willie Francis sitting on the electric chair awaiting death. Look at him strapped to the chair of death, the chair that had already claimed 23 victims, the chair that was later to claim another victim. What chance did he think he had of surviving? Look at him, gentlemen, a beaten animal, do you think there was any hope within that brain? Here you see the picture of a human being facing death, a boy on the threshold of eternity, a picture that speaks a thousand words.

Now almost waving the picture before the board, DeBlanc pleaded,

Here is a boy, who, were it not for a quirk of fate, was about to plunge headlong into the dark abyss of death. What thoughts ran through his mind? Is there any belligerency in that bowed head? Is there anything but humility in those dark features? Is this not a picture of a boy ready and willing to carry out his part of the bargain? Yet the State failed and failed miserably. For this there can be no excuse. The State is to blame and they must shoulder it. Must this boy go through this again? Must he again be strapped to this chair and go through the agony of death for a second time?

Slowly, DeBlanc's voice began to fill with anger, and he spoke sharply to the board:

What assurance, gentlemen, does this boy have that he will go to his death in a humane manner, quickly and painlessly. Supposing that the chair doesn't work a second time? Suppose it doesn't work the third time? That could happen, it's happened once and it could happen again. What is this going to be? An experiment in electricity? An experiment in modern forms of torture? An experiment in cruelty? Is the State of Louisiana trying to outdo the Caesars, the Hitlers, the Tojos, the Nazis, the Gestapo in torture? How long does the State of Louisiana take to kill a man? If we want to make it cruel, let's do it right, let's boil him in oil. Why not burn him at the stake? Or put him on the rack. Then we would be sure that by sundown he would be dead.

Gentlemen, the whole system of capital punishment which is the policy of this State is in jeopardy because of the inhumane method in which it is being inflicted in this case. I say, without equivocation, that unless this Board sees fit to say that this boy will not suffer the torture of death again, the critics of our method of execution shall have ample ground to condemn as a whole our system of punishment.

Gentlemen, I have travelled throughout southern Louisiana since the attempted electrocution on May 3rd, and I can say with certainty that public opinion is against this boy being electrocuted again. If this boy goes back to the chair, they will say that the one and only reason is to satisfy the bestial lust for blood, to satisfy this cry for revenge. If he goes back to the chair, they will say that it is nothing short of murder.

People all over America have written to me expressing their sincere belief that it was the hand of God that stopped the electrocution. They have expressed their horror and disgust at a second attempt. I say in all sincerity that I believe that Willie Francis was not killed because it was not meant that he should be killed, that there was some reason, perhaps not explainable now, but still there was a reason in the design of Fate that this boy should live. Fate acts in strange ways. I, for one, would want no part in his re-execution. When I meet my God face to face, I would not want the stain of his blood on my hands.

DeBlanc paused. Out of the corner of his eye he had seen Lieutenant Governor Veret shift in his chair. He had also noticed the attorney general avoiding eye contact and rearranging the papers before him. DeBlanc wondered if he had struck an exposed nerve. Perhaps, he hoped, the two had begun to feel uncomfortable.

Looking directly at the board, DeBlanc spoke slowly.

You, gentlemen, are the heart and soul of the State of Louisiana in this case. Men and women everywhere are asking: What will Louisiana do in this case? Will they return this boy to the chair? Will Louisiana be fair to the negro? A boy's life is in your hands. I have done my duty. All remedies have been exhausted—the case is in your hands. And may God be your judge.

Three days later, the Pardons Board returned with a unanimous answer.[31] Yes, Willie Francis must be returned to the electric chair. The board gave no reason or explanation for its decision. DeBlanc was stunned. He had thought that the apparent public support for Willie would have turned the tide. He also had hoped that Lieutenant Governor Veret and Attorney General LeBlanc may have been sympathetic to Willie's case.

For DeBlanc, the decision of the Pardons Board left only one recourse: the United States Supreme Court. DeBlanc had taken the precaution of planning for such an eventuality. Recognizing that he did not have the constitutional law background or appellate court experience to handle a case alone before the Supreme Court, DeBlanc early on sought help for Willie's final appeal. Upon the recommendation of Paul Pietri, a friend of DeBlanc's in high school and a book salesman for a legal publishing house, DeBlanc had contacted J. Skelly Wright, a former U.S. attorney in Louisiana now practicing law in Washington, D.C. Pietri lived in New Orleans where he and Wright had been good friends before World War II.[32] It soon became clear to DeBlanc that Wright was the man to prepare Willie's appeal to the Supreme Court. Thus, after hearing the judgment of the Pardons Board, DeBlanc wired Wright simply: "Board refused to commute sentence. File petition and wire me."

On June 4, 1946, DeBlanc and Wright filed a stay of execution and a petition for a writ of *certiorari* with the United States Supreme Court. (A writ of *certiorari* is a pleading filed with the Supreme Court which asks the Court to correct errors made in a lower court. Petitioners must show good reason why the Supreme Court should order the lower court to certify its record for further review.) Francis, they stated, had "already been through the most grueling experience known to man. Appropriate parts of his body had been shaved and wires applied; he was seated in an electric chair and current run through his body."[33] DeBlanc and Wright argued that review of the Louisiana Supreme Court's ruling was appropriate. That same day, Justice Hugo Black issued a stay of execution to allow the Court time to study the petition for *certiorari*.[34] The fate of Willie Francis now rested with the United States Supreme Court in far-away Washington.

IV

Supreme Court Disarray

June 1946 found the Supreme Court in a state of ferment and disarray. The 1945–1946 term completed by the Court was described by one of the justices, Felix Frankfurter, as one of the worst in the Court's history.[1] Public confidence in the badly divided Court had never been lower. A public rift had exploded between Justices Robert Jackson and Hugo Black over judicial ethics.[2] The Jackson-Black feud fueled rumors that the thick marble walls of the Supreme Court building hid similar internal conflicts from the general public.

The Court's problems were not only those of a personal nature. The Court was deeply divided over abstract notions of judicial philosophy. Illustrative of this sharp debate, the 1945–1946 term had been riddled with four to four decisions (Justice Jackson and his ninth vote were missing because of his presence as American prosecutor at the Nuremberg War Crimes Trial)[3] and an unprecedented number of dissenting opinions.[4] The death of Chief Justice Harlan Fiske Stone in April 1946 at the end of the term exacerbated the philosophical differences. The Court was leaderless. By June 1946 a replacement for Stone had still not been named. Many wondered if it really mattered—could any one person be expected to reconcile the differences of the diverse and individualistic membership of the Supreme Court?

The depth of the divisions found on the Court came as a surprise to many. After all, the same president had appointed seven of the nine justices and had elevated another justice, Harlan Fiske Stone, to the Chief Justiceship. Surely, many believed, the Roosevelt appointees would be men cut from the same cloth and would reflect the president's philosophy. The Roosevelt Court was expected to be unlike the "nine old men" of the 1930s when the Supreme Court was unable to agree in a large number of cases.

During that critical period, the Court was locked in battle with the Roosevelt administration and within itself over the constitutionality of New Deal legislation. A bloc of four justices disapproved the economic legislation supported by the Congress and president. On the other side, three justices supported the measures. Two justices were the "swing men" between the blocs. The result was division and inconsistency. The National Industrial Recovery Act, the Agricultural Adjustment Act, the Bituminous Coal Conservation Act and the Municipal Bankruptcy Act were struck down as unconstitutional.[5] Yet, the Court upheld the Tennessee Valley Authority Act and its concept of federal aid to public power projects.[6] The divisiveness was so great that during the 1936–1937 term nearly 20 percent of the opinions issued by the Court were accompanied by written dissents.

Roosevelt was frustrated by the Supreme Court's actions, but without a single Court appointment through his first term, the president appeared powerless to effect a change in the Court's will. Roosevelt decided, however, to secure Supreme Court sanctioning of his New Deal legislation through his famed "Court-packing" plan to enlarge the Court with his own appointments.[7] Both the country and the Congress soundly rejected this plan. Roosevelt ultimately got his way, however, as death and resignation opened the way for his own appointments to the Court. By the end of his presidency, Roosevelt had the unique opportunity to restructure virtually the entire membership of the Supreme Court. It was expected that in a Roosevelt Court dissension would subside and unanimity would increase.

The men appointed by Roosevelt were highly talented and individualistic. His first appointment, Hugo LaFayette Black, strongly criticized at the time, turned out to be one of the best. The son of an Alabama storekeeper and a graduate of the University of Alabama law school, Black practiced law in Birmingham following graduation. In 1927 he was elected to the United States Senate where he became a powerful figure. Black reached national prominence, heading several committees that delved into abuses of marine and airline subsidies and the activities of lobbying groups. More importantly, he was a loyal New Deal Democrat and one of the president's strongest supporters in the Senate.

Black's appointment to the Court caused a furor when he was accused of having been a member of the Ku Klux Klan. The controversy gradually subsided after Black went on nationwide radio, admitting his one-time membership in the Klan but assuring the people that it had long been terminated. He strongly repudiated the prejudice for which the organization stood. By 1946, after only eight years of service, Black was the senior associate justice on the Court. The sixty-year-old Black was recognized as the leader of the liberal or activist wing of the Court.

Less than six months after the Black appointment, President Roosevelt named Stanley Reed of Kentucky as his second appointment. A successful Kentucky lawyer, Reed came to Washington when President Herbert Hoover named him general counsel of the Federal Farm Board; he served there from 1929 to 1932. In a rare move, Reed was retained in the new administration and served as general counsel for the Reconstruction Finance Corporation from 1932 to 1935. In 1935 Roosevelt appointed him solicitor general of the United States, where he diligently, although not too successfully, defended the constitutionality of the experimental New Deal legislation before a hostile Supreme Court. Reed's oral argument style was so ardent that he once fainted in midargument. Nominated to the Supreme Court in 1938, the Kentucky Democrat was seen as the "middleman" of the Court in that he swung the balance on important issues, sometimes taking one side and sometimes the other.

Following the death of Justice Benjamin Nathan Cardozo in July 1938, Viennese-born Felix Frankfurter was appointed to the Court in January 1939. Frankfurter began his legal career as an assistant United States attorney in 1906. During World War I, he was an assistant, in turn, to the secretaries of war and labor, and became chairman of the War Policies Board in 1918. In Washington, Frankfurter became friendly with many notable figures, including Frankfurter's personal hero, Oliver Wendell Holmes. (Frankfurter later filled Holmes's "scholar's seat" on the bench.)

Frankfurter attained national prominence as a professor at the Harvard Law School. He wielded considerable behind-the-scenes influence in the Roosevelt administration. Earlier, Frankfurter had received considerable national attention with his defense of labor and civil liberties, which included the Sacco-Vanzetti and Tom Mooney cases.[8] These activities, combined with his role as a founding member of the *New Republic* and the American Civil Liberties Union and with his work with the National Association for the Advancement of Colored People, earned him a reputation as a leading liberal spokesman. In fact, Frankfurter's reputation as a left-wing liberal was such that at his Senate confirmation hearings he felt it necessary to declare that he was not a communist.

At the time of Frankfurter's appointment the liberal magazine *Nation* commented that "Mr. Roosevelt gave the Court new vitality with the appointment of Justice Black; he gave it new and rich talents for conciliation, adjustment, and statesmanship in Frankfurter. . . . From the time he was instrumental in saving Mooney from execution to his defense of Sacco and Vanzetti, Frankfurter has shown his devotion to justice and his courage."[9] Once on the Court, however, Frankfurter disappointed many of his supporters. He quickly became an outspoken advocate of "judicial self-restraint," and was considered to be a conservative on the bench. Frankfurter urged that the Court defer to the executive and, particularly, the legislative branches of government on many important issues, even when fundamental civil liberties were at stake.

Justice William O. Douglas, who at forty-one was the youngest of the justices, was appointed to the Court by Roosevelt in March 1939, to succeed Justice Louis D. Brandeis. Roosevelt had wanted to place a westerner on the Court, and Douglas, born in Minnesota and raised in the State of Washington, fit the bill. He was a graduate of Columbia law school, and was later a member of the Columbia and Yale law faculties. Douglas came to Washington in 1934 to join the newly created Securities and Exchange Commission (SEC), serving as its chairman from 1936 to 1939. As SEC chairman, Douglas was a vigorous opponent of now outlawed Wall Street business practices. On the Court, Douglas was a liberal whose early record was nearly identical to that of Justice Black. In fact, there was complete unanimity between Douglas and Black during Douglas' first two terms on the Court.

Justice Frank Murphy, a graduate of the University of Michigan Law School, was appointed to the Court in 1940. Murphy had been an early and strong supporter of Roosevelt in 1932. Before reaching the Supreme Court, the bachelor justice had been mayor of Detroit, governor of Michigan, high commissioner to the Philippines, and attorney general of the United States. An infantry captain in World War I and a member of the Army of Occupation in Germany, Justice Murphy was absent from the Court while serving on temporary duty as an infantry officer in Fort Benning, Georgia, just before World War II—much to the chagrin of the chief justice. The tall, gaunt Murphy was a faithful Catholic and actively participated in the affairs of the church. A consistent liberal spokesman, Justice Murphy's opinions displayed such deep sympathy and concern for the constitutional and legal rights of the underprivileged and unpopular that a new maxim was soon coined in the nation's capital: "justice tempered with Murphy."[10]

In 1941 President Roosevelt appointed Robert H. Jackson to the Supreme Court. Regarded as having a brilliant legal mind, Jackson passed the New York bar examination without having graduated from law school. A longtime friend of Roosevelt's, Jackson joined the New Deal government as general counsel of the Bureau of Internal Revenue in 1934, where he had made a name for himself by winning a much publicized lawsuit against the wealthy Mellon family. After two years with the Bureau, Jackson served in rapid succession as assistant attorney general, solicitor general, and attorney general (where he succeeded Frank Murphy) in the Roosevelt Justice Department. As his position in the Justice Department rose, so did Jackson's influence with Roosevelt. Prior to his appointment, Jackson was considered one of the president's closest advisers.

In 1945 Jackson acceded to President Truman's request that he become the United States chief prosecutor at the Nuremberg Nazi War Crimes Trial. Jackson was successful at Nuremberg, but his experience in Germany effected a profound change in his philosophy. The once libertarian judicial activist who had often sided with Black, Douglas, and Murphy became, upon his return, a markedly conservative interpreter of the Bill of Rights. Jackson began to take a restrictive stance on matters affecting state criminal justice procedures. In 1946 his record was relatively close to that of Justice Frankfurter. Yet, his votes on the Court did contain enough surprises to make it difficult to count his vote one way or another.

The last Roosevelt appointment to the Supreme Court was Wiley Rutledge. Born in Kentucky, Rutledge was an open and friendly man who as dean of law at Iowa University was a vocal supporter of Roosevelt's court-packing plan. He thereby caught the president's eye. In 1939 President Roosevelt appointed Rutledge to the United States Court of Appeals for the District of Columbia Circuit. In 1943 he was elevated to the Supreme Court, not because of his judicial credentials but rather for a much simpler reason. As Roosevelt explained to Rutledge: "Wiley, we had a number of candidates for the Court who were highly qualified, but they didn't have geography—you have that."[11]

On the Court of Appeals, Rutledge developed a reputation for reaching decisions clearly illustrating his demand for protection of certain basic human rights. This reputation was reinforced by his opinions on the Supreme Court. Rutledge was one of the Court's liberals and almost invariably could be found voting with Justices Black, Douglas, and Murphy.

The newest member of the bench was Justice Harold Hitz Burton, appointed in 1945 by President Truman to succeed retiring Justice Owen Roberts. Roberts was the only pre-Roosevelt appointee to last through Roosevelt's twelve years in office. By 1945 he had earned a reputation as a conservative member of the Court. To replace him, President Truman chose Burton, a senator from Ohio and the first Republican to join the Court since the Hoover administration. Burton had been a popular mayor of Cleveland and was elected to the Senate in 1940. While in the Senate, he was on a Senate Committee, chaired by then Senator Truman, investigating fraudulent war claims against the government and had gained a warm friendship and the confidence of the future president. After only one term on the Court, Burton already was regarded as one of the Court's most conservative members.

Presiding as chief justice, over perhaps the most impressive collection of judicial talent ever to sit on the Court at one time, was Harlan Fiske

Stone. A New England Republican from New Hampshire, Stone was appointed to the Court in 1924 as an associate justice by a fellow Amherst classmate, Calvin Coolidge. Prior to his appointment, Stone had had a successful career as a Wall Street lawyer, as professor of law and dean at Columbia, and as attorney general in the Coolidge cabinet. In the cabinet post, Stone cleaned up the mess left in the attorney general's office by Harry M. Daugherty and the Teapot Dome Scandal of the Harding administration, reorganized the Department of Justice, and recommended the appointment of J. Edgar Hoover to breathe life into an ineffective Federal Bureau of Investigation. On the Court, Stone found himself on the liberal wing of the Court with Justices Cardozo and Brandeis. In June 1941 President Roosevelt named Stone chief justice to succeed the retiring Charles Evans Hughes. With the number of Roosevelt appointees on the Court, it was expected that Stone would return the Court to an era of consensus and agreement.

By 1946, however, the Supreme Court was badly divided—both personally and philosophically. Perhaps it was inevitable that nine complex, talented, and strong-willed men with disparate backgrounds would eventually engage in personal clashes. Since at least 1941 rumors and hints of infighting among the Roosevelt appointees had been filtering out of the Supreme Court building. Court-watchers began to detect acerbic references in the written opinions of the justices, directed toward one another. Articles began to appear in the press reporting antagonism among them.[12] There were rumors of personal differences between Douglas and Frankfurter; Black and Frankfurter; Black and Jackson; and Murphy and Jackson.

Many of the reports of bitterness between the justices were accurate. For example, Justice Frankfurter complained to his diary that Justice Burton was naive and "hasn't the remotest idea how malignant men like Black and Douglas not only can be, but are."[13] As one journalist commented at the time, "only the fountains seemed serene" at the Supreme Court.[14]

The personal animosity between the justices was aggravated by rumors of political ambitions of several justices. Justices began to suspect that political motives were distracting their brethren from the work of the Court or, worse yet, had begun to influence judicial decisions. In 1944 President Roosevelt considered tapping Justice William O. Douglas as his vice-presidential running mate before settling on Harry Truman.[15] In 1946 there were already rumors that Douglas would become the Democratic vice-presidential nominee in 1948 to aid President Truman with liberal and independent voters. In fact, Truman had already asked Douglas to become secretary of interior following Harold Ickes's resignation, as a prelude to a possible vice-presidential nomination, but

Douglas declined.[16] There was also speculation that Justice Jackson was positioning himself to run for governor of his home state of New York.[17]

The internal problems of the Court exploded in an episode that shocked the country and, in the words of one historian, represented "the most rancorous display of judicial temper in nearly a century."[18] On June 10, 1946, Justice Robert Jackson made a startling and bitter public attack against Justice Hugo Black.[19] Jackson had been considered by President Roosevelt for the position of chief justice in 1941, but the appointment instead went to Harlan Fiske Stone. Roosevelt promised Jackson—or so Jackson believed—the chief justiceship the next time around. In 1946 the office of chief justice was again vacant. Jackson was again a candidate and expected President Truman to honor Roosevelt's previous "commitment."[20] However, when the appointment went to Treasury Secretary Fred Vinson, it was too bitter of a pill for Jackson to swallow quietly.

Jackson had concluded an exhausting year's work in Nuremberg as American chief prosecutor of the Nazi war criminals. Indeed, Jackson's absence had provoked much irritation among his colleagues. In a letter shortly before his death, Chief Justice Stone remarked, "Jackson is away conducting his high-grade lynching party in Nuremberg. I don't mind what he does to the Nazis, but I hate to see the pretense that he is running a court and proceeding according to common law. This is a little too sanctimonious a fraud to meet my old-fashioned ideas."[21] While away, Jackson had heard rumors that Black and friends had frantically lobbied against his promotion. There were even reports that Black, Douglas, and Murphy had gone to President Truman and threatened to resign if Jackson was appointed chief justice.[22] Strained, overworked, and 3,000 miles from home, Jackson lashed out.[23]

In a long letter cabled to the chairman of the House and Senate Judiciary committees, Jackson charged that Black had made "public threats to the President" to resign if Jackson were appointed chief justice.[24] Jackson then implied that Black's opposition to his nomination could be traced to a 1945 case before the Court, *Jewell Ridge Coal Co.* v. *Local No. 6167, United Mine Workers*,[25] in which Black's law partner from twenty years before had appeared as counsel to argue the case. At that time, Jackson, both in private and in a little noted brief opinion, had questioned the propriety of Black's participation in the decision. Yet, Black sat on the case and eventually cast the deciding vote in a five to four decision in favor of his former partner's client.

In his statement from Nuremberg, Jackson contended that Black was getting even with Jackson for Jackson's earlier exposé of questionable judicial ethics. Black had acted as a "stealthy assassin," by "mysteriously and irresponsibly" leaking "stories of feuds" to the newspapers. Jackson objected to these methods and only sought, he said, to give the true facts "to the responsible Committees of Congress." Jackson concluded his statement by complaining that the employment of a justice's ex-law partners as counsel before the Court threatened to "bring the Court into disrepute" and "if it is ever repeated while I am on the bench I will make my Jewell Ridge opinion look like a letter of recommendation by comparison."[26]

It was not surprising, then, that the antagonism between Black and Jackson carried over into the Court's 1946 term. In a diary which he kept throughout his years on the Court, Burton chronicled a small, yet significant incident illustrating the continued cold relations between the two justices. The incident also points out a social trait for which political Washington has always had a particular fondness, namely, the exhibition of superficial compatibility to conceal deeper and contrary feelings. Usually, such cold formal politeness could be found in a strained marriage, a chance social meeting between political rivals, or during acrimonious debates on the floor of the House or Senate. Now, it was plainly present in the Conference Room of the United States Supreme Court.

On October 10, 1946, four months after the Jackson-Black feud first hit the newspapers and less than six weeks before oral argument on the *Francis* case, Justice Burton recorded:

I noticed this morning when we came to conference—where each Justice greets the other—Justice Jackson was sitting beside me . . . when Justice Black came in. Justice Black shook hands with him immediately—and Justice Jackson said, "Good morning, Hugo." Also, during the conference today, Justices Jackson and Black joined in a brief discussion—all in the best of quiet manners. I mention this because of the popular idea . . . that they could not speak to each other.[27]

Yet, all was not right between the two justices, as Burton showed in his next sentence. "These were the first instances of their speaking to each other that I have seen this fall."

The personal discord that existed between the justices not only embarrassed the Court, but also impeded its efficient functioning. Justice Stanley Reed recognized this in a July 8, 1946, letter to Frankfurter: "Bob's statement about the Court will have some unfortunate results. A few sores are hard to heal. He and Hugo will be enemies while both serve."[28]

It was in such a poisoned atmosphere that the 1946 Court grappled with a persistent and difficult question: "What is the proper judicial role of the United States Supreme Court?" With regard to this question, the Court found itself divided into two hostile camps. On the one side were Chief Justice Stone and Justices Frankfurter, Jackson, and Burton who believed in a restrained judicial role. On the other side were Justices Black, Douglas, Murphy, and Rutledge who believed in an active judicial role. In the middle was Justice Stanley Reed who shifted between the two divergent poles deciding which view should prevail.

The Frankfurter-led wing of the Court believed that the judicial process should only give effect "to the will of the law."[29] Judges do not make law; rather, they find it. As Chief Justice John Marshall said in 1824:

Courts are mere instruments of the law, and can will nothing. When they are said to exercise a discretion, it is a mere legal discretion, a discretion to be exercised in discerning the course prescribed by law; and when that is discerned, it is the duty of the court to follow it. Judicial power is never exercised for the purpose of giving effect to the will of the judge; always for the purpose of giving effect to the will of the legislature; or in other words, to the will of the law.[30]

Marshall's judicial philosophy echoes the classic English model of Sir William Blackstone and Francis Bacon. In his *Commentaries*, Blackstone wrote that a judge is "sworn to determine, not according to his own private judgment, but according to the known law and customs of the land; not delegated to pronounce a new law, but to maintain and expound the old one."[31] Similarly, Bacon said, "Judges ought to remember, that their office is *jus dicere*, and not *jus dare*; to interpret law, and not to make law, or give law."[32]

Under this philosophy of judicial self-restraint, the Supreme Court should pay sufficient respect and defer whenever possible to the judgment of the state courts and legislatures. The control of crime and the finding of punishment, according to the Frankfurter point of view, was a legislative concern. A legislature is the true representative of the people's wishes in a democratic society. By contrast, the Supreme Court is not an elected body and not a good reflex of a democratic society. As such, a legislature's judgment regarding social policies should rarely, if ever, be overturned by an unelected Supreme Court.

A Supreme Court justice must be a passionless vehicle for accepting the facts as developed by the trial bench and then applying the law in a "principled" manner using the tools of reason. Little creativity is possible; the rules supposedly preexist, and the facts are said to speak for themselves. There is no room for personal judgment and personal feelings. Justice Frankfurter expressed this view well in his refusal to hold unconstitutional a West Virginia compulsory flag salute in public schools. "Were my purely personal views relevant," Frankfurter said, "I should wholeheartedly associate myself with general libertarian views in the Court's opinion. . . . [But] as a member of this Court I am not justified in writing my private notions of policy into the Constitution, no matter how deeply I cherish them or how mischievous I may deem their disregard."[33]

The other wing of the Court, led by Justice Black, saw a much larger and more active role for the Court in reviewing the judgments of the state legislature. This bloc, which Frankfurter disparagingly referred to as "the Axis,"[34] believed that the Court must at times become an active participant in social affairs, particularly those matters where the executive and legislative branches are paralyzed by concern over their own tenure and individual careers. If an unjust status quo exists with respect to the poor, minorities, or members of unpopular groups as a result a legislative enactment or executive act and the legislature or executive are unable to or unwilling to correct this situation, then the Court must be prepared to fill the breach. Justice Hugo Black believed that "Under our constitutional system, courts stand against any winds that blow as havens or refuge for those who might otherwise suffer because they are helpless, weak or outnumbered, or because they are nonconforming victims of prejudice and public excitement."[35]

The personal and philosophical divisions reached such proportions that during the 1944–1945 term, the Court surpassed its own record for internecine warfare. Cold statistical analysis reveals the depth of the Court's troubled waters. Fifty-eight percent of the Court's opinions were accompanied by dissents. This dwarfed the 20 percent disagreement rate reached during the height of the battle between the president and the Court over the New Deal legislation during the 1936–1937 term. Moreover, thirty of the Roosevelt Court's decisions had been decided by a five to four vote—the greatest number in Supreme Court history. Indeed, the Court was not functioning as one deliberative body.[36]

The Court made little improvement in its record over the 1945–1946 term. Because of Justice Jackson's absence at Nuremberg, the Court was composed of only eight justices. Despite the presence of one less vote to file a dissenting opinion, the intracourt rancor continued. There was only a slight drop in the rate of disagreement—to 56 percent. Moreover, thirteen cases were decided five to three, and in six cases the vote was four to three. And awaiting Jackson's return in the fall of 1946 were sixteen cases over which the Court was deadlocked four to four.[37]

In the 1945–1946 term, there was also a sharp increase in the number of concurring opinions filed by the justices. A concurring opinion is usually filed by a justice who agrees with the result reached by the Court but disagrees with a part of the Court's reasoning and feels compelled to explain the discrepancy. Over the 1945–1946 term, 37 of the 137 majority decisions announced by the Court included a concurring opinion.[38] In many instances, the majority voted together for the same result but for different reasons. In these cases, lawyers found it impossible to tell what the law of the case was or would be in the future. The number of dissenting opinions, concurring opinions, and five to four votes generated by the Court caused a great deal of confusion, not only for the parties before the Court but also for the state legislatures, the Congress, state courts, and federal courts. Lawyers could not predict the results of the Supreme Court's future decisions.

The Supreme Court speaks almost entirely through its decisions and opinions. The decisions rendered by the Court not only resolve the immediate case before it, but also establish principles for the guidance of lower courts and the legislature. A decision reached by a five to four vote or fragmented by multiple concurring or dissenting opinions fails to provide authoritative judicial guidance.

Attempting to hold together this broadly divided Court was Chief Justice Stone. As an associate justice of the Supreme Court, Stone had been a legend. During the 1920s and 1930s the phrase "Holmes, Brandeis and Stone dissenting" seemed to be routinely appended to the conservative Court's decisions—many of which were later overturned in accord with the reasoning of Stone's prescient dissents. As chief justice, however, Stone was at best ineffective.[39]

Although the chief justice is "first among equals," the office carries with it very few formal powers. The chief justice manages the docket, presents cases, conducts conferences, and when he is in the majority, assigns opinions. The influence of a chief justice can only be measured by an elusive standard of leadership skills.

The Court has been compared to a symphony orchestra—the qualities that come out of the individual members depend to no small extent on the qualities that the leader draws out of them. In presiding over the conferences in which the justices discuss and decide cases, Stone's predecessor, Charles Evan Hughes, "was like witnessing Toscanini lead an orchestra."[40] By contrast, Stone conducted his conferences in an easygoing manner as if they were New England town meetings.[41] Discussion was open-ended and seemed to be endless.[42] Stone could not, or would not, cut short discussions and call for the conference to proceed so as to get its work done. He exhibited little, if any, leadership.[43] A consensus at conference was difficult to reach, and dissenting and concurring opinions flourished. Stone himself recognized his difficulties in "getting my team of wild horses to pull together."[44] By 1946 the Court was coming under increasing attack for its inability to achieve agreement in its decisions, while Stone struggled to hold the "wild horses" together despite severe personal and philosophical differences.

On April 22, 1946, Justice Stone collapsed on the bench while Justice Douglas was reading a decision to which Chief Justice Stone had written a dissent. The justices carried Stone off the bench to a nearby couch where three physicians diagnosed the illness as a "slight attack of indigestion."[45] In actuality, Stone had suffered a massive cerebral hemorrhage. Later that afternoon, Stone slipped into a coma and died at the age of seventy-three. Played as the recessional at the chief justice's funeral was the Hymn "The Strife Is O'er."[46] For Stone, the strife of the Court was over, but for his successor it had just begun.

On June 7, 1946, President Truman nominated his friend Frederick M. Vinson of Kentucky to become the thirteenth chief justice of the United States. Vinson had served in the House of Representatives as an influential member of the House Ways and Means Committee and had worked vigorously for passage of President Roosevelt's New Deal programs. In 1938 Roosevelt appointed him a judge on the United States Court of Appeals for the District of Columbia Circuit. By 1943, however, Roosevelt needed Vinson's economic expertise in the executive branch. Over the next two years Vinson served successively as director of the Office of Economic Stabilization, director of the Federal Loan Administration, and as director of the Office of War Mobilization and Reconversion.

During these two years in the executive branch, Vinson worked closely with the then vice-president, Harry S Truman. Vinson became a trusted friend and adviser to Truman, and in 1945 Truman appointed Vinson secretary of the treasury. One year later, Vinson was nominated to replace Chief Justice Stone. In Truman's opinion, Vinson was the one person "capable of unifying the . . . Court and thereby improving its public image."[47] Truman hoped that Vinson, with his years of administrative experience and his skills at negotiation and compromise, might restore harmony to a deeply divided court.

The decision-making process of the Supreme Court, however, is not easily susceptible to backslapping compromise. Deep philosophical differences cannot be solved by force of personality. As a clear intellectual inferior to Black, Douglas, Frankfurter, and Jackson, there was little hope that Vinson would be able to provide the intellectual leadership necessary to end the rash of five to four decisions that had plagued the Court. At best, the new chief justice might be able to soften the Court's convulsive personality clashes and prevent further public outbursts.

The low state of the Supreme Court in mid-1946 is described in this letter from Justice Felix Frankfurter to his colleague, Justice Frank Murphy:

June 10, 1946

Dear Frank:

Today ends another epoch in the history of the Court—the quinquennium of the 1941–45 terms. Of course there have been many shortcomings in the past and some striking instances of what Chief Justice Hughes so aptly called "self-inflicted wounds." But if I were transplanted into a classroom and had to tell my students what I thought about the period just closed, I would have to say the following—assuming, of course that I lived up to Holmes' injunction "never lie to the young":

1. Never before in the history of the Court were so many of its members influenced in decisions by considerations extraneous to the legal issues that supposedly control decisions.

2. Never before have members of the Court so often acted contrary to their convictions on the governing legal issues in decisions.

3. Never before has so large a proportion of the opinions fallen short of requisite professional standards.

It would relieve me of much unhappiness if I did not feel compelled to have these convictions. But they are based on a study of the history of the Court which began from the day I left Law School, just forty years ago and on first-hand and detailed knowledge of what has been going on inside the Court during the last thirty-five years.

Of all earthly institutions this Court seems nearest to having, for me, sacred aspects. Having been endowed by nature with zestful vitality, I still look forward hopefully to the era which will open on the first Monday of October next.

Ever yours,

F. F.[48]

On June 10, 1946, the same day on which Frankfurter issued this stinging appraisal of the Supreme Court and the same day on which the Jackson-Black feud blew up in public, the Supreme Court issued a little noted order. The Court denied DeBlanc and Wright's petition for a writ of *certiorari*.[49] The Court had decided not to review the decision of the Louisiana Supreme Court to send Willie Francis to the electric chair a second time. As a result of the Court's action, Justice Black's June 4 stay of execution was automatically revoked. The State of Louisiana was permitted to begin immediately with its plans for a second execution attempt.

Skelly Wright was notified by phone of the Court's order. Wright was stunned at the news. He had recognized that only one out of ten petitions for *certiorari* are ever granted by the Court; yet, he thought that Willie's unique plight certainly merited Supreme Court review. Deeply disappointed, Wright wired DeBlanc at his office in St. Martinville: "Supreme Court denied writ Francis case today."[50]

DeBlanc immediately left his office to tell Willie the bad news. Ever since DeBlanc and Wright had filed the *certiorari* petition on June 4, Willie had been anxiously hoping that the Supreme Court would take his case. When Willie saw DeBlanc approach his cell at the New Iberia jail, he knew that something was wrong. Usually, DeBlanc brought Willie candy and comic books. This time he bore only a grieving expression.

Hearing the news of the Court's decision, Willie slowly sat down on his small metal cot. Willie was motionless on the outside, but his mind was racing on the inside. He began to think of what he would have to endure for a second time. He was afraid—afraid of the waiting and afraid of the pain of the electric chair.[51]

Willie's thoughts were interrupted by the noise of reporters who had rushed to the jail to get his reaction to the Court's decision. DeBlanc intervened. He would not allow Willie to face the reporters at such a difficult time. Willie motioned with his hand to bring the reporters in. When asked for his comments, Willie said simply, "I'm praying harder than ever. Got myself a new prayer book. All I can do is wait."[52] Wait and pray, that is, while the State of Louisiana made plans to try again.

Within twenty-four hours, Willie's prayers were answered. The next morning, a clerk at the Supreme Court was routinely reviewing the Court orders from the previous day when he discovered, to his dismay, that a horrible mistake had been made. Symbolic of the Court's disarray, the Court had botched its handling of the petition for writ of *certiorari* filed by Wright and DeBlanc. Apparently, an error had been made in the reporting of the Court's order regarding Willie. The Court had actually decided to grant Willie's appeal and held that *certiorari* should be "granted" and not "denied."[53] In addition, a stay of execution had been issued pending final disposition of the case by the Court. The clerk's office immediately called Governor Jimmie Davis in the event the governor should authorize a second execution attempt based on the wrong information. Hearing that the Court's order had been inaccurately reported, Davis told a nervous clerk that Willie had not been executed and that he would abide by the Court's stay of execution.[54]

That afternoon, DeBlanc arrived at Willie's jail cell carrying candy, comic books, and a wide smile. Willie was feeling "pretty good" over the surprising news. Facing yet another rash of reporters, Willie explained, "It's funny, sort of. I was expecting good news yesterday, and I got bad. And now when I'm expecting bad news, its good."[55]

V

Briefs and Oral Argument

Skelly Wright and Bertrand DeBlanc immediately began to plan their strategy for the appearance before the Supreme Court. Although they had persuaded the Court to review the judgment of the Louisiana Supreme Court against Willie, in reality their work had only begun. Now they had to prepare a brief on the merits of the case which had to be filed by late October with the Supreme Court. Such briefs, which are usually fully documented with case law, constitutional interpretation, and policy arguments, are the primary source of information for the justices. Within four weeks of filing their brief, Wright and DeBlanc could expect to appear before the nine justices to present oral argument on Willie's case.

The task awaiting the two was difficult. First with DeBlanc in St. Martinville, Louisiana, and Wright in Washington, D.C., the lawyers had a logistical problem in coordinating litigation strategy. A separation of 1,000 miles caused at least a four- to five-day delay in correspondence by mail. In addition, lengthy telegraphs discussing legal arguments would be at least as expensive as telephone calls. Such expenses represented a hardship for DeBlanc who was struggling to make ends meet while developing a law practice in rural Louisiana.

Expenses were also of concern to Skelly Wright, who was not receiving a fee from the impoverished Francis family for undertaking Willie's appeal. Like DeBlanc, Wright had just returned from World War II and was attempting to build a private law practice. Although taking on Willie's appeal held little or no promise of financial renumeration, Wright was excited about the prospect of his first case before the Supreme Court. The case meant all the more to him because it had arisen in his home state of Louisiana.

Skelly Wright was born in New Orleans. A graduate of Loyola University with degrees in philosophy and law, he had been appointed assistant United States attorney for Louisiana in 1937. In that post, Wright made a name for himself with his prosecution of the "Louisiana Scandal" cases. Wright was regularly in the headlines, with a large percentage of his cases resulting in convictions. He successfully prosecuted narcotics cases with 98 percent convictions. When World War II erupted, Wright was commissioned in the Coast Guard as a lieutenant (j.g.) in January 1942. After a year of sea duty on a submarine chaser, Wright was stationed in London and later landed in France on "D-plus-4" Day on Omaha Beach.

Following the war, Wright resigned his post as assistant United States attorney in New Orleans to begin the private practice of law in Washington, D.C.

Recognizing each other's financial limitations, Wright and DeBlanc decided to avoid the prohibitive expense of long distance telephone calls and began a series of cross-country letters. This method was ponderous and often frustrating; it lacked the spontaneity to be gained in oral communications. Despite these obstacles, the two spent the summer of 1946 exchanging ideas in numerous letters.

Through their correspondence, they slowly began to develop a strategy to overcome their major problem: How to persuade the Supreme Court, in a case for which there was no precedent, to support Willie's cause. In its 150-year history, the United States Supreme Court had never heard a case involving a failed execution attempt. Wright and DeBlanc, in their attempts to convince the Court of the validity of Willie's cause, would have to write their arguments on a *tabula rasa*. This foray into unknown legal territory was complicated by the bitter divisions that existed on the Supreme Court. How could two lawyers fresh out of the service get five justices of this fractured Court to agree on novel, untried constitutional arguments?

Wright and DeBlanc decided to act boldly and present a new argument before the Supreme Court, so that the judgment of the Louisiana Supreme Court could be overturned. On October 28, 1946, Wright and DeBlanc filed a twelve-page brief on the merits before the Supreme Court. Under traditional ideas of constitutional law, Wright and DeBlanc might have been expected to argue only that a second execution attempt would violate the due process clause of the Fourteenth Amendment to the Constitution of the United States. Wright and DeBlanc, however, went far beyond the orthodoxy. They argued that a second execution attempt would deny Willie Francis due process under the Fourteenth Amendment because it would subject him to double jeopardy, prohibited by the Constitution's Fifth Amendment, and cruel and unusual punishment, prohibited by the Constitution's Eighth Amendment. Wright and DeBlanc's approach, while apparently a mere legal subtlety on the surface, actually struck at the heart of the Frankfurter-Black battle over judicial restraint. In other words, the Court was asked, contrary to more than a century of accepted law, to apply parts of the Bill of Rights to Louisiana.

In an 1831 case, *Barron* v. *Baltimore*,[1] Chief Justice John Marshall had written for the Supreme Court that the first eight amendments (often referred to as the "Bill of Rights") applied to and limited only the power of the federal government. The Bill of Rights, which guarantees such important liberties as freedom of press, speech, and religion, and which assures a fair trial, did not apply to the governments of the individual states. As a result, virtually no restrictions were placed on the states with respect to the formulation and administration of penal codes. In the years before the Civil War, states were free to execute their own notions of criminal justice. If a state, for example, wished to give an individual an unfair trial, there was no basis for the Supreme Court of the United States to review and overturn such an occurrence. The matter was entrusted entirely to the state and the state court's interpretation of its own constitution.

In 1868, however, the Fourteenth Amendment was adopted. The first section of the amendment forbids the states to deny its citizens the "privilege or immunities of citizens of the United States," or to deprive any person their constitutional guarantee of "liberty . . . without due process of law," or to deny them "the equal protection of the laws." These limitations apply to the states exclusively and not to the federal government. A means became available by which the Supreme Court could protect a citizen from denial of due process by an oppressive state.

What, however, did due process mean? In 1877 the Supreme Court rejected an argument that it meant that the Fourteenth Amendment was intended to incorporate or automatically extend the Bill of Rights to the states. After 1877 the Court consistently held that the due process clause of the Fourteenth Amendment imposed undefined "civilized" standards on the states which were not applicable to the express guarantees of the first eight amendments. Justice Benjamin Nathan Cardozo wrote in *Snyder* v. *Commonwealth of Massachusetts*: "The due process clause of the Fourteenth Amendment did not withdraw the freedom of a state to enforce its own notions of fairness in the administration of criminal justice *unless* in so doing *it offends some principle of justice* so rooted in the tradition and conscience of our people as to be *ranked as fundamental.*"[2] Cardozo did not divulge how he and the other justices determined those principles of justice. Then, and often now, due process is whatever the Supreme Court says it is.

Frankfurter embraced Cardozo's view of due process, a view that was well suited to Frankfurter's ideas of judicial restraint. The Constitution largely left the domain of criminal justice to the states. Frankfurter believed that the Fourteenth Amendment did not disturb that distribution of power between the states and the central government. Rather, the amendment merely restricted somewhat the previously limitless freedom which the states had in making and enforcing their criminal laws. Certainly, Frankfurter contended, the amendment was not intended to apply the federal Bill of Rights to the several states. Consistent with his philosophy of judicial self-restraint and deference to the states, Frankfurter maintained that the Fourteenth Amendment did not withdraw the responsibility of criminal justice from the states and make it the business of the federal judiciary.

Justice Black disagreed. He disliked Cardozo's general definition of due process and distrusted the idea of justices deciding whether a particular state action violated vaguely defined standards of civilized conduct. As this cordial 1939 letter from Frankfurter illustrates, early in his tenure on the Court Black believed that the Bill of Rights should simply be applied to the states through the due process clause of the Fourteenth Amendment:

> Dear Hugo:
> Perhaps you will let me say quite simply and without any ulterior thought what I mean to say, and *all* I mean to say, regarding your position on the "Fourteenth Amendment" as an entirety.
> (1) I *can* understand that the Bill of Rights . . . applies to State action and not merely to U.S. action, and that *Barron* v. *Baltimore* was wrong. I think that it was rightly decided.
> (2) What I am unable to appreciate is what are the criteria of selection as to the . . . Amendments—which applies and which does not apply.
> This is not written to draw any comment from you—not that I should not have pleasure in anything you may say. But I have written the above merely to state, as clearly as I am capable of, what is in my mind.
>
> F. F.[3]

Black recognized that the Court's interpretation of the Fourteenth Amendment's due process clause had created two different standards of constitutional protection. There could be an action, for example, which violated the double jeopardy or cruel and unusual punishment amendment when performed by the federal government, which, when performed by the state, would not be a denial of due process. Only if the imposition of double jeopardy or cruel and unusual punishment which was performed by the state went beyond that which was forbidden by the Bill of Rights to such an extent that it offended Cardozo's vague concept of due process could the act be forbidden. This made no sense to

Black. Why should there be a double standard? How could a particular action be unconstitutional if performed by the federal government but not necessarily unconstitutional if performed by the states?[4]

Skelly Wright and Bertrand DeBlanc shared Black's concerns in developing their strategy for Willie's appeal. They recognized that the Bill of Rights would impose a very strict and demanding code of conduct on the states unlike the vague and deferential standards of the due process clause in the Fourteenth Amendment alone. Only ten years before, the Supreme Court considered whether an act that was forbidden by the Fifth Amendment should also be forbidden by the Fourteenth Amendment. In *Palko* v. *Connecticut*,[5] the Court affirmed the imposition of the death sentence, even though the second trial was plainly in violation of the double jeopardy clause of the Fifth Amendment. The Court, again speaking through Cardozo, held that the state did not violate the due process clause since the lack of protection afforded by the state against double jeopardy did not offend a "principle of justice so rooted in the tradition and conscience of our people as to be ranked as fundamental."[6] Absent again were any articulated criteria for fulfilling that "test." Cardozo and his colleagues left the determination of whether a given act was "fundamental" to the subjective, uncontrolled decisions of the individual justices.

Wright and DeBlanc believed that if they could persuade the Court to measure the State of Louisiana's behavior by the more demanding Fifth and Eighth amendments, rather than the lenient standards of due process used in *Palko*, the Court might reverse the Louisiana Supreme Court decision. Such an approach would also allow the Court's conservative justices, such as Frankfurter and Jackson, to shed their philosophy of judicial restraint for this one case. The justices would not be forced to defer to the state's notions of criminal justice as required under the due process clause.

The attorneys thus argued in their brief on the merits that a second attempt to carry out the death sentence would violate the Fifth Amendment's prohibition against allowing any person "to be twice put in jeopardy of life or limb . . . for the same offense." Recognizing, however, that the Fifth Amendment did not expressly apply to the states, they urged that through "extension and interpretation of the due process clause of the Fourteenth Amendment," the Fifth Amendment should be held to bind Louisiana.[7]

The two lawyers also argued that a second attempt to execute Willie would be cruel and unusual punishment proscribed by the Eighth Amendment, and, by similar extension, a violation of the due process clause of the Fourteenth Amendment. Wright and DeBlanc posed this question: "How many times does the State get before the due process clause of the 14th Amendment can be used to protect the petitioner from further torture?"[8] They provided their own answer: "The State of Louisiana had a right to execute this man but this right has been forfeited by subjecting the petitioner to the torture, both mental and physical, of being prepared for death, of being placed in the electric chair, of having electricity applied to his body."[9] Wright and DeBlanc decided that they must develop this point and shock the Court with the horror of the electric chair—a horror that had been associated with the chair since its invention late in the nineteenth century.

Ironically, the electric chair was originally designed as a painless and instantaneous means of taking life. Hanging had been recognized in most states as the only allowable form of execution. A number of hangings, however, had been clumsily carried out, and a more efficient method of killing had to be found.[10]

Recognizing this problem, Governor David B. Hill of New York issued the following challenge in his 1885 annual message to the state legislature: "The present mode of executing criminals by hanging has come down to us from the dark ages, and it may well be questioned whether the science of the present day cannot provide a means for taking the life of such as are condemned to die in a less barbarous manner. I commend this suggestion to the legislature."[11] The legislature responded by appointing a commission to investigate and report "the most humane and practical method known to modern science of carrying into effect the sentence of death in capital cases."[12] The commission reported in favor of execution by electricity and accompanied their report with a bill that was enacted in 1888.[13]

The commission believed that execution by electrocution would be more humane than execution by hanging. It found that "the most potent agent known for the destruction of human life is electricity. Death, as a result, is instantaneous upon its application."[14] Moreover, the condemned would feel no pain. The commission confidently concluded that "an electric shock of sufficient force to produce death cannot, in fact produce a sensation which can be recognized. The velocity of the electric current is so great that the brain is paralyzed; is indeed dead before the nerves can communicate any sense of shock."[15]

The commission rejected the possibility that, for some reason, enough electricity might not reach the condemned, and a prisoner might survive the shocks. Buried deep in the commission's report was this concern of a New York City doctor: "lightning may strike an individual and not kill; and no dynamo ever produced a shock as great. . . . If lightning does not always kill, surely we cannot expect death to result [always] from electricity."[16]

Thus, the electric chair was born. Scheduled to receive the dubious distinction of being the electric chair's first victim was William Kemmler. Kemmler had been convicted in 1889 of killing his mistress, Matilda

Ziegler, with an axe[17] and was quickly sentenced to die in the electric chair. Kemmler's lawyers immediately appealed the case, stating that this new method of execution was "cruel and unusual punishment." The New York State Court of Appeals rejected the argument. The court stated that "We have examined this testimony and can find but little in it to warrant the belief that this new mode of execution is cruel, though it is certainly unusual."[18] The New York court held that the testimony before it had "remove[d] every reasonable doubt that the application of electricity to the vital parts of the human body under such conditions and in the manner contemplated by the statute must result in instantaneous and consequently in painless death."[19]

The United States Supreme Court affirmed the judgment of the New York court.[20] Writing for a unanimous Supreme Court, Chief Justice Melville Fuller defined cruel and unusual punishment as follows: "Punishments are cruel when they involve torture or a lingering death; but the punishment of death is not cruel, within the meaning of the word as used in the constitution. It implies there something inhumane and barbarous, something more than the mere extinguishment of life."[21] Pointing out that the Eighth Amendment applied only to the federal government and not to the states, the Court held that electrocution as a means of execution was consistent with the due process of law guaranteed by the Fourteenth Amendment.

On August 6, 1890, Kemmler was strapped into the electric chair at Auburn prison. One electrode was attached to his back and another, in the form of a small metal bowl, was placed over his head and attached with a head band. With a signal from the warden, an electric current of 1,000 volts was unleashed.[22] After fifteen seconds, doctors in attendance ordered that the current be turned off. As doctors began to gather around Kemmler's apparently limp body, they were suddenly startled. According to *The New York World*:

Suddenly the breast heaved. There was a straining at the straps which bound him, a purplish foam covered the lips and was spattered over the leather head band. The man was alive. Wardens, physicians, everybody, lost their wits. There was a startled cry for the current to be turned on again. Signals, only half-understood were given to those in the next room at the switchboard. When they knew what had happened they were prompt to act, and the switch handle could be heard as it was pulled back and forth, breaking the deadly current into jets.[23]

For five minutes, the blasts of electric current continued.[24] Kemmler was then unstrapped and carried into the autopsy room where it was discovered that his brain had been hardened by the heat and "the blood in it was baked into a condition resembling charcoal," and the skin on his back had been burned black.[25]

Public condemnation of the new electric chair came quickly. *The New York Press* editorialized: "It will not mend matters at all to say that there was ignorant bungling on the part of the executioners; that the first current was not kept on long enough or the second current too long. The age of burning at the stake is past, the age of burning at the wire will pass also."[26] *The New York World* similarly commented, "The first experiment in electric execution should be the last. Its result strongly condemns this method of putting criminals to death as very cruel and very shocking. The theory of unconsciousness from the first moment of shock is at best a mere assumption. It was not sustained in Kemmler's case by outward indications. Apparently, the man died in agony, by slow torture."[27] Similarly, the *New York Herald Tribune* ran headlines announcing "Kemmler's Death By Torture."[28] And the *New York Times* commented:

He [Kemmler] died this morning under the most revolting circumstances, and with his death there was placed to the discredit of the State of New York an execution that was a disgrace to civilization. . . . The execution cannot merely be characterized as unsuccessful. It was so terrible that the word fails to convey the idea. It was, as those who advocated it desired that it should be, attended by men eminent in science and in medicine, and they almost unanimously say that this single experiment warrants the prompt repeal of the law.[29]

Despite the uproar over the use of the electric chair, the chair was again put into use.

The next two executions were uneventful but, on July 27, 1893, another bungled execution occurred. William Taylor was subjected to a first jolt of electricity, after which the chair broke down.[30] Semiconscious, Taylor was removed from the chair, carried into the autopsy room, and given a morphine injection and chloroform.[31] Meanwhile, electricians and workmen worked frantically to repair the malfunctioning apparatus. Sixty-nine minutes later current had been restored. Taylor, however, was now dead. Undeterred, state authorities carried Taylor out of the autopsy room, strapped him back into the electric chair, and ran current through his lifeless body for half a minute.[32] Despite these failures and the physical pain caused, the electric chair became a fixture in the American system of justice.

Since Willie Francis had endured the tortuous physical and mental suffering of the electric chair on one occasion, DeBlanc emotionally argued that Willie should not be forced to undergo this suffering a second time simply because the state had made a mistake. Dramatically illustrating the point, Wright and DeBlanc attached to the brief five affidavits of witnesses describing the attempted execution in wrenching detail. Relying on these affidavits, the lawyers recalled the electrocution scene for the Court: "A current of electricity sufficient to cause death was applied.

The petitioner jumped. The chair moved. His lips puckered and swelled. What effect that current of electricity had on this man's mind or upon his soul no one will ever know."[33]

"No one on this earth," Wright and DeBlanc continued, "can tell how close to the hereafter Willie Francis actually was at the time that the current of electricity was applied to his body. No living being can appreciate the suffering, the torture, both physical and mental, that Willie Francis has already undergone. No other living being has been so close to death and through no fault of his own brought back into this life so that the State of Louisiana may get a repeat performance."[34]

Willie's lawyers concluded the Eighth Amendment argument with these words: "It is submitted that in this age of enlightened justice, admitting that a man may be brought to death in expiation of a crime, that death must not be one of torture. If the State of Louisiana had a right to execute Willie Francis she was bound at her peril to make his death as instant and painless as possible. By her failure to do so she has forfeited her right to his life."[35]

In addition to the argument that a second execution attempt would improperly subject Willie Francis to double jeopardy and also cruel and unusual punishment, Wright and DeBlanc had a third arrow in their quiver. They argued that "[t]he trial of Willie Francis was a farce and a travesty on justice." Although Willie had had court-appointed counsel at his trial, they acted in a perfunctory way, taking no steps to protect Willie and offering no evidence. Drawing extensively on the Supreme Court's 1932 decision in *Powell* v. *Alabama*,[36] and various state court decisions, Wright and DeBlanc contended that the Supreme Court of Louisiana had erred in concluding that Willie's trial was "entirely regular" and not a violation of the due process clause of the Fourteenth Amendment.[37] (*Powell* was the case involving the "Scottsboro Boys"; for the first time, the Supreme Court held that a person charged with a capital crime was entitled to a lawyer paid by the state if he could not afford to hire one himself.)

Noting the racially-charged atmosphere in which the trial was conducted, Wright and DeBlanc listed the failings of Willie's counsel. No attack on the initial indictment was made by counsel. No motion for change of venue was introduced at the trial in behalf of Willie Francis. No evidence was introduced in his behalf at the trial. And no appeal whatever was taken from the judgment of conviction—not even a motion for a new trial. Consequently, within eight days after the indictment was returned against him, the petitioner was tried, convicted, and sentenced to death.

Moreover, the lawyers noted, the Supreme Court would never know the full story of the trial of Willie Francis because no stenographic record was taken at the trial. Obviously, no appeal was contemplated, and there was none. "It is submitted," the lawyers wrote, "that the abysmal darkness which surrounds the trial of Willie Francis speaks no less eloquently than the efforts made in his behalf both before and after that trial by the counsel appointed by the Court to represent him."[38]

The facts in Willie's case, they contended, were similar to the facts in *Powell* v. *Alabama*. In *Powell*, the trial court judge had appointed counsel for the accused under circumstances that made counsel's representation ineffective. Nine illiterate young black men between the ages of thirteen and twenty-one were charged with the rape of two white girls on a freight train. The trial court judge had appointed all the members of the local bar to serve as defense counsel. When no defense attorney appeared on the morning of the trial, a local attorney was pressed into service. The new defense counsel undertook his task with considerable reluctance, and the defendants were convicted.

In *Powell*, the Supreme Court reversed the judgment of the Supreme Court of Alabama, recognizing that the effective assistance of counsel was an integral part of the right to a fair trial: "The failure of the trial court to make an effective appointment of counsel was . . . a denial of due process within the meaning of the Fourteenth Amendment . . . and [its] duty [to appoint counsel] is not discharged by an assignment at such time or under such circumstances as to preclude the giving of *effective* aid in the preparation and trial of the case."[39] The Court concluded that "'[t]he record indicated that the appearances (of counsel appointed by the Court) was rather *pro forma* than zealous and active.' Under the circumstances disclosed, we hold that defendants were not accorded the right of counsel in any substantial sense. To decide otherwise, would simply be to ignore actualities."[40]

Wright and DeBlanc declared that, as in *Powell*, the mere *pro forma* representation of Willie Francis by counsel appointed by the court amounted to a denial of due process. "If appointed attorneys are so ignorant, negligent or unfaithful that the accused was virtually without representation, or did not in any real or substantial sense have the aid of counsel, he would be deprived of a fundamental right."[41] This was plainly what happened in the trial of Willie Francis.

Wright and DeBlanc concluded their brief by urging the Supreme Court to reverse the Louisiana Supreme Court and to rule in one of three ways. If the Court concluded that a second electrocution attempt would violate the double jeopardy or cruel and unusual punishment clauses, then the Court should either set Willie Francis free or return the case to the trial court in St. Martinville, Louisiana, with instructions to resentence Willie Francis to a punishment other than death. Furthermore, if the Court believed that there had been a lack of effective representation by counsel, then the Court should send the case back to the trial court in St. Martinville for a retrial.[42]

Two weeks after receiving petitioner's brief, the State of Louisiana filed a thirty-five page brief in opposition. Not surprisingly, the state argued that the double jeopardy clause of the Fifth Amendment and the cruel and unusual punishment provision of the Eighth Amendment were not applicable to the states. Rather, it said, the case must be judged under the due process clause of the Fourteenth Amendment. There was no violation of due process, the state maintained, "as the law has been administered by a competent court of justice of the State of Louisiana." The Court was urged to exercise judicial restraint and to uphold the judgment of the Louisiana Supreme Court.[43]

The state pointed out that under the Fourteenth Amendment, "[t]he Courts of Louisiana have the right to impose a sentence of death upon a conviction for the crime of murder. It is the Governor's mandatory duty to execute the sentence in a manner provided by law—electrocution. The sentence, as well as the petitioner remains unexecuted."[44] The state insisted that its notions of criminal justice must be respected and upheld by the Court under the Fourteenth Amendment. "We know of no law which permits any court to stay the hand of the executive branch of government when executing its full legal duty."[45]

The State of Louisiana also disagreed with Wright's argument that the trial of Willie Francis violated the Fourteenth Amendment due process clause. The state first argued that since this point had not been raised in the Louisiana Supreme Court, it would not be procedurally appropriate to press the point for the first time before the Supreme Court. Moreover, even if the point could be raised before the Supreme Court, the state quoted from the decision of the Louisiana Supreme Court ("there is no irregularity shown in any of these proceedings"), and insisted that "this statement of the Louisiana Supreme Court is unvarnished truth." The state also distinguished the *Powell* decision which Wright and DeBlanc relied on by observing that "the attorney appointed by the [*Powell*] Court was appointed on the *morning* of trial," whereas in the trial of Francis, counsel was appointed six days prior to trial and thus "had ample time for preparation and trial."[46]

Louisiana concluded its brief by praising the performance of the principles in the *Francis* trial. Counsel for Willie were described as "alert," "aggressive," and "men of outstanding legal ability." Judge Simon was described as being singularly astute and conscientious. The state considered Judge Simon to be "an honorable man" and an "eminent jurist." The Supreme Court was assured that "there has been absolutely nothing placed before Your Honors for your consideration that justifies a remand for re-trial."[47]

Supreme Court Rules allow the filing of a reply brief to answer questions that have not been adequately covered in the main brief on the merits. On November 15, 1946—three days before oral argument—

Wright and DeBlanc filed such a reply brief. They defended their use of the Fifth and Eighth amendments and reinforced their double jeopardy argument. As a last point, however, the pair introduced a new argument: A second attempt to execute Willie would be a denial of equal protection of law guaranteed by the Fourteenth Amendment. They argued that a second execution attempt would be a more severe punishment than is imposed on others guilty of a similar offense. In other words, since others did not have to go through the strain of preparing for execution a second time or had not experienced a botched execution attempt, Willie should not be forced to submit to a second.

With the filing of Francis's reply brief, both parties focused on oral argument. Usually, all nine justices listen to lawyers on each side for a half-hour. A lawyer, however, cannot simply read from a written text for thirty minutes uninterrupted. In fact, the Supreme Court Rules specifically warn counsel that the justices look "with disfavor on any oral argument that is read from a prepared text."[48] Rather, counsel must anticipate that his or her presentation will be interrupted with question after question from the justices. Counsel must, therefore, be flexible enough in the presentation to adapt his or her argument to the specific concerns of the justices. Experienced lawyers realize that questions asked by a justice are often clues as to what problems a justice may have with a particular case. The ability or lack of ability of counsel to answer satisfactorily these judicial questions may decide the outcome of a case.

For many justices, oral argument has a strong force beyond what the written words in briefs convey. Conclusive impressions are often formed regarding the merits of a case. Oral argument is the only way for a justice to get answers directly from counsel to questions that are bothersome to the Court in a particular case. As Chief Justice Hughes observed, "the desirability of a full exposition by oral argument in the highest Court is not to be gainsaid" because it provides the Court with an opportunity "to separate the wheat from the chaff."

November 18, 1946, was a raw, cloudy day in Washington, D.C. Skelly Wright's mind was focused intently on his first Supreme Court oral argument. Slowly and purposefully, he climbed the seventy-five steps leading to the main entrance of the Supreme Court building with its gleaming white marble columns. Completed in 1935, the Corinthian-columned building was considered a marble palace and far too opulent for many of the justices at that time. They were reluctant to move into the new "monstrosity" and preferred their much more modest quarters in the United States Capitol across the street. Commented one justice on moving day, "What are we supposed to do, ride in on nine elephants?"

As Wright walked up the steps, he seemed not to notice the grandness of the building or the trappings of justice that surrounded him. Seated on either side of the steps, sculpted in white marble, was a woman symbolizing "the contemplation of justice," and a man symbolizing "law and order." High above the entrance, chiseled into the facade, were the words "Equal Justice Under Law."

The main courtroom of the Supreme Court was similarly laden with formal symbols of justice. On the south wall flanked by figures representing Liberty and Peace and Philosophy were nine historical lawmakers who lived before Christ—Menes, Hammurabi, Moses, Solomon, Lycurgus, Solon, Draco, Confucius, and Octavian. On the north wall were nine lawmakers who lived after Christ—Justinian, Mohammed, Charlemagne, King John of England, St. Louis of Francis, Hugo Grotius, Blackstone, John Marshall, and Napoleon. At the corners of this frieze were figures representing Fame and History.

Precisely at twelve noon, the heavy red velvet curtain draped behind the courtroom bench parted. Clad in formal dress, Clerk of the Supreme Court Charles Elmore Cropley solemnly rose from his seat at the left-hand side of the bench and intoned: "The Honorable, The Chief Justice and the Associate Justices of the Supreme Court of the United States! Oyez! Oyez! Oyez! All persons having business before the Honorable, the Supreme Court of the United States, are admonished to draw near and give their attention, for the Court is now sitting! God save the United States and this Honorable Court!"

In order of their seniority, the justices robed in funereal black entered the high-ceilinged chamber and took their seats. Once seated, the Court announced its decisions in three separate cases involving patent law, interstate prostitution, and the authority of Congress to regulate interstate commerce. Having dispensed with the day's decisions, the chief justice called the first case to be heard in oral argument that afternoon: "Rothensies, Collector of Internal Revenue versus Electric Power Company."[49] Clerk Cropley responded "counsel present," and oral argument commenced with a discussion of some of the intricacies of the Internal Revenue Code.

Following these proceedings closely was Skelly Wright. The Court heard oral argument from 12:00 noon until 2:00, adjourning for thirty minutes for lunch. The Court then returned to the bench to sit from 2:30 to 4:30. Argument of the *Francis* case was scheduled to begin at 2:30 PM. Wright sat through oral argument in both *Rothensies* and the next case, studying the justices and their questions, searching for any nuance that might prove useful for his own oral argument.

Precisely at 2:30, the velvet curtains once again parted. Clerk Cropley announced the Court's arrival, and the justices reappeared. This time, however, Skelly Wright rose from his chair and strode to the speaker's lectern. As petitioner, Wright was the first counsel to address the Court. Before him he saw the nine justices settling into their high-back leather chairs. Peculiarly, no two chairs were alike. Each justice had selected his own style of chair for individual comfort. In front of them was the Court's bench fashioned from the finest mahogany. Behind the justices stood four floor-to-ceiling pillars with a large clock hanging on a chain between the two center pillars.

Wright quickly scanned the faces of the justices, only some ten feet away. At the far left, Justices Rutledge and Murphy chatted casually. To their right, Justice Frankfurter sat in the shortest chair of all the justices. Ironically, Frankfurter sat next to his chief antagonist, Justice Black. In the center, Chief Justice Vinson seemed to be gathering together assorted papers. To the right of the chief sat Justice Reed who was easily recognizable by his bald head. To the right of Reed, Justices Douglas and Robert Jackson sat quietly, with Jackson sitting only four chairs away from his adversary Justice Black. Sitting at the far right-hand side of the bench was Justice Harold Burton.

Wright looked straight ahead at Vinson as the chief justice pulled a slip of papers from the sheaf before him. "Louisiana ex rel. Francis versus Resweber," Vinson read. Wright heard Clerk Cropley once again intone "counsel present." Looking at Vinson, he saw the chief justice nod his head almost imperceptibly. Beginning with the traditional words "Mr. Chief Justice, may it please the Court," Wright launched into his oral argument.[50]

Wright reviewed the facts of Willie's case before beginning his constitutional argument. First discussing the lack of adequate representation by counsel, he pointed out to the Court that Willie was tried, convicted, and sentenced within eight days. No evidence was presented in his behalf, and no appeal was made. Wright then began to discuss the first execution attempt by noting that Willie had waited for eight months from time of conviction until the execution date.

Suddenly, a question came from Wright's left. It was Frankfurter—a man who had a reputation for dealing with counsel in oral argument in much the same manner as he had dealt with his students at Harvard Law School twenty years before. Frankfurter stated Louisiana's argument to Wright that the sheriff had express statutory authority to electrocute Willie Francis "until dead"—even if it required two attempts.

Wright fielded the question flawlessly. An agent of the state, in this case the sheriff, cannot deny a citizen of the state his rights under any circumstances. It made no difference that in this case the sheriff had express authority by statute. Frankfurter jotted down a note, apparently satisfied with the answer.

Wright quickly wrapped up the summary of the facts and turned to his double jeopardy argument. Wright discussed the "anguish of mind" which Willie Francis experienced up to the moment of execution. Willie's head and left leg had been shaved, and he was administered the last rites of the church, Wright told the Court. Punishment consisted of two parts—one of which was everything before the execution and the other was the execution itself. Another execution attempt "would be doubling up on his punishment." Wright summarized his argument this way: "Willie Francis has been punished up to the last moment. A second execution repeats all of the previous punishment up to that point."

Wright heard a voice to his right. It was Justice Reed with a question: "Just as if a man were sentenced to ten years and had served nine and then escaped. Then you would contend that he could not be made to serve all ten over again."

Wright knew that what the justice was actually asking was where the line can or should be drawn between improper and proper punishment. Wright first distinguished Reed's hypothetical case with the *Francis* case. Unlike the prisoner, Willie Francis did not escape punishment by his own actions. Rather, he did not realize punishment because the state botched the execution attempt. Second, each case must be considered on its own facts to decide what is improper punishment; "here it went beyond that point."

Still questioning the double jeopardy argument, Justice Burton at the far right of the bench asked, "How far can doctrine be carried? Suppose they merely had shaved his head before putting him in the chair—would that be double punishment?"

Wright turned to face Burton, but before he could answer, Frankfurter interrupted with a variation of the Burton hypothetical. Would the double jeopardy argument be appropriate if a man's execution were postponed after he had been taken from his cell and started toward the execution chamber?

Wright stood his ground. The facts of the two hypotheticals posed some difficult questions, he admitted, but the facts of the hypothetical were not the facts of Willie's case. Echoing the words of his brief, Wright answered that in this case the state had clearly crossed the line of what was allowable.

"If the State of Louisiana had a right to execute Willie Francis," Wright said, "she was bound to make his death as instant and painless as possible. By her failure to do so, she has forfeited her right to his life."

Wright concluded the double jeopardy argument by urging the Court to remand the case to the Louisiana trial court for resentencing. But, came the question, are you arguing that Willie Francis should be set free? Wright answered that the matter could be left to the discretion of the state which might impose any penalty less than death. Left unsaid to the Court was Wright's strategy. For now, he just wanted to avoid imposition of the death penalty for his client. Later, he could concern himself with a new trial for Willie Francis.

The last half of Wright's oral argument was uneventful. Wright made the same cruel and unusual punishment and equal protection arguments which he made in his brief on the merits and the reply brief. Wright's voice filled the chamber when he said that a second trip to the electric chair would subject Willie Francis "to the most severe punishment the State of Louisiana has ever inflicted upon a person sentenced to die."

The Court became quiet, almost subdued save for one interruption. When Wright mentioned the affidavits from witnesses to the execution which were appended to his brief, Chief Justice Vinson objected.

"Why are the affidavits here," Vinson sternly asked Wright. Wright replied that "the Court might find it necessary to review it for a finding" on the question of whether electricity reached Willie Francis in the first electrocution attempt. Vinson, however, would have none of this. The affidavits were not part of the record received by the Supreme Court from the Louisiana court. As such, the affidavits were not properly before the Court and should not be taken into account by the Court. Vinson's ruling did not disturb Wright. The affidavits were a bound portion of his brief on the merits submitted to the Supreme Court. If the justices had not seen the affidavits before, certainly Vinson's comments now directed their attention to them. And it was unlikely that the new chief justice's remarks would restrain the independent-minded justices from reading or referring to the affidavits.

As soon as Skelly Wright concluded his argument and sat down, Michael Culligan, special assistant attorney general for the State of Louisiana, approached the lectern. Culligan, an Irishman from New Orleans with an obvious brogue, began with a description of the murder of Andrew Thomas. It was, Culligan tried to impress the Court, a most terrible murder. Culligan hoped that, by focusing the Court's attention on the murder victim, he might generate sympathy for the state's cause. Such a tactic may have been successful in Louisiana, but it was of no help before the United States Supreme Court.

Culligan was brought up short by Frankfurter. "Just a minute Mr. Culligan," an impatient Frankfurter snapped, "we know that a terrible crime was committed." "We want the law," Frankfurter demanded, "so get to the law, now."

Accustomed to southern cordiality and manners, Culligan was dazed by Frankfurter's judicial outburst. Pausing for a second to collect himself, a reprimanded Culligan turned to his constitutional law argument and asserted that the double jeopardy clause of the Fifth Amendment and the cruel and unusual punishment provision of the Eighth Amendment applied only to the federal government. Culligan contended that the Supreme Court had no business interfering in the issue of sending Francis back to the chair. Willie Francis's fate should rest with the governor who had the power, Culligan argued, imprecisely, because that power actually rested on the approval of the Louisiana Pardons Board.

"The sentence against Francis has not been carried out because he has not been declared officially dead as is required by Louisiana law," argued Culligan. "No state statute has been attacked," Culligan said, resisting Supreme Court intervention in the case. Culligan continued, erroneously asserting: "No court power of procedure has been attacked; no contention is made that he has been deprived of the protection of the law." Culligan conveniently ignored Wright and DeBlanc's due process and equal protection arguments.

Moreover, Culligan warned, if the Supreme Court should intervene and deny a second execution attempt, the state would be confronted with the unprecedented "question of determining what to do with Francis." Culligan explained that Louisiana had no statutes dealing with such cases and that there was no guarantee that the legislature would enact a special statute in this case. Having talked for nearly ten minutes with but the one interruption, Culligan yielded the balance of his half hour to his co-counsel, L. O. Pecot.

Pecot, district attorney for the Sixteenth Judicial Circuit of Louisiana who had prosecuted Willie Francis in the trial court, told the Court that Willie had been fairly tried and legally sentenced. Taking his cue from Culligan, Pecot asserted that the executive of the state had full authority to see that the sentence was completely carried out. He cited the state statute and death warrant signed by the governor requiring that a current of electricity be passed through Francis until he was dead. The fact that he was alive proved, Pecot said, that the sentence had not been carried out.

At this point, Pecot was interrupted by Justice Hugo Black. Recalling Wright's argument that the State of Louisiana had forfeited its right to Willie's life, Black asked Pecot, "Just how many times does a man have to go to the chair without being killed to suffer sufficient punishment? Would it be 15 times, and would he have to be burned each time?"

Pecot replied that he could not discuss a hypothetical case, but that in Francis's case, he felt that the anguish was insufficient to warrant interference in the state's orderly execution of the sentence.

Pecot picked up his argument and reiterated Culligan's comments concerning resentencing. Confusion might result, Pecot observed, from a Court decision preventing a second execution attempt because state officials would lack legal authority to impose another sentence. Pecot said that Francis would have to be held in custody indefinitely unless and until the Louisiana legislature passed a law to deal with the *Francis* case.

Lending support to Pecot's argument, Jackson commented from the bench that, in the absence of a law under which Francis could be punished, the state might be required to release him. Skelly Wright from his seat at counsel's table winced at Jackson's words. He knew that the Court would never block a second execution attempt if it meant allowing a person described as a "convicted murderer" to go free. Quickly, however, Frankfurter broke in—much to Skelly Wright's relief. Frankfurter suggested that the Supreme Court itself might step in and propose an alternative punishment if it found that a second execution attempt was improper.

By now, the red light on the speaker's lectern had flashed on, indicating that the state's time for argument had expired. Pecot quickly urged affirmance of the Louisiana Supreme Court's decision and sat down. Chief Justice Vinson acknowledged all three counsel with a nod, announced that the case had been submitted, and called the next case scheduled for oral argument. There was no indication of what the Court's decision would be or when it would be announced.

In the great marble hall outside the courtroom, after argument, Wright was uncertain of his performance. DeBlanc, who had flown to Washington that morning for the argument, assured Wright that he had done well. Indeed, in his personal diary for November 18, 1946, Justice Burton wrote down Wright's name and entered next to it the comment "very good."[51] Wright was not concerned about whether he had been eloquent or whether he had given a good impression. He was only concerned about whether he had been effective.

Wright was worried about votes—the votes of the justices. Great oratory meant little if the justices voted to send Willie back to the electric chair a second time. Wright also worried that the conservative members of the Court would blindly accept arguments for judicial self-restraint. Wright left the Supreme Court building with a feeling of helplessness. After a busy and often hectic five months, he could only wait for the judgment of the Supreme Court.

VI

Supreme Court Consideration of Death by Installments

In the years before the Roosevelt New Deal, Supreme Court conferences were described as

dull and starchy affairs during which the late Justice Holmes sat with his face buried in his hands, elbows on the table. And if one of his colleagues took more than five minutes to present his views on the case, Holmes would uncover his face, turn toward the speaker and grunt:
"Christ."
Then he returned to the shelter of his hands. But if his colleague insisted on prolonging his discourse, Holmes would emerge again, this time grunting in all too audible a voice:
"God."
And if by any conceivable chance his colleague did not heed the second warning, Holmes unloosed a flow of profanity that is unprintable.[1]

Conferences for the Roosevelt Court, however, were rarely "dull and starchy" affairs. Justice Robert Jackson once commented that the moment at which oral argument between the parties ended was the same moment at which argument between the justices began.[2] This certainly was true for the Supreme Court as it considered the fate of Willie Francis. The nine judges quickly focused their attention on a question central to its ongoing debate over the extent of judicial restraint: whether a justice may allow personal views to enter into the judicial decision-making process. The battle lines were soon drawn. To the supporters of judicial activism, the answer was a definite yes. The supporters of judicial restraint answered with a firm no.

On November 23, 1946, five days after Skelly Wright's oral argument, the Supreme Court met in Saturday conference to consider, among other legal matters, Willie Francis's case. Every Saturday at noon, the Supreme Court met in its Conference Room to discuss and consider all the cases argued during the past week. Adjacent to the chief justice's suite, the oak-paneled room is ornately decorated; a rectangular table dominates the center. Around the table are nine leather chairs, each personalized on its back with a brass nameplate of an individual justice. A row of tall oak bookcases filled with calf-bound volumes of all the opinions of the federal courts line one wall. A portrait of Chief Justice John Marshall, set over a grand marble fireplace, surveys the Conference Room and, with a watchful eye, the justices in conference.[3]

As the justices entered the Conference Room, they followed court tradition and shook hands with one another. Presumably, this formal gesture is intended to remind them that their heated arguments over legal issues should not interfere with the goal of harmonious working relationships. Perhaps more accurately, one justice compared this customary act to a pair of boxers touching gloves before the beginning of a bout.[4]

After the justices entered the Conference Room, the door was closed behind them. The conference of the Court is not a public meeting, and strict secrecy is maintained. Only the nine justices are present. No secretaries or law clerks are in attendance. No transcript of the conference is kept, although individual justices at times keep their own notes of conference discussions. If a message is to be delivered from the conference, the junior justice goes to the door, knocks for the marshal, and passes the message.

The conference is held for the purpose of discovering the justices' impressions of a particular case. It is at conference where all nine justices first discuss a case among themselves and learn each other's views. Considering one case at a time, each justice discusses in turn the questions presented by the case and casts a vote to affirm or reverse the decision of the court below. While this early vote is only tentative and not binding, it does serve to develop a Court consensus on the case.

Presiding over the conference, as did his predecessors Charles Evans Hughes and Harlan Fiske Stone, was Chief Justice Fred Vinson. The Court's 1946–1947 term had barely begun, and already the early reviews of the new chief were not good. Indeed, after the first conference in which argued cases were taken up, Justice Frankfurter rendered this acerbic judgment of Vinson's performance in his diary: "He [Vinson] is confident and easy going and sure and shallow. He seems to have the confident air of a man who does not see the complexities of problems and blithely hits the obvious points."[5] Frankfurter further recorded that Justice Reed similarly was "rather disappointed by Vinson's performance since he did not do as well as he had expected him [Vinson] to do."[6]

Seated at the conference table for the first time in a year were all nine justices, Jackson having returned from Germany during the summer of 1946. Sitting at the north end of the table was Chief Justice Vinson. At the other end of the table sat the senior justice, Hugo L. Black. Although only on the Court for ten years, Black was already senior justice in terms of years of service. To the left of Vinson sat Justices Reed, Jackson, Burton, and Frankfurter; to the right sat Justices Murphy, Rutledge, and Douglas.

Vinson referred the eight justices to the conference agendas that lay before them on the conference table. The mimeographed agendas consisted of two lists. The first list, two pages long, consisted of eleven petitions for *certiorari* and various miscellaneous matters. The second list, three pages long, consisted of another petition for *certiorari*, two more miscellaneous matters, nine motions to proceed *in forma pauperis*,[7] and eight petitions for rehearing.[8] Only after wading through these agenda items would the Court consider the thirteen cases that had been argued and submitted the previous week.

The second of the argued cases called for discussion by Vinson was No. 142: *Louisiana ex rel. Francis* v. *Resweber*.[9] As was customary, discussion of the merits of the case began with the chief justice. According to notes of the conference taken by Justices Douglas and Murphy, Vinson had little trouble disposing of Willie's case. The chief justice briefly discussed Wright's double jeopardy argument and indicated that "it is clear to my mind that the Louisiana Supreme Court should be affirmed."[10]

Discussion of the case turned to the other justices by seniority. Saying little, both Black and then Reed indicated that they would also vote to affirm the judgment of the lower court. Black's vote was a surprise. Willie Francis's case seemed well suited for Supreme Court intervention and Black's judicial philosophy. In contrast, the vote of the moderately conservative Reed was not unusual. However, as Reed was the "swingman" on the Court, his vote was an important harbinger of which way the Court intended to rule in Willie's case.

When his turn came to speak, Justice Frankfurter began by noting that *Francis* was "not an easy case."[11] Frankfurter had voted to grant *certiorari* because, as he wrote later, it seemed "too serious for this Court to think too unimportant even to consider—particularly when one takes account of some of the really trivial cases that we do take."[12] Justice Murphy noted that, after briefly discussing double jeopardy, Frankfurter turned his attention to the cruel and unusual punishment argument and used an earthy "test" of unconstitutionality which he derived from Justice Oliver Wendell Holmes: "I get to Holmes' statement that certain things make me puke."[13] According to Douglas, Frankfurter found that "though the second execution attempt is hardly a defensible thing for the state to do, it is not so offensive as to make [him] puke,"[14] Frankfurter therefore voted to affirm the judgment of the Louisiana Supreme Court.

Justice Douglas, who had surprisingly voted to deny *certiorari* in the case, also voted to affirm the decision of the Louisiana Supreme Court. Douglas's votes in *Francis* were inconsistent with his usual libertarian activism. Unlike a conservative justice such as Harold Burton, Douglas rarely sided with the government position in criminal cases.

After Douglas's vote, Justice Murphy voted to reverse and Justice Jackson to affirm. Both the Murphy and Jackson votes were predictable. Murphy had been recognized as the Court's great civil libertarian; a second execution attempt would offend these views. In his notes for the conference, Murphy recorded his vote to reverse as a "Loud R."[15] On the other hand, Jackson, the Nuremberg prosecutor, could be expected to uphold the state's position in this death penalty case.

Justice Rutledge then voted to reverse, and, unexpectedly, so did Justice Burton, who originally had objected to the granting of *certiorari*. Recalling Burton's position on *certiorari*, Justice Frankfurter later wrote:

When the petition for *certiorari* in the Willie Francis case first came before the Court, Mr. Justice Burton said it was plain that we ought not to take the case. I was strongly of the contrary view and argued my view as vigorously as I could. As we left the Conference Room, Justice Burton said to me, "Felix, as you know most of the time I agree with you and certainly I can understand why you take the position that you take. But for the life of me I can't see why a man of your intelligence should think that simply because something went wrong with an electric wire, for which nobody was responsible, the State of Louisiana cannot carry out a death sentence imposed after a fair trial."[16]

Now, Burton had inexplicably switched his position. Aligning himself with the most liberal justices on the Court, Murphy and Rutledge, Burton was one of only three justices who wished to save Willie from a second execution attempt. In his first year on the Supreme Court, Burton had been a strong supporter of the government's position in criminal cases—directly opposite to Justice Douglas's record.[17] Yet it was Burton who was now criticizing the decision of the Louisiana Supreme Court and Douglas who was defending the government's position. It was apparent that the plight of Willie Francis had touched the judicially conservative Burton.

As is the custom of the Supreme Court, if the chief justice votes with the majority, he then decides which justice will draft the Court's opinion. If the chief justice is not in the majority, the senior associate justice who votes with the majority makes the assignment. When the justice to whom the opinion has been assigned has prepared it to the satisfaction of the other members of the Court who agreed with him, it then becomes the opinion of the Court.

As a member of the six to three majority, Chief Justice Vinson exercised his privilege by assigning the case to Justice Reed on November 25, 1946. Willie Francis was then seventeen years old. Despite Frankfurter and Reed's disappointment over Vinson's intellectual skills, the assignment of Reed to write the Court's opinion showed a measure of executive competence. Vinson knew that Reed was the Court's swingman—alternating between the Frankfurter and Black wings of the Court.[18] At the conference, Reed had voted with Vinson and the Frankfurter wing of the Court. Yet, that vote was not final and could later be changed. By giving Reed the responsibility of writing the Court's opinion, Vinson had pinned Reed down. It would be difficult for Reed later to change his mind, disavow the majority opinion he was assigned to write, and swing over to the dissenters' side.[19]

Reed drafted the first version of his opinion for the Court in pencil on a yellow legal pad. Influenced in part by the conference discussion, Reed's opinion sought to explain the Court's reason for sending Willie Francis back to the electric chair for a second time. Reed's opinion would have to be written with considerable care, for it would not only have to convince and hold a majority of the justices, but the opinion would eventually be publicly announced and would have to convince the American people of the rightness of the Court's decision.

Once Reed's draft had been typed by his secretary and proofed by his law clerk, it was sent to the Supreme Court printer located in the building's basement. (In August 1946 the Court had approved a plan for on-premises printing. Previously, the printing had been sent out of the building to Pearson's Printing Office.) Under tight security, Reed's draft was printed and returned to his office, where it was reviewed for minor errors. After several printer's proofs, copies of the proposed majority opinion were ready to be circulated among the other justices for comment. In all, the gestation period for the production of the majority opinion, including drafting, legal research, revisions, and printing, was short: a little over two weeks.

On December 11, 1946, Reed circulated his proposed opinion for the Court. Rejecting Wright and DeBlanc's Fifth and Eighth Amendment arguments, Reed relied solely on the due process clause of the Fourteenth Amendment. Reed implied that the Fifth and Eighth amendments were not applicable to the states. In order for the Court "to determine whether or not the execution of the petitioner may further take place after the experience through which he passed," Reed stated, "we must examine the circumstances in the light of the due process clause of the Fourteenth Amendment."[20]

Relying on the 1937 Supreme Court decision, *Palko* v. *Connecticut*,[21] Reed quickly dismissed Wright and DeBlanc's double jeopardy argument. Finding that the Fifth Amendment was inapplicable to the states,

Palko held that giving the state the same right of appeals as the accused did not violate the due process clause of the Fourteenth Amendment. By analogy, Reed wrote, "We see no difference from a constitutional point of view between a new trial for error of law at the instance of the state that results in an execution and an execution that follows a failure of equipment." Reed concluded that "When an accident, with no suggestion of malevolence prevents the consummation of a sentence, the state's subsequent course in the administration of its criminal law is not affected on that account by any requirement of due process under the Fourteenth Amendment. We find no denial of federal due process in the so-called jeopardy of the proposed execution."[22] In short, Reed established a negligence test; since the electric chair failed as a result of an "accident," and not any cruel motive on the part of Louisiana, the due process clause of the Fourteenth Amendment was not violated.

Reed likewise rejected Wright and DeBlanc's "cruel and unusual punishment" argument. Reed relied for support on the 1890 case, *In re Kemmler*, where the Supreme Court had held that death by electrocution was not cruel and unusual punishment and that only those methods involving torture or lingering death were constitutionally forbidden. Citing *Kemmler*, Reed found that the Louisiana state legislature adopted electrocution for a humane purpose, and that its will should not be thwarted.[23] Reed did not accept "petitioner's suggestion that he once underwent the psychological strain of preparation for electrocution, and to require him to undergo this preparation again subjects him to a lingering or cruel and unusual punishment."[24] Rather, he concluded that "We cannot agree that the hardship imposed upon the petitioner rises to that level of hardship denounced as denial of due process because of cruelty."[25] No reason was given for that conclusion. Reed's alleged reasons were nothing more than a restatement of the question before the Court.

Lastly, Reed addressed Wright and DeBlanc's contention that "the trial of Willie Francis was a farce and a travesty on justice."[26] Reed disagreed: "The record of the original trial presented to us shows the warrant for arrest, the indictment, the appointment of counsel and the minute entries of trial, selection of jury, verdict and sentence. There is nothing in any of these papers to show any violation of petitioner's constitutional rights."[27] Moreover, accepting the point made by Culligan at oral argument, Reed asserted that there was a jurisdictional problem. "Review is sought here because of a denial of due process of law that would be brought about by execution of petitioner after failure of the first effort to electrocute him," Reed wrote. That was the only question presented for the Court's consideration and "if there were error in the trial that denied federal constitutional rights to petitioner, those alleged errors should be presented for redress to the state court in Louisiana."[28] Thus, Reed concluded, the judgment of the Louisiana State Supreme Court should be "affirmed."[29]

Left unaddressed by Reed's December 11 draft opinion was Wright and DeBlanc's equal protection argument. Two days later, Reed took care of this omission by amending his opinion with a memorandum to the conference. Reed rejected the contention that a second execution attempt would be a more severe punishment than is imposed on others guilty of a like offense. Reed insisted that "laws cannot prevent accidents nor can a law equally protect all against them. So long as the law applies to all alike, the requirements of equal protection are met."[30] In this case all would be treated alike. For if in the future an individual experienced a botched execution attempt, Reed assured his colleagues that that individual would also be forced to undergo a second execution attempt. "Should other condemned prisoners have a similar unfortunate experience as this petitioner, there is no reason to think that the rule of Louisiana law would be any different."[31]

Reflecting the difficulty of the issues presented, Reed's decision quickly spawned three dissenting and one concurring opinions. A dissenting opinion is written by a justice who disagrees with the result reached by a majority of the Supreme Court in a case. In the case of Willie Francis, the dissenters disagreed with the majority and believed that the decision of the Louisiana Supreme Court should not be affirmed. Although a written dissent opinion is not required when a justice disagrees with the majority's result, nonetheless such opinions are usually written to explain and justify the reasons for a justice's disagreement and protest. As Chief Justice Charles Evans Hughes wrote in 1928 before he joined the Court: "A dissent . . . is an appeal to the brooding spirit of the law, to the intelligence of a future day, when a later decision may possibly correct the error into which the dissenting judge believes the court to have been betrayed."[32]

On December 12, 1946, the day after Justice Reed circulated his proposed majority opinion, Justice Burton circulated the first dissenting opinion. Now in his second year on the Court, Burton had had a difficult first year. There were whispers in Washington that he was neither hard-working nor intellectually capable. Many considered him the Court loafer. Fingers were pointed to statistics showing that during his first year on the Court, Burton had written only six majority opinions—the lowest number on the Court and far fewer than the thirty-one and twenty-eight opinions written respectively by Black and Douglas—the most prolific authors on the Court. Late in Burton's second term, Drew Pearson would write this scathing criticism of the socially visible justice in his newspaper column "The Washington Merry-Go-Round": "Justice Burton seems to think that being on the Supreme Court is not for the purpose of handing down opinions but to enjoy a continued round of parties. There is scarcely a party of any importance in Washington where he does not appear—including some parties not so important."[33]

Similarly, many questioned Burton's ability to tackle the complex legal issues presented for Supreme Court consideration. In a note to Frankfurter commenting on Burton's performance at the Harvard Law School and subsequent appointment to the Supreme Court, Harvard Law Professor Thomas Reed Powell wrote, "Dear Felix: This is to let you know that your new colleague received an average of 68 and a grade of 61 in Constitutional Law. He is photogenic anyway."[34] Frankfurter would later write of Burton, "One has an easy and inviting access to his mind. The difficulty is with what one finds when one is welcomed to enter it."[35]

Unnoticed by his critics were Burton's strong humanitarian instincts. Although he was a strong believer in the Frankfurter philosophy of judicial self-restraint and could usually be found voting with the Frankfurter wing of the Court, Burton did not fall into the same trap that had snared Frankfurter and others. He did not mechanically apply his judicial philosophy to the facts before him in a case. As one Supreme Court law clerk noticed, Burton was "the most open-minded of all the justices. If you were on trial, he would be the one you'd want for a judge."[36] It was this "open-mindedness" that allowed Burton to apply his personal beliefs and humanitarian instincts—emotions that had been aroused by the plight of Willie Francis.

Since the November 23 conference vote, anticipating the Reed opinion, Burton had worked intently on a dissent. In a deeply felt opinion, Burton argued first that a second execution attempt would deny Willie equal protection of the law.[37] In addition, Burton maintained that "the execution of this man [sic] by one or more reapplications of the electric current will amount to the infliction upon him of a cruel and unusual punishment which will deprive him of his life without due process of law, and that such a punishment should be held invalid as in violation of the Constitution of the United States."[38]

Accepting Wright and DeBlanc's argument, Burton concluded that "the execution of this man [sic] by one or more reapplications of the electric current will deny to him the equal protection of the law guaranteed by the Fourteenth Amendment."[39] Burton found that the Louisiana death penalty statute was particularly relevant in answering this question. The statute provided for "the application and continuance of such current through the body of the person convicted until such person is dead."[40] The statutory language, Burton argued, did not provide for electrocution by interrupted and repeated application of current several days or even several minutes apart. Under the death penalty statute itself, Willie Francis could not be made to suffer a delayed death caused by at least two noncontinuous and long separated applications of electric current.

Burton also accepted Wright and DeBlanc's cruel and unusual punishment contention. Echoing the pair's petition for a writ of *certiorari*, Burton asked, "How many more than one deliberate and intentional applications of current does it take to produce a cruel and unusual punishment?"[41] Certainly, Burton continued, if the state officials had deliberately placed Willie in the electric chair five times and each time had applied electric current to his body in a quantity or voltage not sufficient until the final time to kill him, such a form of torture would rival that of burning at the stake. Since five applications were so obviously cruel and unusual punishment, why not rule, Burton asked, that "the uniqueness of the present case is enough to demonstrate that today a second attempt is sufficiently cruel and unusual to be so recognized and to come within the prohibition of our Constitution?"[42] In his view, the Constitution required "instantaneous death" and not "death by installments."[43]

Burton rejected the distinction drawn by Reed between "an accident with no suggestion of malevolence"[44] and intentional torture by the state in violation of due process under the Fourteenth Amendment. "The lack of intent to produce the first failure is not material to the present issue," Burton wrote; "it neither lessens the proposed torture nor justifies the original failure."[45] A second execution attempt should not be permitted since "the equipment failed when it was the duty of the State to be sure that the equipment did not fail."[46] Burton, moreover, was not content to stop there. Even if the Reed "negligence test" were to be applied, a second electrocution would not be justified. There could be no doubt that the first electrocution failed as a result of the state's carelessness and not as a result of an accident. Discussing the mechanics of the first electrocution, Burton found that the equipment "contrasts with the precautions generally taken elsewhere to insure against failures of executions by electricity."[47]

Burton then went on to distinguish the *Kemmler* case relied on by Reed. Burton pointed out that in *Kemmler*, the Supreme Court emphasized the requirement that the electric current was to be applied in such a manner as to cause instantaneous death. The New York electric chair statute was "humane" as long as the resulting death was "instantaneous" and "painless." Without those prerequisites, Burton argued, the New York statute would have been held unconstitutional. Likewise, since the electrocution of Willie Francis was neither instantaneous nor painless, a second attempt would be cruel and unusual punishment.[48]

Justice Burton also implied that serious and cruel mental effects were attendant to a second trip to the electric chair. Burton's argument was prescient; the Supreme Court has since recognized the mental suffering of prisoners awaiting execution. The condemned person undergoes a "fate of ever-increasing fear and distress."[49] This anxiety is so intense that "the onset of insanity while awaiting execution of a death sentence is not a rare phenomenon."[50] Although Burton's argument was new to the marble halls of the Supreme Court in 1946, the mental suffering of a condemned prisoner has long been discussed. Indeed, as Samuel Johnson said in a famous sentence nearly two centuries ago, "Depend upon it, Sir, when any man knows he is to be hanged in a fortnight, it concentrates his mind wonderfully."[51]

In his conclusion, Burton courageously rejected his usual philosophy of judicial self-restraint. He indicated that state executive clemency was the most appropriate means of preventing an unjust execution. However, where the state has failed to act, and the propriety of a second execution attempt becomes an issue in the Supreme Court, then the Court must grant the required relief. Burton concluded that the execution of Willie Francis "by the reapplication of electric current to him under the present circumstance would be in violation of his constitutional rights."[52] Burton urged that the case be returned to Louisiana for the fashioning of a new sentence—not the death sentence.

Justice Burton's dissent was soon followed by draft dissents circulated by Justice Murphy on December 13, 1946, and by Justice Rutledge on December 14, 1946. Both opinions struck a common chord: a judge could not, and must not, completely divorce personal views from the judicial decision-making process. This was the issue, at bottom, in Willie's case. Abstract constitutional theories and notions of due process would become only supporting rationale in this debate.

Described once as a "realistic humanitarian,"[53] Justice Frank Murphy believed that the justices had an obligation to resolve the issues that faced them in a practical manner. Murphy refused to be bound by abstract notions of judicial restraint. It was inconceivable to him that a justice might feel rigidly bound by a philosophy of judging which, when applied, could result in grave injustices. Murphy expressed his approach in 1944 when he wrote in a dissent that "The law knows no finer hour than when it cuts through formal concepts and transitory emotions to protect unpopular citizens against discrimination and persecution."[54] More bluntly, Murphy had once written, "I don't care what the technicalities are, I just won't do it."[55]

Strongly believing that a judge's personal views were indispensable to the decision-making process and especially so in the case of Willie Francis, Murphy wrote in his circulated dissent that "More than any other provision in the Constitution, the prohibition of cruel and unusual punishment depends largely, if not entirely, upon the humanitarian instincts of the judiciary." Murphy concluded that: "to me, it is inhuman and barbarous to subject any person to the torture of two or more trips to the electric chair in the hope that one of them will result in the taking of the person's life."[56] He maintained that in the unique circumstances of *Fran-*

cis, "We have nothing to guide us in defining what is cruel and unusual apart from our own consciences. . . . Our decision must necessarily be based upon our mosaic beliefs, our experiences, our backgrounds and the degree of our faith in the dignity of the human personality."[57]

Justice Murphy found that the mental torture Willie had suffered was sufficient to reverse the Louisiana court. He wrote that with a second electrocution attempt, "the mental anguish which characterizes preparation for execution must be repeated, an anguish that can be fully appreciated only by one who has experienced it."[58] The mental agony of a second attempt, together with physical pain which "may accompany the unsuccessful attempt," was such that it "makes the total punishment cruel and inhuman."[59] Moreover, this process "could go on indefinitely," Murphy warned, "dependent upon the number of times that the executioner bungles his ugly task." "The time to call a halt," Murphy stated, "is when the first attempt fails after inflicting a substantial amount of anguish or pain."[60]

Finally, Murphy addressed Assistant Louisiana Attorney General Culligan's contention at oral argument that death was the penalty to be exacted from Willie Francis and that until death actually occurred, the punishment had not been carried out. According to Murphy, that argument missed the whole point of the case. "Capital punishment may not be imposed, as here, in such a manner as to be cruel and unusual," Murphy wrote.[61] He noted that "Louisiana has attempted once to take petitioner's life and has failed." Disagreeing with Justice Reed's contention that it was only an "accident," Murphy concluded, "(U)nless we are to discard the first principles of humanitarianism, Louisiana must not be allowed an endless opportunity to take human life."[62] Such a result was particularly appropriate in Willie's case: "And it is not without significance that this cruel and unusual punishment is about to be inflicted upon a helpless and inarticulate member of a minority group. The need for utilizing the highest humanitarian ideals is never greater than in a case of this nature."[63] (As of 1988, it may be noted, it is "not without significance" that the majority of the almost 2,000 people on the Death Rows of the nation are black.)

Similarly, the unpublished dissent of Justice Rutledge stressed Willie's mental torture, and also dealt with the negligence test seemingly established in the Reed opinion. Moreover, like Murphy, Justice Rutledge believed that a judge could not separate personal views from judicial decision making. In his dissent circulated to the justices on December 14, Rutledge recognized that the justices were blazing new ground in the unusual circumstances of Willie's plight.

Rutledge, like Burton, scored the Reed opinion for suggestions that the botched execution was excusable because it was an "accident" and not "intentional torture."[64] Louisiana's subjective motivation in attempting the first execution was of no significance in determining whether its action was cruel and unusual punishment. "I do not think the element of torture is removed," Rutledge wrote, "because the state acts carelessly rather than deliberately."[65] For Rutledge, Louisiana had "a duty to see that such failures do not occur."[66] The state has "no right to take chances with faulty or antique equipment, low current or any other risk likely to produce such horror."[67] In the case, Louisiana had not shown that the failed execution was due to factors beyond the state's control.

Rutledge wrote that "(t)orture, for the victim, is not a matter of the executioner's state of mind. It may be inflicted as much by carelessness and bungling or taking a chance as by design."[68] Rutledge refused to accept Reed's presumption that the execution failure was due to an "accident." If the failure was due to carelessness, as Rutledge suspected, and not an accident, then Reed's reasoning should fall. In any case, a question existed, and a life "should not hang upon a thread so slender."[69] Recognizing the mental agony which a Death Row prisoner undoubtedly suffered, Rutledge concluded that "Willie Francis cannot be electrocuted again without undergoing a second time the death pangs he already has suffered and which now I think the state has no right to reinflict."[70]

Dissenting opinions can be multiple, or the authors may join together in a single dissent. Burton realized that a single, strong dissent would be more effective in pointing out the errors of Reed's opinion than would several separate opinions. He also realized that a well-written dissent might even pull in two additional votes. On rare occasions in the past, a dissent has been able, through the force of its arguments, to persuade a member of the Court's majority to change his mind. With two votes, Burton's dissenting opinion would be converted into a majority opinion for the Court, blocking a second execution attempt.

Burton moved cautiously but effectively. First, he convinced the other dissenters to coalesce around his dissenting opinion. Burton knew that Murphy loved nothing more than going off on his own and writing separate dissenting opinions. (Murphy was, in a sense, the Court's Don Quixote.) Yet, with continued cajoling such as that found in this note, Burton persuaded Murphy to drop his own dissent:

> Frank,
> Attached is my redraft of the dissent in the Francis case. . . . I hope that in addition to your separate statement you can also join in this. I am sure it will strengthen our positions if [we] join in at least this much.
>
> H.H.B.[71]

By the end of 1946 Justice Rutledge also dropped his planned dissent and joined Burton. In a New Year's Eve note to Burton, Rutledge revealed the narrowness and uncertainty that now surrounded the Court's consideration: "Please allow me to join in your opinion. It's a good job, right, and I hope will induce the change in the additional necessary vote."[72]

As the Rutledge note reveals, Burton had been making progress in securing the votes necessary to prevent a second execution attempt. Where once two votes were needed, now only a single additional vote was needed. On December 20, 1946, Justice Douglas reversed his original vote at the time of the conference and joined Burton. Burton recorded in his diary that on that date he "conferred with Justice Douglas and got his consent to my dissent in #142 as modified at his suggestion."[73] Later that day, Douglas wrote Reed a terse note in longhand explaining his shift:

> Dear Stanley—
> I have given further study to No. 142, the Willie Francis case, and have decided to go with Burton on vacating and remanding in order for a determination of whether he did in fact receive an electrical charge.
>
> W.O.D.[74]

With Douglas, Burton now had four solid votes for reversing the Louisiana Supreme Court and barring a second execution attempt on Willie Francis. In effect, Willie's life would turn on a single vote.

Meanwhile, Justice Reed was worried about keeping the four other justices, and their votes, in agreement with his majority opinion. The loss of Douglas had been expected for some time. Still, the vote was now only five to four. With a swing of but one vote, Burton's dissenting opinion would become the new majority opinion. Reed could only be sure of his own vote and that of Chief Justice Vinson. Vinson had been the first to support Reed's opinion, sending the justice a typed note stating simply "I agree."[75] Reed was less sure of what Justice Jackson and the unpredictable Justices Frankfurter and Black would do.

Reed's fears were confirmed on December 20, 1946, when Justice Jackson circulated a concurring opinion. A concurring opinion is written by a justice who agrees with the result reached by the majority opinion, but who objects to something that was either said or not said in the opinion. The dissatisfied justice will pen his thoughts describing either of these deficiencies. In the case of Justice Jackson, there were objections both to what Reed said and didn't say.

Jackson responded to the urgings of Justice Murphy which extolled the virtues and courage required of an active judiciary. Surprisingly, the conservative Jackson prefaced his concurrence with a strong denunciation of the death penalty. Jackson wrote: "If I am at liberty, in the name of due process to vote my personal sense of 'decency'; I not only would refuse to send Willie Francis back to the electric chair, but I would not have sent him there in the first place. If my will were law, it would never permit execution of any death sentence."[76] "This is not because I am sentimental about criminals," Jackson explained, "but I have doubts of the moral right of society to extinguish a human life, and even greater doubts about the wisdom of doing so. . . . A completely civilized society will abandon killing as a treatment for crimes."[77]

Unlike Murphy and Rutledge, however, Jackson believed that the justices must suppress their personal feelings and predilections because "judges are servants, not masters of society and it is society's laws that should govern judges."[78] Jackson's position posed a clear dilemma. It was "society's law" that was the very issue before the bar: Did the Louisiana practice comport with the Constitution? Yet, Jackson thought it inappropriate to allow personal feelings to enter into his consideration of this question. How then could Jackson resolve the issue?

For Justice Jackson the answer was clear: By following his notions of judicial restraint, he would merely defer to the state and accept as proper whatever judgment it rendered. He disagreed, however, with Justice Reed who, in his majority opinion wrote that he was guided by "national standards of decency." For Jackson, there were no such standards—only blind acceptance of the state judgment. There was no room for personal feelings or humanitarian instincts in Jackson's legal universe. "Unable to cite any constitutional backing for my prejudice against executing Francis" and finding that he could not "believe that the founding fathers ever intended to nationalize decency," Jackson concluded that he "must vote to leave the case to Louisiana's own law and sense of decency."[79]

In an undated and unsigned memorandum to his file, Justice Rutledge recognized the inconsistencies presented by Jackson's concurring opinion. Rutledge wrote: "I consider it to be more than absurd for the prosecutor at Nuremberg to say that he doesn't approve of capital punishment. If he didn't approve, he should never have taken the job. The remarks at the bottom of page 1 about 'the duty of prosecutors' adds to rather than detracts from the absurdity."[80] The latter reference is to a comment in Jackson's concurrence that "as long as society adheres to its policy of death penalties it is for us in individual cases to apply the policy of the law, as it is the duty of prosecutors, whatever their personal convictions, to advocate it."[81]

Reed was concerned that Jackson's concurrence would only confuse an already difficult case for both the other justices and, eventually, the general public. Reed wanted the Supreme Court to present the appearance of agreement in this already much-publicized case. Having lost Douglas and been reduced to a narrow five to four vote, he knew that

Jackson's concurrence could only serve to highlight the divisiveness that existed in the Court.

Aside from Jackson, Reed was also concerned about Felix Frankfurter's vote and with good reason. The "additional necessary vote"[82] to which Rutledge referred in his December 31 note to Burton was Frankfurter's, who had become the swing vote. And Burton had already recognized, Reed was sure, the importance of Frankfurter's vote.

VII

Reed Struggles to Hold a Majority

Felix Frankfurter was uneasy about his vote in the *Francis* case. Although he had voted with the majority at conference, he personally disapproved of capital punishment. Yet, bound by his philosophy of judicial self-restraint, Frankfurter believed that he dare not disturb the judgment of the State of Louisiana. There was no room for personal feelings in the judicial decision-making process. (Why Frankfurter did not realize that his views on judicial self-restraint were also personal is completely mysterious.) The supposed internal tension between Frankfurter's personal beliefs and judicial philosophy greatly distressed him, if we are to believe his remarks in a series of letters between him and Burton.

On December 13, 1946, one day after Burton circulated his dissent, Frankfurter revealed grave misgivings regarding his vote in the case. In a letter, Frankfurter indicated that he had read Burton's dissent and had "reflected upon it with sympathy."[1] "I have to hold on to myself not to reach your result," Frankfurter wrote. "I am prevented from doing so," he continued, "only by the disciplined thinking of a lifetime regarding the duty of this Court in putting limitations upon the power of a State, when the question is merely the power of a State under the limitations implied by the Due Process Clause." (Frankfurter thus intimated that the four dissenters, in his opinion, had engaged in undisciplined thinking.) The justice then went on to quote once again with approval Justice Oliver Wendell Holmes, who "used to express the relationship between the Supreme Court and the States by saying that he would not strike down State action unless the action of the State made him 'puke.'"[2] It was Frankfurter's judgment that *Francis* had failed to meet the Holmes "test," which, of course, was completely subjective. There are no external crite-

ria by which a judge can evaluate whether a given governmental action is
so bad as to make him vomit.

The conservative Frankfurter stated that "the construction placed upon the State statute by the Louisiana Supreme Court is binding upon
us." In other words, the Supreme Court must assume under Louisiana
law that "in case the electrocution did not succeed through an unexpect-
ed, innocent happening, at least a second attempt to produce death may
be made."[3] Urging judicial self-restraint and deference to the states,
Frankfurter maintained that the United States Supreme Court must pre-
sume the constitutionality of this interpretation of the Louisiana statute.
"For such, and such alone, in view of the relation of the United States to
States and of this Court to State courts, is the exact legal situation before
us."[4]

Frankfurter was willing to leave undisturbed this presumption of constitutionality. "I cannot say that a second execution attempt so shocks
the accepted, prevailing standards of fairness and justice not to allow the
State to electrocute after an innocent, abortive first attempt," Frankfurter
wrote Burton, "that we, as this Court, must enforce that standard by
invocation of the Due Process Clause."[5] By failing to disclose how he
ascertained "the accepted prevailing standards of fairness and justice,"
Frankfurter's conclusion consisted purely of his personal views. Moreover, he slipped from the purely *personal* "standard" of puking to one in
which he stated that *community* standards should prevail. And this he
did even though he knew full well there was *no* way that he, or any of his
colleagues, could determine "the accepted prevailing standards of fairness and justice." Nevertheless, again asserting the difficulty he had in
reaching his decision, Frankfurter found that "after struggling with myself—for I do think the Governor of Louisiana ought not to let Francis go
through the ordeal again—I cannot say that reasonable men could not in
calm conscience believe that a State has such power."[6] By invoking the
test of the "reasonable man," Frankfurter incorporated tort law into the
Constitution. Moreover, to apply such a "test," he also necessarily took
the position that the justices could and should act as a little lunacy
commission to determine the reasonableness and rationality of actions of
state governmental officers. Who, indeed, is a "reasonable man"?

"And when I have that much doubt," Frankfurter continued in the
letter, "I must according to my view of the Court's duty, give the State
the benefit of the doubt and let the State action prevail."[7] Why, one must
ask, should the state have the "benefit of the doubt"? On that question
Frankfurter was silent except to say that abstract principles of judicial
restraint outweighed the facts of the bungled execution. Frankfurter, in
short, exalted a political theory over a teenager's life.

Curiously, Frankfurter ended the letter by complimenting Burton for
listening to his conscience: "it is one of the most cheering experiences

since I have been on this Court to have you, who have felt so strongly against taking the case at all, come out in favor of reversal as a result of your own conscientious reflections."[8] Frankfurter thereby implicitly accused Burton of ignoring his duty to the Court because, like Justices Rutledge and Murphy, he chose to follow his conscience.

Frankfurter was apparently troubled by another aspect of the dissent filed by Burton, which, like Justice Rutledge's dissent, had exposed a weakness that Frankfurter felt Reed should address. Burton had cast a shadow over the manner in which Louisiana had tried to carry out the electrocution in St. Martinville. Nothing had been mentioned in either the briefs for Francis or Louisiana with respect to the allegedly drunken and disorganized electrocutioners. Nonetheless, Burton suspected that the state had botched the electrocution.[9]

Frankfurter felt it important that the state's first electrocution of Willie Francis be portrayed as "an innocent, abortive first attempt." This Reed had not done, at least not to Frankfurter's satisfaction. Troubled by Burton's dissent, Frankfurter sent the following "Dear Stanley" note to Reed on December 14, 1946:

> I assume that you will add something like this to your opinion, even if it is already implied:
>
> "We have not before us a situation where officers of the State acted with malevolence or callousness or carelessness toward human life. Nothing in the record remotely warrants such imputation. On the contrary, the case presupposes the appropriate precautions were taken and the abortiveness of the attempted execution is one of those contingencies which is not the fault of man. Any other consideration is unfair to the State and disregards the very narrow scope of our authority to limit the powers of a State."
>
> Faithfully yours,
>
> F. F.[10]

Wishing to mollify Frankfurter and keep his vote, Reed made changes in his opinion reflective of Frankfurter's concerns.

While Reed thus attempted to retain Frankfurter's endorsement of the majority opinion, Burton sought to swing Frankfurter over to the side of the dissent. In a note responding to Frankfurter dated December 26, 1946, Burton took a novel approach in attempting to place *Francis* outside the boundaries of Frankfurter's due process analysis and its attendant deference to the state courts. Burton asked Frankfurter to "consider that in enforcing the 14th Amendment against these state officials we are enforcing not only the *federal* amendment *but also* the *express* language of the *state* legislature."[11] The Louisiana statute provided:

Every sentence of death imposed in this State shall be by electrocution: that is, causing to pass through the body of the person convicted a current of sufficient intensity to cause death, and the application and continuance of such current through the body of the person convicted until such person is dead.[12]

Justice Burton argued that the statutory language prohibited a second attempt to execute, and that this view had "not been interpreted to the contrary by the Louisiana Supreme Court as that Court merely said that it was an executive matter and that it declined to look at it."[13] In support of his contention that the statute prohibited a second attempt, Burton maintained that the statute did not provide for electrocution by interrupted or repeated applications of electric current so that the victim would recover complete consciousness before being submitted to the next shock. Rather, the statute expressly prescribed the application of a current of sufficient intensity to cause death and the continuance of the application until death resulted. Thus, Burton's implicit message was that Frankfurter could, by his own conception of due process, save Willie Francis without failing to pay the deference he deemed owed to the Louisiana authorities.

Frankfurter responded to Burton's entreaty with a December 31, 1946, "Dear Harold" letter that began with praise of both Burton's efforts and Frankfurter's own conscientiousness. "I think I can say without the slightest exaggeration that, knowing the care that you give to the writing of your opinions, I try to bring the same kind of care to their consideration."[14] "And, in a case like that of Willie Francis," Frankfurter wrote, "my high regard for the quality of your work is reinforced by my feelings regarding the duty of States not to fall short of the standards which it is within the competence of this Court to enforce."[15]

These pleasantries aside, it became clear that Frankfurter's vote had not changed. Once again urging deference to the states, Frankfurter insisted that "[w]hatever scope the State Court gives to a state law is binding upon us even though the State Court gave it a scope which we think it should not have given or gives it a scope which we think it should have given. All this is purely a State question beyond our purview." For Frankfurter, the issue remained: "whether, under the circumstances in which the State court found no violation of the State law, there is a transgression of the Due Process Clause."[16]

"I cannot bring myself to think that if I were to hold there was," Frankfurter answered Burton, "I would not be enforcing my own private view rather than the allowable consensus of opinion of the community which, for purposes of due process, expresses the Constitution."[17] (Again, the learned justice invoked alleged community standards, without saying how a community consensus could be determined.) But enforcing his "own private view" is precisely what Frankfurter did. While stressing a duty to some indefinable, unascertainable "consensus of opinion of the community," Frankfurter nonetheless asserted that he was deeply disturbed by his vote in *Francis*. He concluded the letter to Burton with these words: "I am sorry I cannot go with you, but I am weeping no tears that you are expressing a dissent."[18]

As with Justice Jackson, Frankfurter wanted it both ways. He knew his was the critical vote, yet he relied on something he did not and could not know to vote to send Willie to his death—the "consensus of opinion in the community." Surely, Frankfurter knew that societal consensus was merely a convenient counterpane under which personal predilections could be hidden.

By the end of 1946 it was clear that Burton had lost and that Frankfurter would remain with the Reed majority. Frankfurter formally told Burton of his decision in Burton's chambers on January 2, 1947.[19] Retaining Frankfurter's vote, however, was not a total victory for Stanley Reed, for on the same day Frankfurter conferred with Justice Burton, he also circulated his own concurring opinion. The case of Willie Francis had placed a severe strain on both Felix Frankfurter's judicial philosophy and his loyal adherence to it. A concurring opinion was necessary, Frankfurter felt, to clear up any misunderstanding that had arisen over the application of that philosophy and to justify his vote.

Frankfurter's concurrence began with an apologia for its circulation in the first place: "This case serves to illustrate why it has been the tradition of the Court throughout its history, for more than one opinion to be written even when there is agreement in the result." Frankfurter rationalized that "the more difficult and delicate the issues in a case, the more numerous have been opinions in elucidating a decision."[20] Believing that "[t]he words used [in an opinion] become part of the judicial process in deciding future cases," Frankfurter warned that "judges must be alert against giving verbal hostages to the future."[21] This was particularly true in this case. Frankfurter explained that "we are dealing here with a question the answer to which must exclude unintended implications. The problem, to be sure, is an old problem. But its subtleties constantly reappear."[22]

The problem for Frankfurter involved the Court's application and interpretation of the due process clause of the Fourteenth Amendment. Justice Reed had written for the majority that he was guided by "standards of national decency" in concluding that a second trip to the electric chair would not violate due process. Justice Jackson had criticized this approach for not affording "either an objective or intelligible test of due process." Jackson pointed out that, while Reed had concluded that there was no violation of "standards of national decency," the opposite conclusion could be just as easily reached by a judge with a different personal opinion of what made up these national standards. Indeed, Jackson noted that Justices Murphy and Rutledge had reached such a separate result while using Reed's standard. Reed's standard could too easily fall victim to a judge's "personal bias or dislike."[23] The approach did not reflect "a disciplined and impersonal decency which expresses society's will and the policy of the law."[24] In Jackson's view, the Court should simply defer to the state and "leave the case to Louisiana's own law and sense of decency." (Why he thought a black teenager convicted of murdering a white man would be treated decently was left unsaid.)

In his concurring opinion, Frankfurter attempted to reconcile the divergent positions of Reed and Jackson by blithely concluding: "I read what MR. JUSTICE REED has written to mean what I understand MR. JUSTICE JACKSON to mean by what he has written. Accordingly, I join MR. JUSTICE REED'S opinion by finding in it the gloss of MR. JUSTICE JACKSON'S opinion."[25] Effectively, Frankfurter argued that it was all a simple misunderstanding. Both Jackson and Reed agreed that "Louisiana has not transgressed the limitations imposed by the Due Process Clause."[26] It was only Reed's unfortunate use of the phrase "national standards of decency" which led to a slight matter of misinterpretation. According to Frankfurter, Reed had actually meant to say only what Jackson had more plainly set out in his concurring opinion which was unpublished.[27]

Having seemingly corrected this apparent misunderstanding, Frankfurter then turned to a justification of his vote in the *Francis* case. Frankfurter believed that Louisiana should grant Willie Francis executive clemency and wrote, "I cannot bring myself to believe that, for Louisiana to leave to executive clemency, rather than to require, mitigation of a sentence of death duly pronounced upon conviction for murder because a first attempt to carry it out was an innocent misadventure, offends a principle of justice 'rooted in the traditions and conscience of our people.'"[28] Yet, believing himself bound by notions of judicial restraint, Frankfurter would do no more for Willie than to urge clemency. Apparently, he either did not know or he refused to consider the fact that Louisiana law did not permit gubernatorial clemency.

Faithfully following his inflexible judicial philosophy, Frankfurter found that "this Court must abstain from interference with State action no matter how strong one's personal feeling of revulsion against a State's insistence on its pound of flesh. One must be on guard against finding personal disapproval rooted in more or less universal condemnation."[29] Thus, with respect to the fate of Willie Francis, Frankfurter concluded, "Strongly drawn as I am to some of the sentiments expressed by my Brother Burton, I cannot rid myself of the conviction that were I to hold that Louisiana would transgress the Due Process Clause if the State were allowed, in the precise circumstances before us, to carry out the death sentence, I would be enforcing my own private view rather than the consensus of opinion which, for purposes of due process, is enjoined by the Constitution."[30]

Frankfurter left open the possibility that "a hypothetical situation which assumes a series of abortive attempts at electrocution or even a single, cruelly willful attempt, would . . . raise different questions."[31] Such factual situations may well involve a violation of due process. In the case of Willie Francis, however, Frankfurter was convinced that "the State of Louisiana has not gone beyond its powers."[32]

On the morning on which his concurrence was circulated, Frankfurter's office delivered a short, typewritten letter to Justice Stanley Reed's chambers. "In due course you will see a concurrence of mine in the Willie Francis case,"[33] Frankfurter warned, "It will tell you not only what I have written, but why I have written it."[34]

The mild-mannered Reed was furious when he received Frankfurter's note and, later, concurrence. He had endured a number of editorial suggestions from Frankfurter, including Frankfurter's December 14 note suggesting a lengthy and detailed addition to Reed's opinion. Frankfurter had also returned several circulated drafts of Reed's opinion to the justice with comments scrawled in the margins. Reed had done his best to comply with Frankfurter's suggestions in order to retain Frankfurter's agreement with the majority opinion. Indeed, after Reed adopted one set of changes Frankfurter had proposed, Frankfurter modestly penned on the back of the new set of proofs, "Yes. Thank you for the changes you have made. I am confident history will approve of them. But see p. 2." On page 2 of the proof was a fresh set of changes suggested by Frankfurter.

Reed went to the new chief justice and sought his well-publicized skills at compromise. Perhaps Vinson could intervene and persuade Frankfurter to drop his concurring opinion. After all, if both Frankfurter and Jackson filed concurring opinions, only three justices (Vinson, Reed, and Black) would be left in agreement with the Court's reasoning for sending Willie Francis back to the electric chair. Clearly, the Court would be subject to much public ridicule if more justices were in agreement as to why the Court's result was wrong than there were justices who could agree as to why the Court's decision was right.

Vinson's mission failed from the outset. Almost as a matter of course, Frankfurter had historically felt uncomfortable joining opinions drafted by Stanley Reed. In a note to Vinson concerning another case in 1947, Frankfurter wrote, "Stanley has a way of writing opinions that not infrequently makes me want to dissent even tho I agree with his result. P.S. I have told this to him to his face. F.F."[35] There was no reason to believe that Frankfurter had changed his opinion of Justice Reed's drafting skills in the Francis case.

In a January 4, 1947, letter to Vinson after their meeting, Frankfurter made it clear that he had no intention of withdrawing his already circulated concurrence. "Honest Injun, Fred," a chastised but unrepentant Frankfurter began, "I have thought long and hard about this business of concurring opinions. And I have thought hard about it not only during all the years that I have watched the work of this Court as a mother watches a feverish child. I had to think hard about it very soon after I came on the Court."[36] Relying on his extensive knowledge of Supreme Court history and cases, Frankfurter explained that "[i]n *Graves v. O'Keefe*, Stone wrote an opinion which did not seem to me to be fully adequate to the situation. Now, while Stone never hesitated to write concurring opinions to what Holmes and Brandeis and Cardozo wrote, he was not crazy to have one write concurring opinions in cases in which he wrote. And it was not pleasant for me to have to start off with such a concurring opinion. But I saw no escape."[37]

Similarly, Frankfurter saw no escape in *Francis* and concluded that he was bound to file a separate concurrence. "I really think that the way to deal with an uninformed lay opinion is to try to inform it in the very limited way that we have, by word, but especially by action."[38] "When the occasion is appropriate, as it seems to me especially appropriate in the Willie Francis case," Frankfurter wrote Vinson, "it can only do good, I believe, to make people realize that concurring opinions were not invented by the present crowd and will not cease when they leave the scene."[39]

On January 3, 1947, one day after Frankfurter circulated his concurrence, Reed received more bad news. Prompted into action by the Frankfurter effort, Justice Hugo Black had bolted ranks and circulated his own concurring opinion. The opinion was not even sent down to the Court's printing shop for setting. Rather, it was hurriedly distributed to the other justices in typewritten form. While the activist Black would allow Willie Francis to go back to the electric chair, he would not allow Felix Frankfurter's concurrence extolling the courage required for judicial restraint to go unanswered.

Black's concurring opinion was divided into two parts. In the first part, Black explained his vote to affirm the decision of the Louisiana Supreme Court. Ignoring Wright and DeBlanc's inadequate counsel argument, Black simply asserted that "there is no contention in this case that petitioner has been denied procedural due process."[40] Rather, for Black the only basis for decision should be consideration of whether the Eighth Amendment prohibition against cruel and unusual punishment, and the Fifth Amendment ban against double jeopardy, had been made applicable to the states by the Fourteenth Amendment. If the amendments were applicable to the states, the question became whether the State of Louisiana's planned execution of Willie Francis violated either one.

Black concluded that there was ample support for finding that the Fifth and Eighth amendments were applicable to the states under the Fourteenth Amendment. Black cited and quoted from the 1867 congressional debates considering passage of the Fourteenth Amendment before the amendment was sent on to the states for ratification. These debates, Black observed, "evidence a purpose to protect all persons from state invasion of the freedoms guaranteed by the Bill of Rights. Agreement that the Amendment would accomplish this purpose seems to have been recognized by all." As Black insisted, "that this was its purpose was the common understanding of the times."[41] Moreover, Black maintained, it simply made more sense to refer to the words of the Constitution and the Bill of Rights than "to a mystical natural law which is above and beyond the Constitution, and which is to read into the due process clause so as to authorize us to strike down every state law which we think is 'indecent,' 'contrary to civilized standards,' or 'offensive to our notions of fundamental justice.'"[42]

Once applied, however, Black found that neither the Fifth Amendment nor the Eighth Amendment had been violated. He agreed with Reed that the facts presented to the Court fell short of showing that "wanton infliction of pain" which would amount to "cruel and unusual punishment." "The failure of the electrocution apparatus was purely accidental," Black wrote, "and not because of any desire of the State or any of its agents to prolong or aggravate the painful agonies which nearly always are associated with anticipation of imminent death."[43] In view of these facts, a second execution attempt would not constitute "cruel and unusual punishment."

In rejecting the Fifth Amendment challenge, Black concluded that "the double jeopardy provision was intended to prevent two punishments for the same offense."[44] No support could be found, Black reasoned, for the argument that the purpose of the double jeopardy provision was to prevent execution of a single sentence because a first effort to carry it out had been accidentally frustrated. Accordingly, Black agreed with Justice Reed that the judgment of the Louisiana Supreme Court should be affirmed.

Black disagreed, however, with the reasoning behind the result Reed had reached. In particular, Black objected to the "national standards of decency" test applied by Reed in his opinion. In the second part of his proposed concurrence, Black explained, "I cannot agree that the due process clause of the Fourteenth Amendment, or that Amendment itself, empowers this Court to strike down every state law, or state executive action, or state court judgment under state law, which may 'offend national standards of decency in the treatment of criminals.'"[45]

Sharply criticizing the Fourteenth Amendment due process approach of Frankfurter, Black continued, "If the due process clause means that, we must measure the validity of every state and federal criminal law by our conception of national 'standards of decency' without the guidance of Constitutional language." Recognizing the ultimately "subjective" nature of Frankfurter's concurrence, Black wrote: "Conduct believed 'decent' by millions of people may be believed 'indecent' by millions of others. Adoption of one or the other conflicting views as to what is 'decent,' what is right, and what is best for the people is generally recognized as a legislative function."[46]

To place the Court in such a role was unacceptable to Black. "Our courts move, I think, in forbidden territory, when they prescribe their 'standards of decency' as the supreme rule of the people." "If the Constitution had declared that the Supreme Court of the United States should ordain 'standards of decency,'" Black summarized, "I should, of course, be forced to undertake that monumental task. But it has not."[47]

While disagreeing with the constitutional reasoning of Justices Reed and Frankfurter, Justice Black nevertheless agreed with their result. Black wrote that he "share[d] most of the sentiments of those members of the Court who have so feelingly argued" on behalf of Willie Francis.[48] Yet, bound by his well-known concern for "fidelity to the constitutional text," Black concluded, "I cannot agree with them that any provision of the federal Constitution authorizes us to rule that any accidental failure fairly to carry out a valid sentence of death on the first attempt bars execution of that sentence."[49]

Stanley Reed felt helpless. Black also was charting his own course. Only two justices, Vinson and Reed, were left in agreement on the language in the "majority" opinion explaining why Willie Francis must be sent back to the electric chair. For various reasons, the other three justices believed it was necessary that they individually explain the reasons behind their vote. It was clear that the Supreme Court remained as fragmented as ever. Reed realized that bold action was needed.

Supreme Court opinions, it has been said, are often "desperately negotiated documents";[50] they are the product of a system of bargaining routine in the Supreme Court. One of the duties of the justice who is to write the opinion for the Court is to draft something on which agreement can be had by the majority of the justices which agrees in the result.[51] If there is little support for what a justice has written, the author must rethink the opinion and consider how best to secure additional support.[52] It is through this process of bargaining that Supreme Court opinions are written.

The normal difficulties associated with securing a consensus from nine justices were heightened by the highly independent-minded justices appointed by Roosevelt. Reed concluded that Frankfurter was a lost cause—he would never drop his concurring opinion. Thus, Reed would have to concentrate on persuading Justices Jackson and Black to agree with his majority opinion—an unenviable task considering the bitterness that existed between the two justices.

Reed went to Jackson's chambers and made a personal appeal to Jackson to drop his concurrence. Both Reed and Jackson had worked at the Department of Justice, with Jackson succeeding Reed as solicitor general. The two had always been on friendly terms. Reed explained the obvious importance of securing more than two justices for the Court's opinion. Jackson seemed understanding and on January 9 sent Reed a typewritten note stating only, "I agree. R.H.J."[53]

Justice Black, however, was not as susceptible to personal cajoling. Black had spent over a decade in the United States Senate and well understood the give and take of political and judicial compromise. Reed would be able to gain Black's support only if he was willing to change his opinion in accordance with Black's wishes.

On December 17, 1946, Black had expressed a reluctance to join Reed's opinion because of Reed's "national standards of decency" definition of due process and because Black believed that the Fifth and Eighth amendments should be applied to the states. At that time, Black scrawled on the back of Reed's opinion in sharp, angular handwriting: "Dear Stanley: I expect that I cannot go along on account of your definition of due process of law. Please note that I concur in the result because I do not believe that the judgment of the Mississippi [sic] Supreme Court violates due process of law or amounts to cruel and unusual punishment within the Constitutional meaning of those terms. HLB."[54] Black's views had remained suppressed until they were resurrected by the circulation of the Frankfurter concurrence.

After circulating his fourth draft opinion on January 7, 1947, Reed proposed a major change in his opinion to placate Black. In his first four drafts, Justice Reed relied solely on the due process clause of the Fourteenth Amendment, saying that in order for the Court "to determine whether or not the execution of the petitioner may fairly take place after the experience he passed, we must examine the circumstances in light of the due process clause of the Fourteenth Amendment."[55] Now, however, Reed was ready to cut a deal and meet Black halfway.

Reed proposed to delete the phrase "we must examine the circumstances in light of the due process clause of the Fourteenth Amendment," and substitute in its place "we shall examine the circumstances under the assumption, but without so deciding, that violation of the principles of the Fifth and Eighth Amendments as to double jeopardy and cruel and unusual punishment, would be violative of the due process clause of the Fourteenth Amendment."[56] Reed hoped that by applying the Fifth and Eighth amendments to the *Francis* case, without deciding that the amendments must always be applied to the states through the due process clause, Black might be enticed to drop his concurrence and join the Reed opinion.

Black found the Reed proposal interesting but wanted more. While Reed had deleted one reference to due process in the opinion, there remained other parts of the opinion which relied solely on the due process clause. Such references could be interpreted as a sign that the Court believed that only the due process clause and not the strictures of the Fifth and Eighth amendments should be applied to the states. If all references to the due process test were eliminated, however, the Court's opinion could be seen as a strong indication that the Fifth and Eighth amendments indeed applied to the states and not only the federal government. An opinion written in this manner might also effectively discount Reed's disclaimer that the Court had reached its decision "without so deciding" that the amendments were applicable to the states.[57]

Black responded to Reed's proposal with a receptive, yet firm, note scribbled in pencil:

> I have put in parentheses several clauses which I think would have to be eliminated under your assumption—while I have placed certain phrased substitutes. This I've done only to give you my general idea. I hope you can see fit to make some changes, and really believe it would have to be done in view of the changes you suggest.
>
> HLB[58]

In the margin of Reed's January 7 circulation, Black had penned his proposed substitute language.

Reed immediately incorporated verbatim all of Black's suggested changes. For example, "We find nothing to violate the due process clause of the Fourteenth Amendment in petitioner's further contention that the proposed execution would be so cruel as to offend due process" was deleted and replaced with "we find nothing in what took place here which amounts to cruel and unusual punishment in the constitutional sense."[59] Likewise, "we see no difference from the point of view of due process" became "we see no difference from a constitutional point of view."[60]

On January 11, 1947, Reed circulated his fifth and final draft opinion containing all of Black's suggestions. That same day, Black scrawled "I agree. H.L.B. Jan. 11-47"[61] on his copy of this latest draft and dropped his concurring opinion. Reed now had four justices in agreement with his opinion. Frankfurter would be upset, Reed knew, by such an important and late change in the opinion—a change with whose substance Frankfurter would violently disagree. Reed calculated, however, that Frankfurter would not change his vote which agreed with Reed's result. There would still be five votes for affirming the judgment of the Louisiana court.

Upon receipt of the January 11, 1947, Reed opinion, an angered Felix Frankfurter immediately prepared a "Memorandum for the Conference" also dated January 11, 1947. Frankfurter began the memorandum by noting that "[i]n order that there be an opinion of the Court, I had hoped to join brother Reed's opinion in addition to expressing my own views."[62] This, however, was no longer possible. "The reason," he wrote, "I cannot do so, *inter alia*, is that I do not think we should decide the case even on the assumption that the Fifth Amendment as to double jeopardy is the measure of due process of the Fourteenth Amendment."[63] Frankfurter maintained that "[i]t makes for nothing but confusion in the consideration of constitutional issues under the Due Process Clause to cite cases that construe the scope of the double jeopardy provision of the Fifth Amendment."[64] Consequently, Justice Frankfurter concluded that he could not join in Reed's opinion for the Court.

Bound by his inflexible judicial philosophy of self-restraint, Frankfurter nevertheless cast the deciding vote to send Willie back to the electric chair at the Court's January 11, 1947, Saturday conference. Amending his earlier concurrence to rebut the Reed-Black compromise, Frankfurter wrote that "great tolerance toward a State's conduct is demanded of this Court," and he approved a second attempt to execute only under the Fourteenth Amendment's due process clause which itself "expresses a demand for civilized standards."[65] Where he located those "civilized standards" remains completely mysterious. Frankfurter wrote that "a State may be found to deny a person due process by treating even one guilty of a crime in a manner that violates standards of decency more or less universally accepted though not when it treats him by a mode about which opinion is fairly divided."[66] What *that* statement means is also mysterious: What is "more or less"? Frankfurter viewed his task as sensing, apparently intuitively, the consensus of society.

Frankfurter agreed with Reed that since the first attempt had failed because of an "innocent misadventure," the second attempt would not violate these "standards of decency" and thus would not be "repugnant to the conscience of mankind."[67] As a result, he could not vote to alter the action of the state court. While still expressing a "personal revulsion" at the idea of a second attempt to execute and the state's "insistence on its pound of flesh," Frankfurter asserted that if he voted to overturn the state court's decision he would be enforcing his "private views rather than the consensus of society's opinion."[68] That means, although he did not say so, that Frankfurter was accusing the dissenters of enforcing *their* private views, and also that he knew what they did not—how to determine a societal consensus under the Fourteenth Amendment's due process clause. He neglected to note that constitutions are written to prevent, at least in part, a societal majority from imposing its views on minorities. Implicitly at least, Frankfurter repudiated the basic idea of American constitutionalism—that the majority can be tyrannical.[69]

VIII

Critique of Frankfurter's Concurring Opinion

As we have seen, in his decisive concurrence in the *Francis* case, Justice Frankfurter asserted that Supreme Court justices should not enforce their private views, but rather should determine "the consensus of society's opinion which, for purposes of due process, is the standard enjoined by the Constitution." Stressing that under the due process standard, personal views should not be imposed, Frankfurter wrote:"[w]e cannot escape acknowledging that [the problem of a second electrocution attempt] involves the application of merely personal standards of fairness and justice very broadly conceived. They are not the application of merely personal standards but the impersonal standards of society which alone judges, as the organs of law, are empowered to enforce."[1]

That would be a noble sentiment were it accurate, but it is not. Frankfurter left unanswered the question as to how he ascertained the "consensus of society's opinion" in a case for which there was no precedent. Nor did he say why that "consensus" was the appropriate standard in a Constitution that was drafted to protect minorities from the tyranny of the majority.

Frankfurter vouchsafed no clue as to how the justices could divine public opinion on due process questions. As Justice Black observed in a later case, modern technology has "not yet produced a gadget which the Court can use to determine what traditions are rooted in the [collective] conscience of our people."[2] The Supreme Court certainly "has no machinery with which to take a Gallup Poll."[3] Furthermore, Frankfurter failed to indicate whether the society he referred to was the United States as a whole, the State of Louisiana, or perhaps only the Parish of St. Martin's or the town of St. Martinville.

Although he made no mention of how the Court should have determined the societal consensus, by no means would Frankfurter have accepted a public opinion poll as an acceptable barometer. Indeed, if such a poll had been taken of both blacks and whites, the Supreme Court would undoubtedly have voted to block a second trip to the electric chair. It was reported that in the week after the first electrocution attempt, the governor of Louisiana was "deluged with an unprecedented flood of mail. . . . Thousands of letters, telegrams and postcards poured in from all parts of the United States urging clemency for Willie Francis."[4] One can only infer that Frankfurter had his personal radar finely tuned to "society's" wavelength, and thus was able to pick up signals that Burton and the other dissenting justices could not.

The difficulty with the Frankfurter position is in large part caused by a problem inherent in the vagueness of the meaning of due process in specific circumstances. As the opinion of Justice Reed illustrates, it is difficult to define with precision when a particular action violates the cruel and unusual punishment clause found in the Eighth Amendment. In rejecting Wright and DeBlanc's argument that the psychological strain of preparing to face a second execution subjected Willie to a lingering and, therefore, cruel and unusual punishment, Reed stated, "The cruelty against which the Constitution protects a convicted man is cruelty inherent in the method of punishment, not the necessary suffering involved in any method employed to extinguish life humanely."[5] Based on this standard, he concluded that the unforeseeable events that caused the first execution attempt to fail did not, as a matter of constitutional law, add to the inherent cruelty of a second execution attempt. Reed's distinction between pain inherent in the means of execution and pain actually suffered by an individual illustrates the difficulty of determining, and the Court's unwillingness to define, the exact scope of the phrase "cruel and unusual."

Furthermore, without the application of personal views it was well-nigh impossible for the Court to discern when a particular state action was proscribed by due process of law. Prior to Justice Frankfurter's "consensus of society" definition, Justice Benjamin Nathan Cardozo had formulated the generally accepted definition of the elusive due process concept in *Snyder* v. *Massachusetts* (1934).[6] Cardozo held that a state may enforce its own notions of fairness in the administration of criminal justice unless "in so doing it offends some principle of justice so rooted in the tradition and conscience of our people to be ranked as fundamental."[7] The imprecision of that "test" is manifest. Frankfurter's version of the due process standard articulated in *Francis* did not improve or clarify the Cardozo model. In fact, both so-called standards are covert invitations to the Justices to legislate what Chief Justice Earl Warren called in his valedictory their "own consciences."[8] Indeed, even Cardozo recognized that "We may try to see things as objectively as we please. None the less, we can never see them with any eyes except our own."[9]

Frankfurter allegedly sought to formulate an objective standard against which could be measured particular factual situations, but his standard falls on its own weight. It was something quite different—a subjective determination. In *Adamson* v. *California*,[10] argued before the Supreme Court on the same day that the *Willie Francis* opinion was announced, Justice Black for the first time publicly articulated his view that the Fourteenth Amendment was intended "to extend to all people of the nation the complete protection of the Bill of Rights"[11]—views that Black resisted publishing in *Francis*. The *Adamson* case became a focal point for two divergent constitutional philosophies—Justice Frankfurter's reliance on the vague due process standard and Justice Black's belief that the Fourteenth Amendment made the Bill of Rights applicable to the states.

Adamson had been convicted of first degree murder and sentenced to death in California. At his trial, he did not take the witness stand and therefore did not explain or deny any of the facts or evidence presented against him. Consistent with the California constitution, the prosecutor explained to the jury in his summation that the defendant's failure to take the stand could be considered as an admission of guilt by Adamson. Adamson's lawyers took the case to the Supreme Court, arguing that the Fifth Amendment privilege against self-incrimination ("no person shall be . . . compelled in any criminal case to be a witness against himself") applied to the states and that the California constitution was unconstitutional.

Justice Reed, again writing for the Court, upheld the constitutionality of the California law. Reed relied on the Supreme Court's 1908 decision in *Twining* v. *New Jersey*,[12] in which a judge had called the jury's attention to the defendant's failure to testify in his own defense, implying that this silence was an admission of guilt. Reed, like the 1908 court, found that the Fifth Amendment self-incrimination guarantee was not binding on states and that California was free to follow its own practice.

The real battle in the case was between Frankfurter and Black. In another of his separate concurring opinions, Frankfurter strongly supported the *Twining* decision and relied on "canons of decency and fairness which express the notions of justice of English-speaking peoples."[13] In Frankfurter's opinion, this "'natural law' has a much longer and much better founded meaning and justification than such subjective selection of the first eight amendments for incorporation into the Fourteenth."[14] Frankfurter concluded his concurrence with an endorsement of judicial restraint and urged "an alert deference" to the judgment of state courts.[15]

In a blistering dissent, Black accurately asserted in *Adamson* that Frankfurter's "natural-law-due-process formula" provided the Court with a "license . . . to roam at will in the broad expanse of policy and morals and to pass, all too freely, on the legislative domain of the States as well as the Federal government."[16] Black contended that "one of the chief objects" of the Fourteenth Amendment "was to make the Bill of Rights applicable to the states."[17] "I cannot consider the Bill of Rights," an outraged Black wrote, "to be an outworn eighteenth-century strait-jacket."[18] The Frankfurter approach, Black concluded, gave the Supreme Court "boundless power under 'natural law' periodically to expand and contract constitutional standards to conform to the Court's conception of what at a particular time constitutes 'civilized decency' and 'fundamental principles of liberty and justice.'"[19] (Why Black did not take that position in *Francis* is an unresolved mystery.)

Similarly, as early as 1948, soon after *Francis* and *Adamson* were decided, one commentator saw through the Frankfurter standard, asserting that:

Tentatively, it can be argued that Frankfurter's objective standard is a way of expressing two things: his own set of values for his society and his own conception of the safe limits of his functions. Some things he believes in strongly enough to use his power to protect them. Others he may believe in but not strongly enough to risk the charge of abuse of office.[20]

So much, one might say, for Frankfurter's *verbal* opposition to capital punishment. So much, moreover, for the mental anguish he claimed to have suffered in making his decision in *Francis*.

A decade later, in *Rochin* v. *California*[21] Frankfurter again found himself defending the philosophy of judicial self-restraint in the course of defining due process:

We may not draw on our merely personal and private notions and disregard the limits that bind judges in their judicial functions. . . . To practice the requisite detachment and to achieve sufficient objectivity no doubt demands of judges the habit of self-discipline and self-criticism, incertitude that one's own views are incontestable and alert tolerance toward views not shared. . . . These are precisely the presuppositions of our judicial process. They are precisely the qualities society has a right to expect from those entrusted with ultimate judicial power.[22]

Frankfurter went on to find in *Rochin* that the forcible use of a stomach pump by police officers was conduct "that shocks the conscience . . . [and is] too close to the rack and the screw."[23] Whose "conscience," his or society's, he did not say. Nor did he inform us as to why pumping a man's stomach was far worse than a second execution attempt.

Although he agreed with Frankfurter's result in *Rochin*, Black could not approve Frankfurter's reasoning. Criticizing the "accordion-like qualities of" the Frankfurter approach, Black asked "what avenues of investigation are open to discover 'canons' of conduct so universally favored that this Court should write them into the Constitution."[24] For Black, Frankfurter's approach was just "high-sounding rhetoric. . . . You may understand what this means; I do not."[25] Indeed, how Frankfurter's opinions in *Francis* and *Rochin* can be reconciled, insofar as constitutionally permissible action is concerned, is a mystery.

Even Justice Frankfurter had difficulties with his own due process standard. In *Haley* v. *Ohio*,[26] for example, decided a year after *Francis*, Frankfurter provided the swing vote in another five to four decision. Haley, a fifteen-year-old black youth suspected of murder, had been questioned by relays of police until 5:00 AM, at which time he confessed to the slaying. For Haley, Frankfurter concluded that a confession made without benefit of counsel had been coerced and that its admission into evidence violated due process. On the basis of that confession, Haley had been convicted of first degree murder and sentenced to life imprisonment.

In *Haley*, Justice Burton also changed his position from that in *Francis*. Reverting to his judicial philosophy of deferring to the government in criminal cases, Burton argued that the Court should place greater trust in the law enforcement community.[27] He concluded that the five-hour midnight interrogation of Haley was not unreasonable and thus, not a violation of the due process clause of the Fourteenth Amendment.

Frankfurter appeared to be troubled by his decision in *Haley*. Justice Burton again sought to change Frankfurter's mind. Frankfurter declined, but not without reservations in a letter to Burton exactly one week before the Court's decision was announced:

You charged my conscience last Saturday for an independent reconsideration of the *Haley* case. Accordingly, I put in the whole of yesterday on that case—reading the entire record, rethinking the problems that it raises, worrying about it (I am still worrying about it) and sleeping on it. For it is one of those cases which for me is a case of inherent difficulty in view of the inherent difficulties of applying the concept of "due process" to state convictions. The upshot of the best understanding of my judicial duty in a situation like this is that I find it necessary to write an opinion of my own, setting forth as candidly as I can why an admission of the confession of Haley under the circumstances in which it was made falls short of the requirements that judicially we have a right to attribute to what due process implies.[28]

As in the *Francis* case, a concurring opinion was again required to bare the innermost feelings of Frankfurter's judicial soul.

In his *Haley* concurrence, Frankfurter disagreed with Burton's conclusion, but not without struggling, once more, with the question of due process. Frankfurter conceded the "doubts and difficulties" associated with applying the due process standard. "They arise frequently when this Court is obliged to give definiteness to 'the vague contours' of Due Process, or, to change the figure, to spin judgment upon State action out of that gossamer concept." Frankfurter found that application of the due process standard "[e]ssentially . . . invites psychological judgment that reflects deep, even if inarticulate, feelings of our society. Judges must divine that feeling as best they can . . . "[29] "As best they can" is an open invitation to make a subjective judgment.

In possible reference to Willie Francis, Frankfurter again stated in *Haley* his opposition to the death penalty, especially where fifteen-year-old boys were involved. Frankfurter went on, however, to reiterate his unwillingness to impose those views on the states: "A lifetime's preoccupation with criminal justice, as prosecutor, defender of civil liberties and scientific student, naturally leaves one with views. Thus, I disbelieve in capital punishment."[30] Yet, as a judge, Frankfurter wrote, "I could not impose the views of the very few states who through bitter experience have abolished capital punishment upon all the other states, by finding that 'due process' proscribes it."[31] "Again, I do not believe that even capital offenses by boys of fifteen should be dealt with according to the conventional procedure." Frankfurter declared, "[i]t would, however, be bald judicial usurpation to hold that the States violate the Constitution in subjecting minors like Haley to such a procedure."[32]

Without giving reasons, Frankfurter wrote that the "Court must give the freest possible scope to the States in the choice of their methods of criminal procedure. But these procedures cannot include methods that may fairly be deemed to be in conflict with deeply rooted feelings of the community." Frankfurter admitted that his due process test suffered from "inherent vagueness." While "this is a most difficult test to apply," Frankfurter decided, "apply it we must, warily, and from case to case."[33]

For the fifteen-year-old Haley, Frankfurter concluded that the "deeply rooted feelings of the community" dictated a reversal of the youth's conviction for murder and the penalty of life imprisonment. At the time of the murder of Andrew Thomas, Willie Francis was also fifteen. For Francis, however, Frankfurter found that the "consensus of society" condemned the youth to a second trip to the electric chair.

One of Frankfurter's former law clerks has argued that Frankfurter's opinion in the *Francis* case "stands as a personal monument to judgment over feeling."[24] Indeed, a Frankfurter biographer has written that "Frankfurter always thought that the Court's actions in the case of *Francis v. Resweber* in 1948 [sic] provided a classic proof of the judicial process at its very best."[35] Frankfurter saw his vote as an act of judicial courage: "Frankfurter said no one could ever really understand what it meant to be in the grip of the judicial function, and to refuse to write one's personal opinions and values into the law."[36]

It is simply not enough to speak of "society" and the "consensus of society's opinion" as if those terms mean something precise—which emphatically they do not. If the terms had some precise meanings in Frankfurter's mind, he never revealed them. Nor did he ever disclose how he determined the societal consensus. How could Frankfurter's vote, despite his professed reliance on the "consensus of society's opinion" be anything but his own private view?

The only possible conclusion is that Frankfurter in the *Francis* case used the term as a means of covering up his own personal predilections—an approach for which he castigated the dissent for adopting. There was a crucial difference between Frankfurter's concurrence and the dissent in the case. The dissent relied on their private views to advance humanitarianism and to save Willie Francis. Frankfurter relied on his private view to advance an abstract judicial philosophy. That philosophy was more important to Frankfurter than an impoverished youth's life.

IX

Reaction to the Court's Decision

Willie Francis had suffered greatly in the months after the botched execution attempt. In his cell at the New Iberia jail, the thought of returning to the electric chair was ever present. On three occasions Willie was told of a date on which he was to be executed. Three times the sixteen-year-old had to prepare himself mentally to die. And three times he was granted a stay of execution. How many more times, Willie wondered, would a second trip to the electric chair be delayed? The mental turmoil of the teenager can only be imagined, but surely it was present.

Willie had waited anxiously for the decision of the Louisiana Supreme Court, only to be disappointed by its ruling. Encouraged by DeBlanc's optimism, Willie had raised expectations over his prospects before the Louisiana Pardons Board, but again was disappointed. Finally, Willie endured a roller coaster of emotions by being first told that the United States Supreme Court would not hear his case, and then being told that the Supreme Court would consider it after all. The pressure on young Willie was immense, for the stakes were nothing less than life itself.

Following the filing of the petition for *certiorari*, the brief on the merits, and Skelly Wright's oral argument, Willie could only wait and pray. He was a hapless pawn of a slow-moving legal system. There was nothing he could do for his cause or contribute to his legal defense. His fate rested completely on the abilities of Skelly Wright and Bertrand DeBlanc, and on the insights and compassion of the nine men on the Supreme Court. An inevitable feeling of uncertainty and helplessness enveloped Willie as he awaited the Court's decision. It was his last chance to escape being killed by Louisiana.

During these difficult and anxious days, Willie tried to keep busy and fill the idle time in his cell. Each day, he faithfully read a Bible his father brought to him from his ill mother. Occasionally, he broke into song, singing the spirituals he had learned as a child. Willie spent many hours discussing the Bible and his faith in the daily visits of Father Hannegan. Willie's father and family and a few friends would also visit him, as would Bertrand DeBlanc, to keep him company.

Friends and family brought magazines for Willie to page through. He struggled over the text of many of the magazines, but the pictures and scenes of distant places provided him with an opportunity to mentally escape his small jail, if only for a few minutes. Willie often thought that if he were freed he would go to Los Angeles and work—"any kind of work." A sister lived there: He hoped to make a new life away from the South and Louisiana.

In addition to these activities, Willie spent a great deal of time with his mail. Soon after the first execution attempt, Willie began to receive letters and telegrams from all over the country. He had become a national figure and provided copy for newspapers. Willie said that he "felt just like a movie star" and "didn't have any idea [he] had so many friends."[1] Although he could write after a fashion, his minimal skills were not adequate to respond to the flood of mail. With the tutoring and help of Father Hannegan and DeBlanc, however, Willie read most of the letters and personally answered many of them.

Most of the letters Willie received expressed support and encouragement. The writers strongly criticized Louisiana for not sparing Willie from a second trip to the electric chair. One correspondent, a preacher from Chattanooga, Tennessee, believed that Willie was saved by God to become a famous minister.[2] Enclosed in many of the letters were small gifts, including cash contributions and rosary beads.[3]

He also received a number of quite unusual letters, one of the strangest of which came from Mrs. Wilmer Cox of Dallas, Texas.[4] Mrs. Cox began her letter with a request: her brother Rufus had been blind since childhood, so would Willie will his eyes to Rufus if Willie had to die in the electric chair? Mrs. Cox said that she didn't want Willie to die and was embarrassed because the request was dependent on his death. But if Willie had to die, could she have his eyes for her brother Rufus?

Curiously, Willie was deeply touched by the woman's request. When he was a child in St. Martinville, he played games with an elderly blind neighbor in his front yard. When they finished their games, the old man would kiss Willie on the forehead. Years later, Willie remained touched by the kindness of his neighbor. He had developed a great deal of sympathy for the blind. As long as he must go to the "Great Beyond," Willie resolved, he would be glad to help someone who was blind by giving them his eyes.[5]

With the assistance of Bertrand DeBlanc, Willie drew up this simple will: "This is my last will and testament knowing life is not sure and God may call me to life everlasting. I want to atone for my life. I leave and bequeath to Rufus Allen of Dallas, Texas, my eyes and that being all that I will dying, have left, I have no other things to will." It was signed, "Yours truly, Willie Francis."[6]

Within a week, however, Willie was forced to break the will. His bed-ridden mother had heard about the promise and would not allow Willie to give up his eyes, even in death. Willie obeyed his mother's wishes, but his disappointment was evident in a letter written to a friend of Mrs. Cox who also lived in Dallas. The letter was dated June 2, 1946, two days before Wright and DeBlanc filed the petition for *certiorari* with the Supreme Court:

Dear Mrs. Taylor,

I received your letter and really was glad to hear from you. About my past, I didn't mean no harm. I received a Rosary. I didn't know who sent it. Since you mentioned about it that you sent it I really do thank you. I didn't receive the magazines yet. I think I will get them Monday. I have written to Mrs. Cox and explained to her about the will I made for my eyes. I had to make my mind up for me to break the will. I hope Mrs. Cox will understand. I had made a promise to her. My mother had wrote to me and told me to break the will up. It took four days for me to write to her and explain everything. I was sorry to break my promise.

Things are not going so good in my case—I am not afraid to die. Only one thing I am worrying about is my soul. Now that I am going to die Friday, I am prepared to meet the Lord. This may be my last letter to you. I won't say "goodbye," because we will meet in Heaven.

Your friend in Christ,

Willie Francis.[7]

Although Willie's disappointments and worries were relieved temporarily by the announcement on June 11, 1946, that the Supreme Court had decided to take his case, the news of impending Supreme Court review served only to increase the amount of mail arriving daily for Willie in his tiny cell.

Among them was a strange offer from Mrs. John F. Kenney of Washington, D.C. An ex-army captain's wife, Mrs. Kenney offered her husband as a substitute for Willie Francis if Willie had to go to the electric chair for a second time. Mrs. Kenney stated that her husband was "probably permanently and totally disabled . . . and unable to obtain any consideration from the Veteran's Administration."[8] Through a letter from

DeBlanc, Willie politely and firmly declined to accept the woman's generosity with her husband's life.

The months of Bible reading and letter writing kept Willie busy but failed to keep his mind off the pending death sentence. The sting of the electric current "like thousands of needles" remained with him. The prospect of Louisiana finishing off what it had started was emotionally draining. Through it all, Willie held on to the hope that somehow his prayers would be answered—that he would not have to return to the electric chair.

On January 13, 1947, one day after his eighteenth birthday, the Supreme Court ended Willie's hopes by the barest of margins. The Court's decision removed all obstacles to Louisiana's plan for a second electrocution. All that remained was for Governor Davis to issue a new death warrant. By all indications, that warrant would come quickly. On the day of the Court's decision, the governor's executive counsel, George Wallace, announced that Davis planned to issue another death warrant fixing the date of execution as soon as the Supreme Court forwarded the "mandate" or certified copy of the decision.[9] According to Supreme Court Rules, a mandate would issue twenty-five days from the date of the Court's decision.

When the news reached Willie, he was staring out of the window of his cell. Directly below him were the simple rooftops of New Iberia, and the above-ground graves of St. Peter's Cemetery. His thoughts, however, dwelled on his family and life back in St. Martinville. He had heard speculation that the Supreme Court might rule in his favor and prohibit a second electrocution. It had now been nearly two months since oral argument. Surely, if the Court was going to affirm the lower court's decision, it would have done so by now. There was talk that the length of time the Court was taking in reaching its decision must be an indication that the Court was grappling with the more difficult task of explaining its reasons for reversing the decision of a lower court.

Willie did not fully understand the reasons, but he detected an increased optimism about his chances with the Supreme Court. This optimism was reflected in his behavior. Indeed, Sheriff Ozenne noticed that Willie appeared quite cheerful since the first days of 1947.[10] He also noticed that the skinny youth was eating better and had begun to add weight on his slender frame. For the first time, Willie was talking and joking with other inmates on the top floor of the jail.[11]

As Willie looked at the world outside of his cell window, he believed there was a chance that someday, somehow, he might be back home with his family. In an instant, these thoughts were dashed forever. Willie was standing at the window when Sheriff Ozenne broke the news of the Supreme Court's decision. At that moment, the song "You Are My Sunshine," being played on a radio at the guard's station, haunted the cell block. Willie slumped to his cot. After a moment he got up and started walking around his cell.

"It's the same thing again," Willie told Sheriff Ozenne. "I got to start worrying again, and boss, I thought I'd got out of it. But I guess a man's got to d-d-die some time," he stuttered, "and I reckon' my time has plumb done come."[12]

Willie had given up hope. "This time it'll be different," Willie told the sheriff. "That electric chair is going to work."[13]

Ozenne asked Willie if there was anything he could do for him. Should he notify members of the Francis family of the Court's decision?[14]

"No, thanks," Willie said, trying to manage a smile. "I'll let you know if I need any help." Willie wanted to be alone.[15]

Willie had always been superstitious; the Court's decision only reinforced these feelings. He was the thirteenth child of Fred and Louise Francis. And he was convicted of murder in St. Martinville on the thirteenth of September 1945. Now, the Supreme Court ruling was announced on the thirteenth day of January. Willie was convinced that he was doomed to return to the electric chair.

Resigned to his fate, Willie bore no ill-feelings toward the nine Supreme Court justices: "Five of the Justices voted against me and four for me. That's pretty close to happiness, I guess. I'm not complaining or anything like that 'cause I know down in my heart, everybody's tried to do the right thing for me and for everybody else. It's just that there's never been another case like mine before and I see how hard it is to say what is the right thing in my case. If I ever get to heaven, I guess, I'll get to know."[16]

Although Willie would not criticize the Supreme Court's decision, the nation's newspapers were not as understanding or forgiving.[17] Press comment was highly unfavorable. Editorial writers across the country were dismayed by the result reached by the Court. Within a day of the Court's pronouncement, editorial pages were filled with columns roundly condemning the decision. Justice Reed had accurately predicted that the decision would generate a public firestorm.

Perhaps the most moving and eloquent commentary was written by Walter White, secretary of the National Association for the Advancement of Colored People. "William Shakespeare should have been in the United States Supreme Court on Jan. 13. Had he been there he most surely would have ruefully remembered his famous line, 'The quality of mercy is not strained,'" White began.[18] "For on that day five Justices of the Court . . . hewed bitterly close to the line of 'justice' and the 'law' while humanity and equity hung their heads in shame." "But humanity's sad visage must have been lightened," White wrote, "by the warm hearts" of four justices led by Justice Harold Burton.[19]

The victim of the Court's "cold justice untempered with mercy" was seventeen-year-old Willie Francis. "When he was fifteen he was arrested, tried and sentenced to death for the alleged murder of a Louisiana druggist. Poverty stricken, virtually illiterate, knowing from the day of his birth only the contumely to which a black skin condemns its possessor in the Deep South, Willie Francis spent many long days and longer nights awaiting death."[20]

White described the mental and physical suffering endured by Willie in the first execution attempt. Willie's suffering, White pointed out, was not enough for the Supreme Court: "And now five men wrapped snugly in the silken robes of the high court and seated in the marble aloofness of the building in Washington dedicated to equity and human kindness as well as the strict letter of the law have said that Willie Francis must sit again in the Louisiana electric chair—and again, and again, and again until the sentence of the court that electric current be made to pass through his body until he is dead has been finished."[21]

White was appalled by such a result, as were other newspapers in the country. Columnist Max Lerner wrote, "In a world that has all but forgotten the human impulse it is a wise thing to heed a cry from the human heart. Even for Justices of the United States Supreme Court."[22] Lerner recalled how Willie "passed through terror once and slipped away from death." "Where five men weigh the legal arguments in one fashion and four in another," Lerner declared, "the margin of legal doubt should surely have been great enough to allow a sense of humanity to operate."[23] Lerner's point is all the more appropriate when one considers Reed's difficulty in even getting five justices to "weigh the legal arguments in one fashion."

Likewise, the *Pittsburgh Press* was critical of the narrowness of the Court's decision. The *Press* observed "a crowning irony" in the "separate opinion of one of the majority—Mr. Justice Frankfurter—who said he was "strongly drawn" by the views of the minority, but voted the other way because the Supreme Court has no legal right to interfere with a 'state's insistence on its pound of flesh.'"[24] All this legal maneuvering meant little, for "if the chair works the next time, Willie Francis will be just as dead as if the high judges had agreed 9-to-0 on what the law requires and permits. Then he won't have to worry about ironies."[25]

Taking another tack, the *Norfolk State News* directly disagreed with Justice Frankfurter's assertion that the "consensus of society" condemned Willie to a second execution. The paper stated that the Court's decision "does not find widespread public acceptance."[26] Despite the complex and sophisticated legal reasons put forward by the majority and Frankfurter, "it still does not alter the wide and justifiably held opinion that to subject a convicted man to a second attempt at electrocution after failure of the first attempt, does in fact, if not constitutionally, subject him to that kind of punishment."[27]

Rather than the death sentence for Willie Francis, the *Norfolk News* suggested that "the national conscience would be eased if the governor of Louisiana were to commute the youth's death sentence to life imprisonment. . . . We strongly commend this view to the governor of Louisiana."[28] This view was also expressed editorially by the *New York Law Journal*: "It would be unfortunate, indeed, if this young colored boy should now be put to death over the protests of four Justices of the Supreme Court of the United States. Any chance for the further inflictions of injuries upon society could be eliminated by his permanent incarceration."[29]

Of course, editorial condemnation of the Court's opinion was by no means universal. The *Washington Post*, for example, found it "difficult to follow the mental processes which have led to criticism of the Supreme Court for its decision in the Willie Francis case." The *Post* explained that "mercy has a useful and rightful place in any democratic system of law enforcement."[30] Willie Francis, however, was not an appropriate candidate for this mercy because "mercy ought to be applied on some other basis than mere mishap. We do not think the Court can be expected to write a mercy concept into the due process clause."[31] The *Post* concluded that "if the Court is to be criticized for straightforward and legally impeccable decisions of this sort, the public understanding of this function is likely to become increasingly distorted."[32]

A number of southern newspapers also applauded the Court's decision. The Greenville, South Carolina, *News* said that "the Supreme Court has delivered an entirely logical judgment in the case of Willie Francis of Louisiana."[33] Praising the Court's decision, the Birmingham, Alabama, *Age Herald* noted the debt of gratitude owed by "Willie Francis, 18 years old, colored, and not too bright."[34] "So long, Willie," the unsympathetic editor wrote, "You're going to die again. But the people of America have given a lot of their time thinking about your case. It's cost the country a good bit of money, more than you could ever earn if you lived to be a hundred." "When you go this time, Willie," the paper urged, "walk in straight and sit down and smile and say 'good-bye' in a strong voice. . . . Take it strong and easy boy."[35] In that same vein, Arthur Krock of the *New York Times* saluted the Court for the "care given the most lowly at bar."[36]

Despite the occasionally negative editorials, Bertrand DeBlanc was impressed by the renewed outpouring of sympathy for his client in the aftermath of the Supreme Court's decision. A song entitled "De Lord Fool'd Around Wid Dat Chair" had even been published depicting Willie's escape from death. It seemed apparent to DeBlanc that the public believed that the physical and mental pain of the electric chair should not be visited on Willie Francis a second time.

DeBlanc recognized the value of this public support. First, popular opinion might be useful in another plea before the Louisiana State Pardons Board. Indeed, one newspaper reported that, "a California mother, whose doctor had given her only four months to live, spent part of that time in a futile trip to Baton Rouge to plead for 'Willie's life.'"[37] Second, the public support for Willie might be used as a source of contributions for Willie's legal defense fund, namely, Bertrand DeBlanc. He had never billed the Francis family for the months he had spent on Willie's case. But with a wife and children to support, DeBlanc needed to generate some income from the case.

For these reasons, DeBlanc wasted no time in seeking to capitalize on this public support. Under Willie's signature, DeBlanc sent out a form letter to dozens of the then popular weekly black newspapers. For example, on January 25, 1947, the following letter was reprinted by the editor-publisher of the *Chicago Defender*:

> Dear Sir:
>
> I was sitting in my cell hoping for some good news. But when they told me that the Supreme Court of the United States said I have to go back to the chair, I just about gave up hope. I sat in that chair once and I was ready to sit in it again. But yesterday my lawyer told me he's going to ask the Court to hear the case again. He says the decision was so close maybe we'd have a chance to win. Mind you, I'm not afraid to die if the good Lord wants me to, but I do want to live if I can.
>
> My lawyer never took a cent from me or my family because he knows we're poor. The expenses in all those courts ate up the money sent in from some good people, and money is needed now. There are still lots of expenses and no society ever gave my lawyer any money.
>
> I ask the good people to help me please. If anybody who reads this paper wants to help save me from going back to the chair, I ask them to please send whatever money they can here to me at the jail. I'll answer and thank them all myself. Thank-you, Sir, for printing this. May God bless you all.
>
> Willie Francis[38]

By this appeal for funds to carry on the fight for his life, the message would be spread in the black community. Often, a plea for mercy and funds would be preached in the family-oriented black churches along with a lesson on the value of forgiveness. A church might then take up a special collection which the newspaper could send to DeBlanc. The appeal proved popular, and the cash contributions were significant.

Willie Francis's cause was a popular one. By contrast, the image of the Supreme Court suffered. It was considered as unmovable and cold as the white marble from which the Court building was shaped. Walter

White summarized these impressions in the concluding paragraph of his comment on the *Francis* case:

Gentlemen, you have done your duty. Cold justice has been upheld. Only if there be pity in the heart of the Governor of Louisiana can Willie Francis's second—or, maybe third or fourth—long walk of the last mile be stayed. We hope, gentlemen of the majority of the United States Supreme Court, that you will not jump also in pain in your warm, comfortable beds in Washington the night Willie Francis again jams his feet against the floor when the switch is thrown. Messrs. Burton, Douglas, Murphy and Rutledge need fear no such bad dreams the night Willie Francis crosses Jordan because they tempered justice with mercy in their dissenting opinion.

Swing low sweet chariot.[39]

X

Frankfurter's Extrajudicial Machinations

Within days of the announcement of his decisive concurring opinion, Justice Felix Frankfurter began to receive letters criticizing his decision. One letter exclaimed, "It is almost impossible to believe that a human being, who does not happen to be a Jap or a Nazi should condemn Willie Francis to death a second time!!!"[1] A letter from Adrian Conan Doyle, son of famed British author Arthur Conan Doyle, read simply, "May God forgive you. Man will not."[2] And a woman from Albany, California, wrote the childless Frankfurter, "Such would not likely happen to your son. He is white and Willie is black."[3]

Most of the letters, however, appealed to Frankfurter's sense of mercy. One, from a Laurenceville, Illinois, woman, read: "You are men of learning and culture. No one can change your final decision. But four of you differ. Then there is a chance that they may be right. Underneath your black robes are hearts. It isn't too difficult, is it, to reconsider this case, that of underprivileged Willie Francis."[4]

The most compelling letter came from Mrs. Harold Evans of New York City on January 20, 1947: "That Boy committed the crime at 15 and since has gone through the valley of the shadow of death and God gave him another chance and you took it away from him. As a white mother please help this boy. Had he been white he could have been sent to a reformatory in the first place, or perhaps gotten a suspended sentence. Perhaps you could instruct their governor to help him. Thanks for what you will do to help this child."[5]

Touched by the obvious sincerity of Mrs. Evans's letter, Frankfurter departed from his usual rule of not acknowledging letters or communications that discussed opinions of the Court. Frankfurter believed that a

justice should not discuss judicial actions and opinions with members of
the general public, but must leave them to speak for themselves.[6] A
justice must keep quiet, no matter how much an opinion might be mis-
understood. By practice, Frankfurter would refer such communications
to the clerk of the Court to acknowledge receipt of the letter on behalf of
the justice.

For Mrs. Evans, however, Frankfurter sent a short response on January
24, evidencing the emotional tug of Willie's case: "You will permit me to
say that I quite appreciate your compassionate feeling on the Willie Francis case. I share it. But a judge of this Court isn't God—he is not even the
Governor of the State, in whom is vested the power of executive clemency. You may care to see the opinion of the Court in this case."[7]

Justice Frankfurter was clearly frustrated by the result of his and the
Court's decision in *Francis*. He would later say that the case "told on my
conscience a great deal. . . . I was very much bothered by the problem,
it offended my personal sense of decency to do this. Something inside of
me was very unhappy, but I did not see that it [the second execution
attempt] violated due process of law."[8] As a result of his dissatisfaction,
and perhaps prompted by Mrs. Evans's letter, Frankfurter sought to
overturn the Supreme Court's *Francis* decision in an extraordinary example of extrajudicial intervention.

Operating through a Harvard classmate and influential member of the
Louisiana bar, Monte E. Lemann, Frankfurter secretly tried to secure
executive clemency for Willie Francis from the governor of Louisiana.
Throughout this attempt, Justice Frankfurter's activities and involve-
ment were kept secret from the governor, the Board of Reprieves and
Pardons of the State of Louisiana, and, apparently, from all but one of
Frankfurter's fellow justices.

One cannot reconcile Frankfurter's vote as a justice to send Willie back
to the electric chair with these secret extrajudicial activities to spare
Willie. Did he think he wore the dual hats of justice and private citizen
and could keep these activities separate? Surely, it perverts the judicial
process for a justice to try to reverse a Supreme Court decision by secret
efforts to manipulate state politics. Would it not have been more honest
for Frankfurter to vote for his self-asserted conviction that Willie should
not take a second trip to the electric chair?

On February 3, 1947, three weeks after the Supreme Court issued its
opinion in *Francis*, Frankfurter wrote Monte Lemann in New Orleans,
soliciting his assistance in commuting Willie Francis's death sentence to
life imprisonment.[9] Lemann and Frankfurter had roomed together at
Harvard and had graduated from the Harvard Law School the same year.
After graduation, Lemann returned to Louisiana where he quietly became a leader in both the civic and legal communities.

Lemann gained national prominence in 1929 when President Hoover named him to the National Commission on Law Observance and Enforcement, generally known as the Wickersham Commission.[10] The commission spent the next two years studying the question of prohibition, before recommending in an 80,000-word report further and stricter efforts to enforce prohibition. Lemann was the only one of the eleven-member board who refused to sign the report stating, instead, that there was "no alternative but repeal of the Eighteenth Amendment"—a dissent popular with both the Democratic party which advocated such a repeal and its future presidential candidate, Franklin Roosevelt.[11] Felix Frankfurter also took notice of his former classmate's strong stand. In a January 22, 1931, letter to Lemann, Frankfurter praised Lemann's action with these words: "seldom has courageous action been so fittingly expressed as in your report. Its calm temper, the sober sense of intellectual responsibility that pervades the whole, make it stand as a notable document."[12]

Through the years, Frankfurter and Lemann continued to follow each other's careers and maintained a friendly, personal correspondence. In fact, in 1938 Frankfurter recommended to President Roosevelt that he name Lemann to the United States Court of Appeals for the Fifth Circuit—a post which Roosevelt later offered but which Lemann declined. Frankfurter described Lemann to Roosevelt as "about the best lawyer south of the Mason and Dixon line" and a person who "really cared about the social reforms of the New Deal," including "securing the effective sympathy" of a southern industrialist for the Roosevelt administration.[13] "By a few such appointments you would not only prevent judicial obstruction," Frankfurter wrote Roosevelt in the midst of the court-packing controversy, "but perpetuate your social outlook in the administration of law for the next twenty years. With men like Monte Lemann in the Fifth Circuit . . . you would be creating judges mindful of the basic function of the law as the body of arrangements for realizing social needs. Such men have not only a progressive outlook now, but they would be openminded to needful changes ten and fifteen years hence."[14] Strangely, Frankfurter himself was not open to progressive social needs nine years later in the *Francis* case. As a consequence, Frankfurter was forced to seek Lemann's help to do politically what Frankfurter was unwilling to do judicially.

Heading the February 3 letter to Lemann "Strictly Confidential," Frankfurter sent a copy of the letter to Justice Burton with the following note: "H.H.B., For your information, F.F."[15] Frankfurter began his letter with a lecture on the general responsibilities of the bar. If there was a legal or judicial "mess" in a state requiring government attention, it was the responsibility of the bar to persuade the state to "clean up the . . . mess." Action by the bar "would be true to the best traditions of our profession and save the State much future misery." Such was the case with respect to Willie Francis. "I have little doubt that if Louisiana allows Francis to go to his death," Frankfurter warned Lemann, "it will needlessly cast a cloud upon Louisiana for many years to come, and, what is more important, probably leave many of its citizens with disquietude."[16] (Strange words, those, from a man who cast the deciding vote in Willie's case.)

In addition to that warning of possible racial discontent, Frankfurter cited policy and equitable considerations as support for clemency. Frankfurter noted that "in New York, when there is a real division in the Court of Appeals, such as there was here, the death sentence is as a matter of course commuted to life imprisonment. There is no formal law about it but it is a settled tradition." Moreover, he asked, "Is there any possible reason for saying that, if Francis is allowed to go to his death instead of imprisonment for life, the restraints against crimes of violence will be relieved?"[17]

The strain which the judicial decision-making process in *Francis* may have inflicted on Frankfurter is visible in the letter's conclusion: "This cause has been so heavily on my conscience that I finally could not overcome the impulse to write you."[18] Frankfurter ended by asking whether the State of Louisiana could show "humaneness" and "compassion" in granting clemency—an action Frankfurter was quite unwilling himself to take by voting with Burton. "It is difficult for me to believe that clemency would not be forthcoming, whatsoever may be the machinery of your state for its exercise," Frankfurter wrote, "if leading members of the bar pressed upon the authorities that even to err on the side of humaneness in the Francis situation can do no possible harm and might strengthen the forces of goodwill, compassion, and wisdom in society."[19]

Unknown to Frankfurter, Louisiana trial court Judge James Simon had been a student of Monte Lemann's at Tulane University Law School. On the surface, it might appear that the former law professor would exercise some influence over his former student. Lemann, however, was less than sure of any effect he might have on Simon. The judge had come from a prominent family in St. Martinville. Indeed, Simon was the third generation to have been a judge in the area and was said to harbor ambitions for statewide elective office—ambitions that might not be advanced if it was contended that he was "soft on blacks." Despite doubts over the prospects of success for the clemency plea, Lemann wrote Judge Simon on April 19, 1947.

Lemann first called the judge's attention to English practice where "considerations of humanity" would dictate against a second execution. Noting that "the English are not soft people and have a deserved reputation for the recognition of fundamental human rights," Lemann recommended that the Louisiana Pardons Board decide against a second electrocution for Francis. Lemann hoped that the reference to the English as not being "soft people" might alleviate fears that Simon might have of being called "soft" in a future political campaign. In addition, Lemann argued to his former student that "it does not seem to me to be a determining factor whether electric current passed through Willie Francis' body or not. The controlling circumstance would be the fact that he was exposed to the ordeal of an abortive execution."[20]

With an oblique reference to Justice Frankfurter, Lemann impressed on Simon the importance of the case before the Louisiana Pardons Board: "I realize that the eyes of the world are in a sense upon us in this case, because I have myself had communications from lawyers of high standing, for whose opinions I have great respect, one of whom wrote me recently that he felt it would be a serious blot upon our State if Francis was permitted to be executed."[21] "These considerations," he continued, "do not, of course, relieve the Pardons Board of its responsibility of reaching its own decision, but I imagine that you and the other members of the Board will feel as much influenced as I have been by opinions so entitled to respect."[22] Lemann then pleaded that, "where at the very least there is so much room for doubt as to what is the proper course to adopt, the further punishment of Francis is not as important as adherence to the highest standards of decency and humaneness which a large and informed body of public opinion feels would be betrayed by Francis's execution."[23]

It is ironic that Lemann's plea to Judge Simon, made at Frankfurter's request, cannot be reconciled with Frankfurter's concurring opinion in *Francis*. Lemann's argument that clemency was warranted by the "highest standards of decency and humaneness" and a "large and informed body of public opinion" is obviously incompatible with Frankfurter's conclusion that a second attempt would not be "repugnant to the conscience of mankind" or the "consensus of society." Indeed, Lemann's letter provides a number of compelling reasons as to why Frankfurter should have voted to block a second execution attempt.

On April 23, 1947, Frankfurter circulated to his fellow justices a copy of Lemann's letter to Judge Simon. The accompanying note from Frankfurter clearly indicates that, other than Justice Burton, they had been told nothing of the letter's conception and parentage: "Dear Brethren: Monte Lemann is, I suppose, unexcelled at the Louisiana bar. He happens to be an old and close friend so it is natural for him to send the enclosure. I thought it might interest the Brethren. F.F."[24] Frankfurter did not mention his role in generating Lemann's letter; nor, apparently, did Burton enlighten the other seven. The obvious question is this: If Frankfurter's extrajudicial actions to try to save Willie's life were proper for a Supreme Court justice, why the secrecy?

On April 22, 1947, Frankfurter wrote a letter of appreciation to Lemann: "You could not have made a better plea for saving Francis from death than by your letter to Judge Simon. . . . Your letter may perhaps be more effective than a formal association as counsel for Francis."[25] "For more than forty years, if I can count straight," Frankfurter continued, "you have chided me for excessive enthusiasm about this or the other thing."[26] "If I tell you that Marion [Frankfurter's wife] is as impressed as I am by your whole procedure in connection with the Willie Francis case, you cannot charge me with excessive appreciation."[27] Thus, it is plain that Frankfurter saw nothing improper in trying to do politically what he would not do judicially.

Justice Frankfurter's attempt to secure executive clemency for Willie Francis had been foreshadowed in his concurring opinion. While "strongly drawn" by the sentiments expressed in Justice Burton's dissent, Frankfurter nevertheless believed that the political solution of executive clemency was constitutionally more attractive than the judicial solution of mitigation of a sentence of death. This approach was consistent with Frankfurter's life-long philosophy regarding the role of the courts in the federal system, but was inconsistent with his verbalized sentiments about the death penalty. He, therefore, had a choice to make between contrary personal principles.

Throughout his career, Felix Frankfurter advocated judicial self-restraint, believing in a quiescent judiciary that leaves litigants no other option than to try to influence the political process. That approach, however, is fatally flawed when the political process cannot adequately meet the demands or aspirations of numerous people and groups. In his 1962 dissent in *Baker* v. *Carr*,[28] Frankfurter told voters in urban areas of Tennessee that they should not invoke the Constitution to eliminate the state's "rotten borough" system, which ensured dilution of the black vote. Rather, they should go to the state legislature and ask that it enforce the state's constitution—in other words, ask the legislators from the rural areas to vote themselves out of office.[29] In both *Francis* and *Baker*, Frankfurter exalted form over substance. If, therefore, Willie Francis were to avoid the electric chair, it would have to be as a result of compassion on the part of Louisiana officials and not Supreme Court decree.

Frankfurter was quite aware of the political realities that existed in the United States in 1947. As a professor at Harvard Law School, Justice Brandeis enlisted him as a paid political lobbyist.[30] Later as a counselor to President Roosevelt and even as a Supreme Court justice, Frankfurter placed loyal friends and former students in positions of influence throughout the country and labored for enactment of desired programs. The near appointment of Monte Lemann to the Fifth Circuit was but one example of Frankfurter's political influence. How, then, could the politically astute Frankfurter have seriously entertained much hope for the success of his extraordinary enterprise?

In 1947, the annual income of black families in the United States was far below that of white families. Segregation of schools and public facilities was lawful, and the "universal practice in the South."[31] And 1947 was the year that the color barrier in baseball had finally been broken when Jackie Robinson joined the Brooklyn Dodgers—a fact that resulted in a threatened rebellion by some baseball players. What blacks lacked most in 1947, however, was political leverage and influence.

In his classic study of racial problems in the United States, *American Dilemma* (1944), Gunnar Myrdal wrote:

From the point of view of the American Creed, the status accorded the Negro in America represents nothing more and nothing less than a century-long lag of public morals. In principle the Negro problem was settled long ago; in practice the solution is not yet effectuated. The Negro in America has not yet been given the elemental civil and political rights of formal democracy, including a fair opportunity to earn his living, upon which a general accord was already [reached] when the American Creed was first taking form.[32]

The lack of "political rights of formal democracy" was evident in voting statistics. Black voter turnout in the South was virtually nonexistent. In the 1946 Mississippi Democratic primary, for example, approximately 3,000 out of the 5,000 registered black voters went to the polls. Yet, according to the 1940 census, there were 1,074,578 black residents in Mississippi.

The reasons for these statistics were several. Until 1944, the white primary, by which participation in the Democratic primary was limited to white citizens, was used in Texas, Alabama, Arkansas, Georgia, Louisiana, and Mississippi as the most effective modern "legal" device for disenfranchising blacks. In 1944 the Supreme Court in *Smith* v. *Allwright* held this practice unconstitutional.[33] Even after 1944, however, voter turnout was low—no doubt attributable to the venomous discouragement of state officials. In one recorded example, United States Senator Theodore Bilbo of Mississippi, in the week before the Democratic primary, inflamed his audience with these words: "White people will be justified in going to any extreme to keep the niggers from voting. You do it the night before the election—I don't have to tell you any more than that. Red-blooded men know what I mean."[34]

Louisiana was little different. Justice Douglas would later write in his judicial autobiography that he considered Louisiana in the 1940s to be "dominantly racist, at least as far as its leaders were concerned."[35] Furthermore, the black population in those oppressive times had very little, if any, political power. The Louisiana constitutions of 1898 and 1921 had effectively disenfranchised the black voter.

To vote in a general election or a primary, an individual had to meet a number of requirements listed in the two constitutions. The parish registrar of voters administered these requirements in a racially discriminatory manner. For example, in the March 1940 Democratic primary for governor, there were 653,087 literate white registered voters. By contrast, there were only 884 black registrants who were considered "literate."[36] The disparity could usually be traced to the more difficult literacy tests that were administered to the blacks.

The members of the Louisiana Pardons Board could read and understand these voting statistics. Lieutenant Governor Emile Veret was mentioned prominently in the state's newspapers as a probable candidate for governor in the 1948 election.[37] There was also talk of Attorney General LeBlanc as a possible gubernatorial candidate. If not, LeBlanc certainly planned to run for reelection as attorney general. And Judge Simon was concerned with both the future (election to the Louisiana State Supreme Court) and the present (winning reelection to his post as a Louisiana trial judge in St. Martin's Parish). With virtually no black political influence, recommending a pardon or commutation of sentence for Willie would generate few votes. Indeed, under the stark political realities of 1947, such a decision could only lose votes of disenchanted supporters. Clearly, amid such an adverse environment a black youth convicted of slaying a white man stood little chance of securing executive mercy.

From the court record, Justice Frankfurter knew that the pardon process had already failed once, but he still chose to place his hopes for Willie in that hopeless process. Meanwhile, Frankfurter would twice vote to deny Wright and DeBlanc's further attempts to have the Supreme Court reconsider its decision. Inasmuch as Frankfurter was deeply troubled by the consequence of his decisive vote and enmeshed in an intellectual swamp, his attempt to gain clemency for Willie Francis can only be recognized for what it was: a pitiful attempt by a jurist to assuage his conscience for allowing a youth to be put to death in the name of abstract principles of judicial self-restraint.

XI

Wright and DeBlanc's Last-Ditch Attempt

Skelly Wright, though disappointed by the Supreme Court's decision, was determined to continue Willie's fight. Wright was convinced that the wording contained in Burton's dissent indicated that it had originally been written as the majority opinion.[1] Burton had written: "The remand of this case to the Supreme Court of Louisiana . . . does not mean that (Willie) is entitled to a complete release."[2] Wright was wrong—a majority of the Court never had agreed to block a second electrocution. But at the time, his theory of a last-minute switch on the Court gave him encouragement.

On January 29, 1947, Wright and DeBlanc filed a petition for rehearing[3] with the Court, arguing that, by amending the electrocution statute, Louisiana had effectively conceded that the failure of the first execution attempt resulted from the incompetence of execution officials. Under the statute in force at Willie's scheduled execution, there was no statutory requirement that the operator of the electric chair be a competent electrician. Two weeks after the failure of the electric chair in St. Martinville, the statute was amended to provide that the operator of the electric chair "shall be a competent electrician who shall not have been previously convicted of a felony."[4] The bill's author, State Senator Aubrey Guinnie of New Orleans, acknowledged that the legislation was inspired by the *Francis* case.[5]

Both of Willie's would-be executioners would have been barred from operating the electric chair under this statute. Wright and DeBlanc contended that "the State of Louisiana has publicly confessed her error and has made provision to eliminate a repetition thereof."[6]

Wright and DeBlanc further argued that a hearing before Louisiana courts was necessary to reveal the state's considerations for changing the statute. Such questions as why the attempt at execution failed and whether the failure was caused by the negligence of the state remained unanswered. The record of such a hearing would show that the Supreme Court erred in assuming that Louisiana had been "careful" when attempting to execute Francis.

The lawyers concluded by bringing to the Court's attention the lack of success they had had with the Louisiana Board of Pardons: "The opinions of the Court indicate that this is a case to be handled by executive clemency [yet] the Board of Pardons and Reprieves had already rejected petitioner's plea for clemency."[7] Wright and DeBlanc urged that a rehearing be granted in the case and that it be remanded to the Louisiana courts for a finding of facts surrounding the botched first execution attempt.[8]

In 1947, just as today, the Supreme Court Rules provided that a petition for rehearing would not be granted "except at the instance of a Justice who concurred in the judgment or decision and with the concurrence of a majority of the Court."[9] Justice Frankfurter did not vote to grant Wright's petition, and thus, on February 10, 1947, the Court entered an order denying this petition.[10]

With the Supreme Court ruling against Willie a second time, DeBlanc was left with no apparent legal options. Not willing to give up, DeBlanc sought to make a second plea before the Louisiana Pardons Board. Reluctant at first to grant a second hearing, the board eventually relented out of courtesy to the Supreme Court and its reference to executive clemency.[11] Notified of a hearing date before the board, DeBlanc began his preparations.

Late one afternoon, three weeks before the hearing, an acquaintance from New Orleans stopped by DeBlanc's office. Louie M. Cyr, a former city judge in New Iberia, found DeBlanc reviewing a case at his desk and asked DeBlanc what he was working on. Scarcely looking up from his desk, DeBlanc responded that it was the *Francis* case. Cyr let out a brief sigh. It was a shame, he said, that Willie had to suffer so much at the hands of the two drunken executioners.[12]

Drunk? DeBlanc looked up quickly from his desk. Yes, it was true, Cyr assured him. On the day following the attempted electrocution of Willie Francis, a friend of Cyr's, George Etie, came by Cyr's office. In the course of the conversation, the subject of the Willie Francis electrocution came up. Etie stated that he had witnessed the attempted electrocution and that, while he had witnessed several other electrocutions, this was the most horrible thing he had ever seen. Etie told Cyr that the executioner and other persons connected with the carrying out of the execution "were so drunk that it was impossible for them to have known what they were doing."[13]

Etie described the execution scene to Cyr. As soon as the switch was pulled, he knew that something was wrong since Willie did not react in the same manner as others he had seen. Willie Francis's nose began to flatten on his face, and in a short while it was so flat that it was impossible to detect that he had a nose on his face. Willie's lips began to swell and continued to do so until they were several times their normal size. Etie told Cyr that the current was left on for about three minutes and that during this time, Willie remained conscious and suffered intense pain. Etie remembered that the pain was so great it caused Willie to jump and kick. At times, the reaction from his body caused the electric chair, which weighed at least 250 pounds, to be lifted from the floor as much as six inches. When the switch was finally turned off, the electric chair had made a full quarter turn from the position it had originally occupied.[14]

According to Cyr, Etie believed that the sole reason for the failed execution was the drunken condition of the executioners. It was, he remarked, the most "disgraceful and inhumane exhibition" he had ever witnessed.[15] Etie recalled that as soon as the switch controlling the current that went through Willie was turned off, the drunken executioner at the switch cursed Willie Francis. Etie also remembered that on the morning of the attempted electrocution, the executioner and other persons with him visited several saloons in New Iberia, and while drinking there extended open invitations to various individuals to go with them to attend the electrocution.[16]

DeBlanc was both elated and disappointed by Cyr's news. Cyr's account of the electrocution would discredit the Supreme Court's official version of the electrocution. No longer could the Court justify a second execution attempt because the first was "an innocent misadventure." Maybe the allegation of drunken executioners being responsible for the botched execution would change the minds of the Pardons Board and, if not them, certainly the Supreme Court.

On the other hand, DeBlanc was upset with both Wright and himself. This was information which they might have uncovered months ago. They had continually stressed to the United States Supreme Court the importance of investigating the facts behind the failed first execution attempt. Yet, the two lawyers had not fully carried out this task themselves. Perhaps if they had done so, DeBlanc wondered, they might have gotten the one additional vote they needed from the Supreme Court.

DeBlanc tried not to dwell on what should have been done in the past. He spent the next several weeks gathering more information about the first execution attempt. He asked George Etie to swear out an affidavit describing what he saw on that day in St. Martinville. Apparently fearing possible retaliation from unknown quarters, Etie refused. Cyr, however, stepped forward and described his conversation with Etie in a sworn affidavit. Continuing his investigation, DeBlanc found an eyewitness to the alleged drinking of the executioners who, unlike Etie, would swear to what he saw.

Ignace Doucet, a resident of St. Martin's Parish, was in St. Martinville on May 3, 1946, and witnessed the attempted electrocution of Willie Francis. Doucet arrived at the St. Martinville courthouse late that morning and stated that the officials working on the electric chair were "drinking during the whole last part of the morning."[17] Doucet swore that "the man who pulled the switch to electrocute the prisoner Willie Francis was the same tall large man whom I saw drinking."[18]

Armed with the sworn affidavits from Cyr and Doucet, DeBlanc again made the long trip to New Orleans and pleaded for Willie's life before the Pardons Board. It seemed clear that Louisiana had fallen down in its responsibilities, DeBlanc argued. Certainly, Willie Francis deserved a commutation from the death sentence to life imprisonment. Once again, however, the Pardons Board was unmoved. On April 22, 1947, the board ruled that Willie Francis must make a second trip to the electric chair.[19]

Willie was hunched over his noontime meal of potatoes and boiled meat when a newspaperman brought Willie the disappointing news. Next to Willie on his cot was his Bible. Willie glanced over at his Bible and said softly, "I'm gonna die. There ain't nothin' I can do. I've gotta die."[20]

"It's pretty tough," the newspaperman said, not quite knowing how to console Willie.

"It ain't tough," Willie replied, "I've gotta die."

Unlike their client, DeBlanc and Wright were in no mood to concede the fight. The pair recognized that time was running out for Willie. On April 28, 1947, Lieutenant and Acting Governor Emile Veret (Jimmie Davis was out of the state) signed a death warrant calling for the execution of Willie Francis on May 9, 1947, between the hours of noon and 3:00 PM. Nevertheless, two possibilities remained for blocking a second electrocution. The first would be handled by DeBlanc in St. Martinville and the second by Skelly Wright in Washington, D.C.

On April 23, 1947, DeBlanc filed papers with Judge Simon requesting that Willie Francis be given a new trial.[21] DeBlanc argued that Mrs. Van Brocklin, Andrew Thomas's next door neighbor, was a necessary witness who should have been called at Willie's first trial. Van Brocklin had testified at the Coroner's inquest that she had heard the shots fired on the night of the murder and had seen a mysterious car with its lights on parked in front of the Thomas house. Arguing that "her testimony would have been material, valuable and of a nature to serve the ends of justice," DeBlanc concluded that "justice would be served by granting a new trial."[22]

Since the day on which he had taken the case, DeBlanc had resolutely refused to raise the question of Willie's guilt or innocence. In order to win Willie's case, DeBlanc felt that all attention should be focused on the question of whether a youth should be sent back to the electric chair a second time. Certainly, a civilized society would answer "no" to that question.

There was also a second consideration. It was one thing to argue on general terms that any second execution attempt was cruel and unusual punishment. It was a completely different matter to argue in 1947 Louisiana that a jury had erred in finding a black guilty of murdering a white. And this would be exactly what DeBlanc would have to argue if granted a new trial. As a tactical matter for his client, this approach could well turn the tide of public opinion in Louisiana against Willie and jeopardize DeBlanc's primary goal—to block a second execution attempt. The white community might unreasonably view the youth as a symbol to the black population that it was acceptable to murder a white without fear of punishment.

On May 5, 1947, Judge Simon heard oral argument from DeBlanc and District Attorney Pecot on DeBlanc's motion. Pecot argued that Louisiana's Code of Criminal Procedure provided that every motion for a new trial must be filed and disposed of before sentence. Since Willie was sentenced on September 13, 1945, Pecot argued that DeBlanc's April 23, 1947, motion was filed too late and should be denied.

To no one's surprise, Simon agreed and, ruling from the bench, denied DeBlanc's motion for a new trial.[23] Simon had already voted against Willie twice when he had an opportunity to extend mercy on the Louisiana Pardons Board. It was not to be expected that he would extend mercy on the St. Martinville bench.

Undeterred, DeBlanc immediately asked the court to suspend Willie's sentence pending an appeal to the Louisiana Supreme Court. Again, Simon ruled from the bench and denied DeBlanc's motion.[24]

The next morning, May 6, DeBlanc filed a third set of papers with the St. Martinville court. In a petition for a writ of *habeas corpus*, DeBlanc argued that the Louisiana statute under which Willie Francis had been sentenced to death was null and void. DeBlanc maintained that the death penalty statute had been "repealed and superseded" by a new statute that required the presence "of a competent electrician, who shall not have been previously convicted of a felony." Because the statute had been "repealed," DeBlanc insisted that Willie's death "sentence is without force and effect and cannot be carried out."[25]

DeBlanc's statutory argument was less than convincing. In passing the new death penalty statute, the Louisiana legislature specifically stated that the legislation merely "amended and re-enacted" the previous statute. DeBlanc's petition for a writ of *habeas corpus* was quickly dismissed that same day.[26]

That afternoon, DeBlanc telephoned Skelly Wright in Washington,

D.C. Wright had been working for two weeks on a petition for *habeas corpus* to be filed with the United States Supreme Court. The lawyers discussed Simon's rulings and considered filing papers with the Louisiana Supreme Court asking for a stay of execution pending an appeal of the new trial motion. The idea was quickly dropped. Clearly, the lawyers were making no impact on the Louisiana courts with their legal arguments, so it was decided that they should go ahead and file their papers with the United States Supreme Court.

On Thursday morning, May 8, 1947, the last full day of oral argument for the October 1946 term and the eve of Willie's execution, Wright and DeBlanc (who flew in from New Orleans earlier that morning) filed a petition for a writ of *habeas corpus* and moved the Supreme Court to stay execution.

In the papers, it was obvious that Wright had pinned this last-ditch attempt at a reprieve on changing Felix Frankfurter's mind. In his concurring opinion, Frankfurter had intimated that if the execution had failed as a result of intention or wanton recklessness, due process would be denied: "The fact that I reach this conclusion [affirming the Louisiana Court] does not mean that a hypothetical with a series of abortive attempts at electrocution, or *even a single willfull attempt would not raise different questions."*[27] Wright believed that his petition showed that that was exactly what happened in an execution bungled by the allegedly drunken state of the executioners. Wright also held out hope that he might pick up the support of one of the justices who had previously agreed with Justice Reed that the first electrocution had merely been "an innocent misadventure."

Relying extensively on the Cyr and Doucet affidavits, Wright told the Court in his petition that "the executioner and other persons connected with carrying out the execution were so drunk that it was impossible for them to have known what they were doing."[28] Wright added that "the scene was a disgraceful and inhumane exhibition, that as soon as the switch controlling the current was taken off, the drunken executioner cursed Francis and told him that he would be back to finish electrocuting him, and if the electricity did not kill him he would kill him with a rock."[29] If the execution was not botched by the drunken negligence of the executioners, Wright alleged that the executioners must have been motivated by "sadistic impulses and either willfully, deliberately or intentionally applied less than a minimal lethal current, for the purpose of torturing the petitioner. As a consequence, the petitioner was cruelly, inhumanely and excruciatingly tortured."[30] Wright asked the Court to stay the execution and suggested that the Court appoint a special commissioner to determine the facts surrounding the first execution attempt or order the Louisiana courts to undertake such an investigation.

The *habeas corpus* petition was circulated to the justices late Thursday morning by the clerk of the Supreme Court. At 11:50 AM, just before the traditional 12:00 noon starting time for oral argument, the justices hurriedly met in the Conference Room to consider Wright's petition. It soon became clear to the justices, however, that they would be unable to discuss the petition and reach a decision in a little less than ten minutes. When the Court convened at noon to hear argument in other cases, Chief Justice Vinson immediately called an unusual recess and the justices trooped back into the Conference Room to consider the petition.

A little over an hour later, shortly after 1:00 PM, the justices filed back into the courtroom.[31] Holding a typewritten statement in his hands, Vinson read the Court's decision: "The petition for leave to file an original petition for writ of habeas corpus is denied for reasons set forth in *Ex parte Hawke*, 321 U.S. 114."[32] Wright slumped forward. He had feared that the Court might rely on the 1944 *Hawke* case which held that a defendant must exhaust all state remedies and then petition a federal district court for *habeas corpus* relief before resorting to the Supreme Court.

For that very reason, Wright explained in his *habeas corpus* petition that Willie might be dead by the time his plea would finally wind its way to the Supreme Court through the federal court system: "Should petitioner seek to vindicate his rights, or even to assert his claims of right, in the courts of Louisiana, state or federal, and should that court deny his relief, he could be electrocuted before he or his counsel could possibly seek even *supersedeas* in that court, particularly if a bond were to be required; and thereby petitioner would die without having had this Court's judgment upon the question that it has already indicated is decisive."[33] Wright was disappointed that the Court appeared more concerned with abstract procedures then with legal practicalities.

Wright's disappointment soon turned to surprise and then to hope as Chief Justice Vinson, after a slight pause, continued with the announcement. This was unusual, for it was the Court's customary practice to dispose of matters such as a *habeas corpus* petition in a simple, one-sentence order. Wright's eyes quickly looked up at Vinson.

"In view of the grave nature of the new allegations, set forth in this petition," Vinson read, "the denial is expressly without prejudice to application to proper tribunals."[34] Vinson then added that Justices Murphy and Rutledge voted for intervention by the Supreme Court on the basis of Wright's motion. Justice Murphy favored granting the *habeas corpus* petition. Justice Rutledge believed, Vinson said, that the request for *habeas corpus* should be treated as a petition for rehearing of the Court's January 13 decision to return Willie to the electric chair. Vinson explained that Rutledge wanted the earlier decision "vacated" or thrown out, and have the case returned to the Louisiana Supreme Court for proceedings to determine the issues of fact presented in the petition for *habeas corpus*. Sick in a Washington, D.C., hospital, Justice Douglas took no part in the consideration or decision of the matter.

Despite their failure to gain Frankfurter's vote, Wright and DeBlanc were encouraged by the language which Vinson and the Court used. Vinson's reference to the "grave nature" of the allegations contained in the petition seemed to Wright to be a judicial hint that the Court was genuinely taken aback by the allegations of drunkenness on the part of the executioners. Wright also found hope in the Court's language that the case was dismissed "expressly without prejudice to application to proper tribunals." Wright read the Court's language to mean: "While we're sorry we can't help you now, we strongly encourage you to pursue the matter in the lower courts."[35]

Among those voting to deny Wright's petition was Felix Frankfurter. The justice had sought a political reversal of the Court's decision through Monte Lemann. Now on the eve of the May 9 execution date, it was clear that Lemann's efforts to win clemency had failed. Frankfurter still refused, however, to do judicially what he wished to do politically: block a second execution attempt. On two occasions he could have acted on petitions filed by Skelly Wright requesting that the Court reconsider its decision. Yet, Frankfurter inexplicably opposed both the February petition for rehearing and the last-minute petition for a writ of *habeas corpus* filed by Wright and DeBlanc.

DeBlanc and Wright decided to try to file a desperate last-hour appeal with the Louisiana Supreme Court to save Willie from a second trip to the chair. They believed that the concerned language of the United States Supreme Court might persuade the court to stay the electrocution and begin an investigation of the facts surrounding the failed first execution attempt. There was, of course, the chance that Willie might be executed while the court was studying the legal papers. This seemed to them to be Willie's only hope for avoiding a return to the electric chair in less than twenty-four hours. They did not follow up on Vinson's hint (in the denial of the *habeas corpus* petition) that the federal district court in Louisiana would be the appropriate tribunal to refile the petition. Why they did not do so is an unanswered mystery. Certainly, in light of subsequent decisions, they could have done so—and perhaps saved Willie's life.

While on his evening flight from Washington to New Orleans, DeBlanc drafted the necessary papers to be filed with the Louisiana Court. On the morning of the execution, DeBlanc visited Willie in the St. Martinville jail to explain plans for continuing the litigation. Willie had been moved from his New Iberia jail cell to the execution site earlier that morning. To DeBlanc's surprise, Willie announced that he had had enough. He did not want DeBlanc to pursue any further litigation.[36]

DeBlanc told Willie that he thought he could go back to the courts and get still another stay. Willie slowly shook his head which was already shaven in preparation for the execution that was less than two hours away.

"No, Mr. B-B-Bertrand. No, don't go back," Willie said, "I'm ready to die. I'm ready to go. I don't want you to do nothing."[37]

DeBlanc began to explain the improved chances of success on the issue of negligence on the part of the executioners. Willie interrupted. "No. No. I don't want you to do nothing."

Willie was determined. "O.K. Are you sure?" DeBlanc asked.

Willie nodded his head. "Leave it alone. Thank you, but leave it alone. I'm ready to die."[38]

DeBlanc did not resist Willie's stated wish. The two embraced and said goodbye. DeBlanc's eyes were filled with tears as he left Willie for the last time.

Willie was weary of the waiting and uncertainty. For eight months he had suffered the pain of knowing that he would soon die (only to have the first execution attempt fail). In the twelve months since then, he had his hopes for living dashed once by the Louisiana Supreme Court, twice by the Louisiana Pardons Board, and three times by the United States Supreme Court. For eighteen-year-old Willie Francis, fatigue and twenty months of mental torture had exacted a dreadful toll.

Willie was convinced that his suffering was for a purpose. He believed that the Lord had let him live through his first trip to the chair because "He wanted me to get my hell on earth."[39] Willie knew that the Lord was with him and the Lord had punished him. Now, Willie thought the Lord had decided that the punishment must end. He had suffered enough. "I have been in this jail sweating it for a year," Willie told a reporter at a cell door press conference the day before the execution, "now I'm ready to go. I want the machine to work this time—I want to die because as soon as I do I am going to the Lord."[40]

These feelings were reinforced in a meeting Willie had with Father Charles Hannegan just before DeBlanc's visit. Father Hannegan saw Willie and told him, "Willie, at 12 o'clock sharp they're going to pull that switch and you're going to die just like this [snap of fingers]. The minute you die, Willie, you're going to be walking to the Lord. And when you meet him now, Willie, he'll be there to welcome you."[41]

Trying to relax Willie, Father Hannegan continued, "now listen, Willie, there are several things you've got to do. When you go to the Lord, you've got to talk to him about your family. The next thing is to put in a good word for your lawyer." "Finally, and do listen," Father Hannegan said with a smile, "don't forget to put in a few good words for me, too."[42]

Father Hannegan's words, though welcome, were not needed. For some time, Willie had been preparing himself emotionally for the execution day. He even knew what he wanted to wear when he returned to the electric chair. "I'm wearing my Sunday pants and my Sunday heart to the chair," Willie declared. "Ain't going to wear no beat-up pants to see the Lord. Been busy talking my way into heaven for this past year. Them folks expecting me to come in style."[43]

Willie also was determined that he would "die like a man." For the last several weeks, he had been practicing the way he wanted to walk the few yards to the death chamber. He told Father Hannegan that he was "going to walk it steady. I'll be darned if I'm going to act like a cry-baby."[44] Father Hannegan believed him.[45]

Outside the small, two-story, red-brick jail gathered a crowd of about 500 persons, mostly white, which had been assembling since 8:00 AM. They were openly hostile to Willie Francis's plight. At one point in the morning, several of Willie's brothers and sisters arrived at the jail to say goodbye to him. As they left the jail, one of the men in the crowd pushed against them and said, "They ought to do away with all of the niggers."[46]

Inside the St. Martinville jail, Willie was unaware of the commotion outside.

After DeBlanc left his cell, Willie concentrated on his last meal—a big plate of catfish caught in the bayous of Evangeline country. A Catholic who was true to his faith, Willie had almost ordered fried chicken before realizing that his execution day fell on a Friday.[47] Fried fish and potatoes, however, was a good second choice. Willie had always liked catfish, and he particularly liked it the way the wife of the jailer cooked it.

After lunch, Willie was joined by Father Hannegan and Father Rousseve from Willie's home parish. Once again, Father Rousseve administered the last rites of the Catholic church. Once again, Willie rose from his cell cot and began to walk the dozen steps across the hallway to the execution chamber.

As Willie began to walk his "last mile" in his Sunday-best dark pin-striped trousers, spoiled only by a slit placed in the left leg for the attachment of an electrode, Father Hannegan placed his hand under Willie's elbow for steadying support. Willie waved aside Father Hannegan's assistance and motioned for the priest to precede him. He wanted to walk these final steps courageously, without the help of others. Steady and without hesitation, Willie made his way out of the small cell at the rear of the jail.

Awaiting him in the execution chamber was the same portable electric chair from which he had once walked away. Louisiana state authorities had taken every precaution to ensure that the chair was in perfect order this time. It had worked perfectly the day before when it electrocuted hitchhiker slayer Alonze (Blackie) Jones in nine minutes after the switch was pulled.[48] Also crowded into the tiny room were about two dozen whites, including Claude Thomas, brother of Andrew Thomas, who was chief of police of St. Martinville at the time of Andrew's slaying. The witnesses watched the proceedings closely, making sure that Louisiana would not botch the execution a second time.

All eyes were on Willie as he walked firmly and erect into the room. Willie paused in front of the electric chair and twice wiped the palms of his hands against the legs of his good trousers. Smiling, he settled into the chair at 12:02 PM. The governor's death warrant had dictated that Willie should be executed between noon and 3:00 PM. Louisiana was wasting no time.

While the officials were busy fixing the leather straps and electrodes, Willie turned to Sidney Dupois, a local barber in St. Martinville who was standing two feet from the electric chair on Willie's right. Dupois, a white, had been an official witness to the first electrocution and was appalled by what he had seen. Indeed, Dupois's wife was very upset when she learned that her husband had been, in a small way, even connected with that first attempt. Now, against her wishes he was a witness to the second attempt. Sheriff Resweber had met him on the street that morning and asked him to be a witness. Because of a sense of civic responsibility, Dupois felt compelled to undertake once again this difficult duty.

Willie asked Dupois how "little Sid," Dupois's nine-year-old son, was doing. Dupois responded, "Fine, Willie, just fine," to which Willie replied, "Well, you tell him to be a good boy now, ya hear."[49]

Willie looked at the other witnesses and recognized a reporter who had frequently visited him in the New Iberia jail. As the broad chest strap was being adjusted, Willie caught the reporter's eyes and attempted to wave—but couldn't—with a hand already strapped down into place by leather binds. Willie mouthed "hello" silently, moving his lips slowly to form the word.[50]

Willie closed his eyes for a moment and then opened them for the final time. Before the dark rubber mask was once again put on, the executioner asked if the straps were too tight. Responding with a wan smile, Willie said, "everything is all right."[51] With those last words, the mask was placed over Willie's head.

At 12:08, the switch was thrown. The first jolt of 2,700 volts of electricity hit Willie's body for 30 seconds. A second charge of electricity was applied for another 15 seconds.

Looking small in the big wooden chair, Willie took the hot stream of electricity without a tremor. The customary arching movement of the body against the leather straps usually seen in electrocutions was absent.[52] Willie's fingers remained motionless on the well-worn arms of the chair.

At 12:12, Willie Francis was pronounced dead and was carried away from the electric chair he had once walked away from. There was no cheating the electric man a second time.

When the signal came to the throng waiting outside the jail that Willie Francis was dead, a woman at the edge of the crowd burst into tears. Left standing alone, sobbing on the courthouse steps, was Willie's aged mother.[53] The triumph of exalted notions of due process and abstract philosophies of judicial self-restraint in the Supreme Court could not console her grief. On that Friday just before Mother's Day, the heart of Louise Francis had been broken. Willie was gone.

Epilogue

Willie Francis is long since dead; his bones are mouldering in some forgotten Louisiana grave. Whether justice was done on that day more than forty years ago when Willie was executed will never be known. His guilt or innocence is an unsolvable mystery.

There are residents of St. Martinville, however, who to this day believe that Willie Francis was innocent. They believe that the confessions were not voluntary and that the confessions were not later disavowed by Willie Francis because of the threat of reprisals upon his family. In addition, they believe that the incriminating evidence found on Willie Francis—the wallet of Andrew Thomas—was unwittingly accepted by Willie as part of a set-up. If Willie committed the murder, they argue, why would he throw away the murder weapon, but keep the wallet? Unfortunately, these and other questions such as the mysterious presence of car lights after the shots were fired on the night of the murder, as well as the disappearance of the alleged murder weapon, were never raised and explored at the trial by Willie's defense counsel.

The many shortcomings of Willie's "trial" are a dark reminder of our recent legal past.[1] If Louisiana did try and convict an innocent youth—a recent study has asserted that at least twenty-three people have been electrocuted, hanged, or gassed in the past eighty-five years for crimes they did not commit—we have reason to hope that such a travesty would not occur today.[2] In the past forty years, the Supreme Court has expanded the rights of the accused in an effort to prevent convictions of the innocent. *Miranda* warnings, exclusion of coerced confessions, and a retrial for ineffective counsel may have led to a verdict of innocent for Willie Francis.

Just as the question of Willie's guilt or innocence remains unanswerable, so too does the question of what would have happened had Francis's lawyers sought *habeas corpus* relief in federal district court. After all, the Supreme Court, in denying the writ of *habeas corpus*, had expressly done so "without prejudice." Indeed, the Court had virtually invited the refiling of the case in the federal district court. Yet, Willie Francis asked that further legal proceedings on his behalf be halted. Since Francis was a minor, should the lawyers have sought to persuade Francis's father to file a suit for *habeas corpus* in federal district court where Francis would have been given another chance? If the matter had been pursued, would the allegations of drunken conduct on the part of the executioners eventually have caused the Supreme Court to reverse itself?

The *Francis* case also poses a crucial, as yet unanswered, constitutional question. If Willie was convicted of the murder of Andrew Thomas today, there is reason to believe that Louisiana would again require him to suffer the torture of a botched electrocution and the agony of a second trip to the electric chair a year later. For in one sense, Willie Francis still lives. His case is central to a question, newly emergent in the debate over capital punishment: Do the *methods* of execution violate the cruel and unusual punishment provision of the Eighth Amendment?

The Supreme Court has never fully confronted the question. In a little noted but important dissenting opinion to *Glass* v. *Louisiana* (1985),[3] Justice William Brennan asked "whether electrocution is a 'humane' method of extinguishing life or is, instead, nothing less than the contemporary technological equivalent of burning people at the stake." Brennan wrote that "Louisiana's execution of Willie Francis remains the most notorious example of the botched manner in which so many electrocutions have been conducted."[4] Although the Supreme Court refused to hear oral argument in *Glass*, the *Francis* case and Brennan's dissent raise a disturbing question about American methods of killing felons. From 1977 through the end of 1985, fifty persons were executed by the various states. Consider the following grisly episodes from five of those executions:

- On October 16, 1985, the seventy-two-year-old Indiana electric chair took five jolts and 17 minutes to kill thirty-seven-year-old William Vandiver. Vandiver was still breathing after receiving the first jolt of 2300 volts for 10 seconds and five hundred volts for 20 seconds.

  Vandiver survived a third surge before being killed by a fourth and fifth jolt. A spokeswoman for the Department of Corrections insisted that the electric chair "was not malfunctioning in any way."[5]

- On December 12, 1984, Alpha Otis Stephens was strapped into Georgia's electric chair. For two minutes electricity rushed into his body, which arched against the straps. As expected, Stephens slumped forward limp when the electricity was stopped.

All had apparently gone according to plan until witnesses noticed Stephens was still breathing. After waiting for six minutes until Stephens's body had "cooled off," before examining it, a doctor confirmed that he was alive. During this six-minute period, witnesses noticed that "Stephens took about 23 breaths." Only after a second two-minute charge was administered did doctors pronounce Stephens dead.[6]

- On October 3, 1983, James David (Cowboy) Autry laid strapped to a gurney in the Texas death chamber as "medical assistants" (doctors do not participate because killing would violate a physician's Hippocratic oath) began to connect the needle and tube necessary for a lethal injection. Their work did not go smoothly. By the time the needle had been inserted into Autry's veins, blood covered his exposed forearm and matted the gurney's sheet.

  In the background, Autry could hear a crowd gathered outside the prison chanting "Kill him!" "Kill him!" Autry remained strapped to the gurney for an hour with an intravenous needle and tube dangling from his arm waiting for the fatal solution. Eventually, however, he was returned to his cell. A last-minute stay of execution had been granted—twenty-four minutes before the poison was to flow.[7]

  Five months later, after a series of legal appeals had run their course, Autry was once again returned to the Texas death chamber. This time, however, there was no last-minute reprieve and he was executed.[8]

- On September 2, 1983, Jimmy Lee Gray died in the Mississippi gas chamber after a desperate and fitful struggle for breath. Witnesses stated that Gray "convulsed for eight minutes [and] his head kept striking a steel pole on the back of the chair."[9] Gray's moans during the execution echoed off the chamber's walls and were described as "blood chilling."[10]

- On April 22, 1983, 1,900 volts surged into John Louis Evans as he sat in the Alabama electric chair. White smoke spurted from beneath the hood over his head and from one leg where an electrode had been placed. Evans quivered and fell back into the chair as the current subsided. Two doctors examined Evans expecting to pronounce him dead, but instead found a heartbeat. A guard quickly reattached the power lines and an electrode that had fallen away when a leg strap had burned through.

  A second burst jolted Evans, and again smoke rose from his head and leg. Once again doctors examined Evans only to find his heart still beating. Suddenly, Evans's attorney, who had remained silent after the first failed attempt, exclaimed, "Commissioner, I ask for clemency. This is cruel and unusual punishment." The prison commissioner conveyed the attorney's request over a previously opened telephone line to the office of Alabama Governor George C. Wallace. Before any reply was received, the guards administered a third charge to Evans. After the third jolt, Evans's leg and head again smoldered—this time with small flames and smoke escaping from the hood that covered Evans's face. Fourteen minutes after the first of three interspersed shocks were administered, he was pronounced dead.

Witnesses walked away from the death chamber convinced that Evans had been burned alive in the chair.[11] "Based on what I saw, I would think that everybody would rather have a different [execution] method," said Ron Tate, a spokesman for the Alabama Department of Corrections, who did not see the actual execution, but saw Evans's charred body afterward. "It wasn't a pretty sight to see, I'm sure, but it's the only thing we have," he commented.[12]

Through the years, the means of execution in America have evolved from hanging to electrocution to the gas chamber to lethal injection—although the electric chair is used more often than any other form of capital punishment.[13] From colonial times to 1890, death by hanging was the allowable form of execution. Because hanging often involves slow, tortuous strangulation, states began to search for an alternative and more humane means.[14] And, as the killing of John Louis Evans and others has shown, death by electrocution is an extremely violent act. So, too, is the gas chamber. Witnesses have observed the "extreme evidence of horror, pain, and strangling. The eyes pop, they turn purple, then drool. It is a horrible sight."[15]

All three forms of capital punishment are painful and, in some cases, brutally so. Perhaps Utah's firing squad is the least brutal. Yet, the firing squad, like the other forms of execution, is fraught with misadventure. In 1951, for example, a Utah firing squad hit the condemned man with four slugs but failed to hit the heart-shaped target pinned to the man's chest. As a result, the doomed prisoner slowly bled to death.[16]

Americans are ambivalent about the death penalty. Although they support capital punishment, many insist that death should be as painless as possible. The desire for a humane death falls far short of the mark. That presents the emergent constitutional question.

Where should the line be drawn between an improper and proper method of punishment? The Supreme Court has yet to give a definitive answer or even directly to confront the question. The closest the Court came was in the *Willie Francis* case. The Court's holding "that Francis has already been subjected to a current of electricity does not make his subsequent electrocution any more cruel in the constitutional sense than any other electrocution"[17] has far-reaching consequences. A condemned person may therefore be forced to sit through jolts of electric current again and again, if need be, until the death sentence has been carried out—which is exactly what happened to Vandiver, Stephens, and Evans. The Court has corrected many constitutional shortcomings since 1947, but the *Francis* case remains undisturbed.

The search continues for a "humane" way of killing. Recognizing the failures and the physical pain caused by the electric chair, several states have recently turned to the gas chamber and, more recently, to lethal injection. As the experience of Jimmie Lee Gray in Mississippi shows, however, the gas chamber is no answer. Moreover, relatively new evidence is available that shows execution by lethal injection poses a serious risk of cruel and protracted death.[18] Even a slight error in dosage can leave a prisoner conscious but paralyzed while dying, an unmoving but sentient witness of his (or her) slow, lingering asphyxiation.[19]

The stark realities of executions are politely shielded from the public eye. They are not public. If pictures are taken, they are kept secret. Albert Camus once observed that "no one dares speak directly of the ceremony. Officials and journalists who have to talk about it, as if they were aware of both its provocative and its shameful aspects, have made up a sort of ritual language, reduced to stereotyped phrases. Hence we read at breakfast time in a corner of the newspaper that the condemned 'has paid his debt to society' or that he has 'atoned' or that 'at five a.m. justice was done.'"[20] Camus concludes that "The man who enjoys his coffee while reading that justice has been done would spit it out at the last detail."[21]

With the sure prospect of an accelerated rate of executions—a surge led by Louisiana—and more than 2,000 men and women now on Death Row,[22] the gruesome facts about any form of capital punishment should no longer be hidden. Indeed, as Judge J. Skelly Wright has written, "in a civilized society, if we assume as we must that the state may take the life of a person as punishment, decency demands that the life be taken without cruelty."

Fundamental decency is the core of the cruel and unusual punishment clause of the Eighth Amendment. The means of punishment cannot be barbarous or tortuous. Such historical forms of execution as crucifixion, burning at the stake, boiling alive, or the rack are beyond the pale. The Eighth Amendment gives even to those on Death Row the right to a punishment that is not cruel.

Today's means of capital punishment make the amendment a hollow guarantee. There is no method of capital punishment which fulfills the *Kemmler* Court's expectation of the "mere extinguishment of life."[23] Indeed, Kemmler's own tortured death nearly a century ago quickly disproved this basic premise of the Supreme Court's initial sanction of the death penalty. Yet, the executions have continued.

In 1958 the Supreme Court said in a noncapital punishment case that the ban on cruel and unusual punishment draws its meaning from the "evolving standards of decency that mark the progress of a maturing society."[24] No one can validly argue that the grotesque executions of Vandiver, Stephens, Autry, Gray, and Evans fell within the limits of civilized standards. They were indecent by any criterion.

Sooner or later, the Supreme Court will have to address the matter of the unavoidable cruelty attendant to all methods of execution. Most Americans support the idea of capital punishment. But how many would approve the ritual of agony and torment found today in the imposition of the death penalty? Certainly, the repulsion of an enlightened, contemporary society against such barbarous methods of capital punishment requires their abolition. Until that time, botched executions and death by installments remain constitutionally acceptable. Sadly, the legacy of the *Willie Francis* case survives.

Notes

CHAPTER I

1. W. Francis as told to S. Montgomery, "My Trip to the Electric Chair" (1947). In this short pamphlet, Willie Francis gave a jailhouse interview to a local resident in which he detailed the hours just prior to the May 1946 execution attempt. This chapter's description of Willie Francis's thoughts immediately before, during, and after the execution attempt are derived, in part, from the account in this pamphlet.

2. Harnett T. Kane described the social atmosphere in the St. Martinville region this way: "I thought I detected an easier relationship between white man and Negro than in other parts of the South." Harnett T. Kane, *The Bayous of Louisiana* (New York: W. Morrow and Co., 1943), p. 263. Yet, in the 1940s, violence often still erupted. Recalling the work of the Civil Liberties Unit of the Department of Justice, Solicitor General Francis Biddle quoted from a letter sent to President Roosevelt by a young black soldier distraught by recent events in his hometown of New Iberia:

I am a corporal in the U.S. Army. I have been in the Army for seventeen months and in England for eleven months. I am a Negro with an American heart, and have been doing my duties as an American soldier. . . .
I was sent some papers from the states a few days ago. And I read where colored people in my home, New Iberia, La., were being beaten up and chased out of town. Included in them was my sister's husband. . . . They are being beaten up because they succeeded in getting a welding school for the colored, so they could build the tanks and ships we need so badly. They forced them to leave their homes, and also beat up the colored doctors and ran them out of town. I thought we were fighting to make this world a better place to live in. . . . I am giving the USA all I got, and would even die, but I think my people should be protected. I am asking you, Sir, to do all in your power to bring these people to justice and punish the guilty ones.

F. Biddle, *In Brief Authority* (Garden City, N.Y.: Doubleday, 1962), p. 156. New Iberia is ten miles from St. Martinville.

3. Works Project Administration in the State of Louisiana, Louisiana 357 (1941).

4. *New Orleans Times-Picayune*, May 4, 1946.

5. Interview with Bertrand DeBlanc, Esq., Lafayette, La., September 25, 1982.

6. Appendix to Brief for Respondent at 71 *Louisiana ex rel. Francis v. Resweber*, 329 U.S. 459 (1947) (from record of Louisiana Pardons Board Hearing, testimony of Vincent Vinezia) (hereinafter cited as Appendix to Brief for Respondent).

7. Appendix to Brief for Respondent at 66 (testimony of Captain E. Foster).

8. Ibid. at 74–75 (testimony of U. J. Enault, Chief Electrician).

9. *The State Times*, Baton Rouge, La., May 3, 1946.

10. Petition for a Writ of Habeas Corpus, *Louisiana ex rel. Francis v. Resweber*, 329 U.S. 459 (1947) (affidavit of Ignace Doucet) (hereinafter referred to as Habeas Corpus Petition).

11. Ibid.

12. Ibid. (affidavit of Louie M. Cyr).

13. Appendix to Brief for Respondent at 71 (testimony of Vincent Vinezia).

14. Interview with Dr. Bernard DeMahy, St. Martinville, La., September 24, 1982.

15. Appendix to Brief for Petitioner, *Louisiana ex rel. Francis v. Resweber*, 329 U.S. 459 (1947) (affidavits of Sheriff Harold Resweber and Sidney J. Dupois) (hereinafter Brief for Petitioner).

16. Interview with Dr. Bernard DeMahy, St. Martinville, La., September 24, 1982.

17. Brief for Petitioner (affidavit of Ignace Doucet); Appendix to Brief for Respondent at 72 (testimony of Vincent Vinezia).

18. Appendix to Brief for Petitioner (affidavits of Rev. Maurice Rousseve and Willie Olivier).

19. Interview with Dr. Bernard DeMahy, St. Martinville, La., September 24, 1982.

20. *Miami Herald*, May 5, 1946.

21. See *Newsweek*, January 18, 1960; *Newsweek*, January 31, 1944. Years later, Governor Davis and Judge Skelly Wright would do battle over Davis's plan to preserve segregation in the schools of New Orleans. Jack W. Peltason, *Fifty-Eight Lonely Men—Southern Federal Judges and School Desegregation* (New York: Harcourt, Brace and World, 1961), pp. 223–243. Despite its position on social issues, the Davis administration did receive high marks in one area—improvement of the state economy. Miriam G. Reeves, *The Governors of Louisiana* (New Orleans: Pelican, 1972), pp. 112–114.

22. Appendix to Brief for Respondent at 62 (testimony of Warden Dennis J. Bazer).

23. *New Orleans Times-Picayune*, May 10, 1946.

24. Ibid., May 4 and 5, 1946.

25. Habeas Corpus Petition (affidavit of Ignace Doucet); see also Brief for Respondent (affidavit of Ignace Doucet).

26. *Time*, July 15, 1946.

27. *Miami Herald*, May 5, 1946; *The State Times*, Baton Rouge, La., May 4, 1946.

28. *Time*, July 15, 1946.

29. *Philadelphia Tribune*, May 11, 1946.

CHAPTER II

1. See Fred B. Kniffen, *Louisiana: Its Land and People* (Baton Rouge: Louisiana State University Press, 1968); Harnett T. Kane, *The Bayous of Louisiana* (New York: W. Morrow and Co., 1943), pp. 256–263.

2. Works Project Administration in the State of Louisiana, Louisiana, 353–359 (1941).

3. Huey Long, *Every Man a King* (New Orleans: National Book Co., 1933), p. 99.

4. *The Weekly Messenger*, St. Martinville, La., November 10, 1944.

5. Record of Coroner's Inquest Before Dr. S. D. Yongue, Coroner of St. Martin's Parish, La., at 7 (November 8, 1944).

6. Ibid. at 4.

7. Ibid.

8. Appendix to Brief for Respondent at 94 (testimony of District Attorney L. O. Pecot).

9. Ibid. at 78 (testimony of Sheriff E. L. Resweber, Sheriff, St. Martin's Parish).

10. *The Weekly Messenger*, St. Martinville, La., August 10, 1945.

11. Interview with Bertrand DeBlanc, Esq., Lafayette, La., September 25, 1982.

12. *New Orleans Times-Picayune*, October 25, 1982. Simon resigned on August 23, 1960, and was later fined $10,000. He was given a six-month jail sentence, which was suspended, and was put on two years' probation. Ibid.

13. Record Before the Supreme Court in *Louisiana ex rel. Francis v. Resweber*, 329 U.S. 459 (1947) at 3 (hereinafter cited as Supreme Court Record). All references to the Record will be to page numbers in the bound version of the United States Supreme Court Briefs and Records rather than to page numbers of the original record.

14. Louisiana Code of Criminal Law and Procedure, Chapter I, Article 740-30 (Dart 1932 and Supp. 1942).

15. Supreme Court Record at 3.

16. Ibid. at 4.

17. Appendix to Brief for Respondent at 99 (testimony of District Attorney L. O. Pecot).

18. The Report of the President's Committee on Civil Rights 25 (1947).

19. Supreme Court Record at 5.

20. Ibid.

21. *Roberts* v. *Louisiana*, 428 U.S. 325 (1976). See also *Eddings* v. *Oklahoma*, 455 U.S. 104 (1982). (All mitigating factors, including defendant's age and family history, should be considered before imposition of a death sentence.)

22. *Miranda* v. *United States*, 384 U.S. 436 (1966) (due process requires that suspects be informed of their right to remain silent and that anything they say may be used against them).

23. *Chambers* v. *Florida*, 309 U.S. 227 (1940).

24. 309 U.S. at 338–340.

25. Supreme Court Record at 7 (from death warrant signed March 29, 1946).

CHAPTER III

1. Motion to Proceed In Forma Pauperis, *Louisiana ex rel. Francis* v. *Resweber*, 329 U.S. 459 (1947) (affidavit of Frederick and Willie Francis) (available in National Archives, Washington, D.C.).

2. Interview with Bertrand DeBlanc, Esq., Lafayette, La., September 24, 1982.

3. *New Orleans Times-Picayune*, May 8, 1946.

4. Supreme Court Record at 9 (from Petition for Writ of Habeas Corpus, filed May 7, 1946).

5. Supreme Court Record at 12.

6. Ibid. at 12–17.

7. *The State Times*, Baton Rouge, La., May 9, 1946.

8. *New Orleans Times-Picayune*, May 8, 1946.

9. *Miami Herald*, May 9, 1946; *New Orleans Times-Picayune*, May 10, 1946.

10. *The State Times*, Baton Rouge, La., May 9, 1946.

11. *New Orleans Times-Picayune*, May 9, 1946.

12. *The State Times*, Baton Rouge, La., May 8, 1946.

13. *New Orleans Times-Picayune*, May 12, 1946; See also *The State Times*, Baton Rouge, La., May 8, 1946.

14. *New Orleans Times-Picayune*, May 8, 1946.

15. Ibid., May 9, 1946.

16. Ibid.

17. Ibid.

18. *The State Times*, Baton Rouge, La., May 7, 1946.

19. Ibid., May 8, 1946.

20. See ibid., May 7, 1946.

21. Ibid.

22. *The Weekly Messenger*, St. Martinville, La., May 17, 1946.

23. *State ex rel. Francis* v. *Resweber*, 212 La. 143, 31 So. 2d 697 (1946) (per curiam).

24. Id. at 150, 31 So. 2d at 699.

25. Ibid., 31 So. 2d at 699.

26. *Philadelphia Tribune*, May 18, 1946.

27. Louisiana Constitution of 1921, Article V, Section 10.

28. The entire text of the May 31, 1946, Louisiana Pardons Board Hearing is reprinted at the Appendix to Brief for Respondent at 59–101.

29. E. Barrett Prettyman, Jr., *Death and the Supreme Court* (New York: Avon Books, 1961), p. 128.

30. Address of B. DeBlanc to Louisiana Pardons Board, May 31, 1946, at 1–14.

31. *New York Times*, June 5, 1946. By not explaining its decision, the actions of the Louisiana Pardons Board were similar to those of the General Court of the Massachusetts Bay Colony when it banished Anne Hutchinson:

Ms. Hutchinson: I desire to know wherefore I am banished.
Gov. Winthrup: Say no more. The court knows wherefore and it is satisfied.

Rummel v. *Estelle,* 587 F.2d 651 (5th Cir. 1978).

32. Interview with Bertrand DeBlanc, Esq., Lafayette, La., September 25, 1982.

33. Petition for a Writ of Certiorari at 4, *Louisiana ex rel. Francis* v. *Resweber,* 329 U.S. 459 (1947).

34. Stay of Execution in *Louisiana ex rel. Francis* v. *Resweber,* 329 U.S. 459 (1947) (available in National Archives, Washington, D.C.).

On June 4, 1946, before granting the stay, Justice Black circulated the following memorandum in a preliminary effort to discuss the matter with the Court:

A petition for stay has been filed with me in No. 1302, State of Louisiana, ex rel. Willie Francis, Petitioner, against the Sheriff of the Parish of St. Martin, Louisiana.
The Petitioner was sentenced to death, and the judgment was affirmed by the Supreme Court of Louisiana. The Sheriff attempted to execute him in accordance with the judgment, and for some reason the electrical apparatus failed to work. Petitioner now claims that to carry out the death sentence would be placing him twice in jeopardy for the same offense and that this is prohibited by the due process clause of the federal Constitution. I shall wish to take it up with the conference at 11:00 this morning. H.L.B.

Black, J., Memorandum for Conference (June 4, 1946) (available in Library of Congress, Black Papers, Box 283).

CHAPTER IV

1. Felix Frankfurter to Frank Murphy (June 10, 1946) (available in Library of Congress, Frankfurter Papers, Box 28).

2. See Hugo L. Black, Jr., *My Father, A Remembrance* (New York: Random House, 1975), pp. 190–191.

3. The United States, for some strange reason, named a judge as prosecutor and its chief prosecutor, Attorney General Francis Biddle, as a judge.

4. Herman C. Pritchett, *Civil Liberties and the Vinson Court* (Chicago: University of Chicago Press, 1954), p. 21.

5. See *Panama Refining Co.* v. *Ryan,* 293 U.S. 388 (1935); *Schechter Poultry Corp.* v. *United States,* 295 U.S. 495 (1935); *United States* v. *Butler,* 297 U.S. 1 (1936); *Carter* v. *Carter Coal Co.,* 298 U.S. 238 (1936); and *Ashton* v. *Cameron County District,* 298 U.S. 513 (1936).

6. *Ashwander* v. *TVA,* 297 U.S. 288 (1936).

7. Roosevelt, unhappy with a number of Court decisions (see note 5, supra), said that the justices were too old and didn't have the energy or stamina to keep up with their docket. He proposed to add some younger justices to the bench to help the "nine old men"—justices to be appointed by Roosevelt. For accounts of the episode, see Leonard Baker, *Back to Back: The Duel Between F.D.R. and the Supreme Court* (New York: Macmillan, 1967); Joseph Alsop and Turner Catledge, *The 168 Days* (Garden City, N.Y.: Doubleday, Doran and Co., 1938); and Alpheus T. Mason, *Harlan Fiske Stone: A Pillar of the Law* (New York: Viking Press, 1956), pp. 442–452.

8. In 1917 Frankfurter served as counsel to a presidential commission investi-

gating the Mooney case. Tom Mooney was a labor leader who had been convicted and sentenced to death for his alleged involvement in a San Francisco bomb explosion that had killed a number of people. President Wilson accepted the conclusion of the commission that Mooney had been convicted on the basis of perjured testimony. Later, the governor of California commuted Mooney's sentence to life imprisonment. In 1927 Frankfurter wrote an article in the *Atlantic Monthly*, and later a book, detailing injustices of the Sacco-Vanzetti case.

9. *Nation*, January 14, 1939.

10. Fred Rodell, *Nine Men, A Political History of the Supreme Court of the United States from 1790 to 1955* (New York: Vintage Books, 1955), p. 277.

11. *Congressional Quarterly*, Guide to the U.S. Supreme Court 855 (1979).

12. Drew Pearson, "The Washington Merry-Go-Round," *Washington Post*, June 14, 1946.

13. Joseph Lash, *From the Diaries of Felix Frankfurter* (New York: W. W. Norton and Co., 1975), p. 343.

14. *The State Times*, Baton Rouge, La., June 12, 1946.

15. See John P. Frank, *Marble Palace* (New York: Alfred A. Knopf, 1961), p. 275; Francis Biddle, *In Brief Authority* (Garden City, N.Y.: Doubleday, 1962), p. 356.

16. *Washington Post*, November 7, 1982. See also *The United States News*, May 3, 1946.

17. Drew Pearson, "The Washington Merry-Go-Round," *Washington Post*, June 14, 1946.

18. J. Woodford Howard, Jr., *Mr. Justice Murphy: A Political Biography* (Princeton, N.J.: Princeton University Press, 1968), p. 392–395.

19. For a full description, see Gerald T. Dunne, *Hugo Black and the Judicial Revolution* (New York: Simon and Schuster, 1977), p. 224–249.

20. Black, *My Father, A Remembrance*, pp. 190–191.

21. Mason, *Harlan Fiske Stone*, p. 716.

22. Lash, *From the Diaries of Felix Frankfurter*, p. 262. See also *New York Times*, June 12, 1946.

23. Arthur Schlesinger accurately characterized the outburst as "the act of a weary and sorely beset man, committed to a harassing task in a remote land, tormented by the certainty that the chief justiceship had now passed forever out of his reach." Schlesinger, "The Supreme Court: 1947," *Fortune* 73 (January 1947).

24. *Washington Post*, June 11, 1946. See also *New York Times*, June 11, 1946.

25. 325 U.S. 161 (1945).

26. *Washington Post*, June 11, 1946. See also *New York Times*, June 11, 1946.

27. Burton Diary (Entry of October 10, 1946) (available in Library of Congress, Burton Papers, Box 171).

28. Letter from Justice Reed to Justice Frankfurter (July 8, 1946) (available at the Harvard Law School Library, Frankfurter Papers, Box 170).

29. *Osborn v. Bank of the United States*, 22 U.S. (9Wheat.) 738, 846 (1824).

30. Ibid.

31. 1 W. Blackstone, *Commentaries* 69.

32. Bacon, *Of Judicature*, quoted in Arthur S. Miller and Alan W. Scheflin, "The Power of the Supreme Court in the Age of the Positive State," *Duke Law Journal* (1967): 522.

33. *West Virginia State Board of Education* v. *Barnette*, 319 U.S. 624, 646 (1943) (Frankfurter, J., dissenting).

34. Lash, *From the Diaries of Felix Frankfurter*, p. 197.

35. *Chambers* v. *Florida*, 309 U.S. 227, 241 (1940).

36. Pritchett, *Civil Liberties and the Vinson Court*, p. 2; Herman C. Pritchett, *The Roosevelt Court* (New York: Macmillan, 1948), p. 25.

37. *United States News*, May 3, 1946.

38. Pritchett, *The Roosevelt Court*, p. 48.

39. Mason, *Harlan Fiske Stone*.

40. Frankfurter, "Chief Justices I Have Known," *Virginia Law Review* 31 (1953): 7.

41. Schlesinger, "The Supreme Court: 1947."

42. Lash, *From the Diaries of Felix Frankfurter*, p. 207. ("We had been at it [in Conference] from 9:30 without interruption which is sheer madness—nearly nine continuous hours. . . . The long hours of our Conferences seem to me a very bad way of doing business.")

43. Lash, *From the Diaries of Felix Frankfurter* p. 228. ("Roberts went on to say, 'Of course, one difficulty is that the present Chief [Stone] is not strong at the helm—you were on the Court long enough to see with what mastery Hughes presided over our Conferences.'")

44. Mason, *Harlan Fiske Stone*, p. 580.

45. *Philadelphia Record*, April 23, 1946.

46. Mason, *Harlan Fiske Stone*, p. 807.

47. Henry J. Abraham, *Justices and the Presidents* (New York: Penguin, 1975), p. 227. In the 1946 term, Vinson's first year of stewardship, the rate of nonunanimous decisions reached a then record-breaking 64 percent. Pritchett, *The Roosevelt Court*, p. 43. By the 1952 term, Vinson's last on the Court, an all-time high of 81 percent was recorded. Pritchett, *Civil Liberties and the Vinson Court*, p. 21.

48. Felix Frankfurter to Frank Murphy (June 10, 1946) (available in Library of Congress, Frankfurter Papers, Box 28).

49. *New York Times*, June 12, 1946.

50. E. Barrett Prettyman, Jr., *Death and the Supreme Court* (New York: Avon Books, 1961), p. 110.

51. W. Francis as told to S. Montgomery, "My Trip to the Electric Chair" (1947).

52. *New Orleans Times-Picayune*, June 12, 1946.

53. *Louisiana ex rel. Francis* v. *Resweber*, 328 U.S. 833 (1946). Because of both the death of Chief Justice Stone and Justice Jackson's absence owing to his participation in the Nuremberg War Crimes Trial, only seven justices participated in the consideration of the petition for a writ of *certiorari*. Voting to grant *certiorari* were Justices Frankfurter, Murphy, and Rutledge. Justices Burton, Black, Douglas, and Reed voted to refuse *certiorari*. Douglas Papers, Box 189 (available in Library of Congress). Yet, because only seven justices were available, the petition was granted on the basis of three votes rather than the usual "rule of four." See Robert L. Stern and Eugene Gressman, *Supreme Court Practice* (Washington D.C.: BNA, Inc., 1978), pp. 346–348.

54. *The State Times*, Baton Rouge, La., June 11, 1946.

55. *New York Times*, June 12, 1946.

CHAPTER V

1. 7 Pet. 243 (1833).

2. 291 U.S. 97, 105 (1934) (emphasis added).

3. Gerald T. Dunne, *Hugo Black and the Judicial Revolution* (New York: Simon and Schuster, 1977), p. 258.

4. See discussion of *Adamson* v. *California*, 332 U.S. 46 (1947) in Chapter 8, infra.

5. 302 U.S. 319 (1937).

6. 302 U.S. at 325 quoting *Snyder* v. *Massachusetts*, 291 U.S. at 105.

7. Brief for Petitioner at 4–7, *Louisiana ex rel. Francis* v. *Resweber*, 329 U.S. 459 (1947) (hereinafter cited as Petitioner's Brief).

8. Ibid. at 7.

9. Ibid. at 8.

10. See Elinor Horwitz, *Capital Punishment, USA* (Philadelphia: J. B. Lippincott Co. 1973), p. 54.

11. See *In re Kemmler*, 136 U.S. 436, 444 (1890).

12. Ibid.

13. "Sentence of Death in Capital Cases," Report of the Commission to Investigate and Report the Most Humane and Practical Method of Carrying into Effect, Transmittal to Legislature of the State of New York, January 6, 1885.

14. Ibid.

15. Ibid.

16. Ibid.

17. Lee W. Sheridan, *I Killed for the Law* (New York: Stackpole Sons, 1938), p. 16.

18. 136 U.S. at 443.

19. 136 U.S. at 443–444.

20. *In re Kemmler*, 136 U.S. 436 (1890).

21. 136 U.S. at 447.

22. Robert G. Elliott, *Agent of Death* (London: J. Long, 1941), p. 16.

23. *The New York World*, August 7, 1890. See also *The New York Press*, August 7, 1890.

24. George Bishop, *Executions* (Los Angeles: Sherbourne Press, 1965), p. 20.

25. *The New York World*, August 7, 1890.

26. *The New York Press*, August 7, 1890.

27. *The New York World*, August 7, 1890.

28. *New York Herald Tribune*, August 7, 1890.

29. *New York Times*, August 7, 1890.

30. Elliott, *Agent of Death*, p. 30.

31. Bishop, *Executions*, p. 22.

32. Elliott, *Agent of Death*, p. 30.

33. Petitioner's Brief at 3.

34. Ibid. at 8.

35. Ibid.

36. 287 U.S. 45 (1932). See, for example, *Williams* v. *State*, 192 Ga. 247, 257–259,

15 S.E. 2d 219, 225 (1941) (meaningful counsel must be provided); *Wilson* v. *State,* 222 Ind. 63, 79, 51 N.E. 2d 848, 854–855 (1943) (defendant entitled to adequate counsel in criminal case).

37. Petitioner's Brief at 9–11.

38. Ibid. at 9.

39. 287 U.S. at 71.

40. 287 U.S. at 58.

41. Petitioner's Brief at 11 quoting *Williams* v. *State,* 192 Ga. 247, 257–259, 15 S.E. 2d 219, 225 (1941).

42. Petitioner's Brief at 12.

43. Brief for Respondent at 24–25, 34, *Louisiana ex rel. Francis* v. *Resweber,* 329 U.S. 459 (1947) (hereinafter cited as Respondent's Brief).

44. Ibid. at 27.

45. Ibid. at 28.

46. Ibid. at 31 (emphasis in the original).

47. Ibid. at 30–31, 32.

48. Supreme Court Rule 38.1 (formerly Rule 44(1)) (1980).

49. 329 U.S. 296 (1946).

50. No transcript or recording of the November 18, 1946, oral argument exists in the National Archives or the Supreme Court Law Library in Washington, D.C. Nor was a summary of the argument prepared by *United States Law Week.* However, portions of the argument have been reconstructed from press reports, papers of the justices, and interview with counsel. See, for example, *Baltimore Sun,* November 18, 1946; *New Orleans Times-Picayune,* November 19, 1946; Bench Notes of Justice Jackson (available in Library of Congress, Jackson Papers, Box 138); interviews with Bertrand DeBlanc, Esq., Lafayette, La., September 24–25, 1982; interview with Judge Wright, August 1982.

51. Burton Diary (Entry of November 18, 1946) (available in Library of Congress, Burton Papers, Box 171).

CHAPTER VI

1. Drew Pearson and Robert S. Allen, *The Nine Old Men* (Garden City, N.Y.: Doubleday, 1936), p. 39.

2. Alan F. Westin, *The Anatomy of a Constitutional Law Case* (New York: Macmillan, 1958), p. 125.

3. See Alan F. Westin, *An Autobiography of the Supreme Court* (New York: W. W. Norton, 1961).

4. James F. Byrne quoted in Westin, *An Autobiography of the Supreme Court,* p. 154.

5. Joseph Lash, *From the Diaries of Felix Frankfurter* (New York: W. W. Norton, 1975), p. 274.

6. Ibid.

7. Latin for "in the manner of a pauper." Supreme Court Rules provide for the waiver of certain procedural requirements for such parties. Supreme Court Rule 46 (formerly Rule 53) (1980).

8. Supreme Court Rules allow "a petition for rehearing of any judgment or

decision . . . (to) be filed" with the Court. Supreme Court Rule 51 (formerly Rule 58) (1980).

9. 329 U.S. 459 (1947).

10. Murphy Papers, Box 72 (available at the University of Michigan).

11. Douglas Papers, Box 189 (available in Library of Congress).

12. See Letter from Justice Frankfurter to Justice Burton (December 13, 1946) (Burton Papers, Box 171, Library of Congress).

13. Murphy Papers, Box 72 (available at the University of Michigan).

14. Douglas Papers, Box 189 (available in Library of Congress).

15. Murphy Papers, Box 172 (available at the University of Michigan).

16. Letter from Justice Frankfurter to *Harvard Law Review* (date unavailable), quoted in "Note, In Memoriam—Harold Hitz Burton," *Harvard Law Review* 78 (1965): 799, 800.

17. See, for example, *Haley* v. *Ohio*, 332 U.S. 596, 607 (1948) (Burton, J., dissenting) (believed that confession obtained from a fifteen-year-old boy arrested for murder, after extensive questioning and without benefit of counsel did not violate due process guarantee); *Ballard* v. *United States*, 329 U.S. 187, 203 (1946) (Burton, J., dissenting) (argued that fact that no women were members of a grand jury did not render a woman's indictment invalid); *Duncan* v. *Kahanamoku*, 327 U.S. 304, 337 (1946) (Burton, J., dissenting) (supporting invocation of martial law and suspension of civil privileges during wartime).

18. See *United States Law Week*, June 26, 1945, at 3493–94 as cited in Alpheus T. Mason, *Harlan Fiske Stone: A Pillar of the Law* (New York: Random House, 1956), p. 639.

19. Lawrence Baum, *The Supreme Court* (Washington, D.C., 1981, Congressional Quarterly Press) pp. 138–139.

20. Justice Reed draft opinion of December 11, 1946 at 2, Box 100 (available at the University of Kentucky).

21. Ibid. at 3.

22. Ibid.

23. Ibid. at 4.

24. Ibid.

25. Ibid.

26. Ibid. at 5.

27. Ibid.

28. Ibid. at 6.

29. Ibid.

30. Memorandum to the Conference from Justice Reed (December 13, 1946) (available at the University of Kentucky, Reed Papers, Box 100).

31. Ibid.

32. Charles Evans Hughes, *The Supreme Court of the United States* (New York: Columbia University Press, 1928), p. 68.

33. *Washington Post*, June 23, 1947.

34. Letter from T. R. Powell to Justice Frankfurter (September 20, 1945) (available in Library of Congress, Frankfurter Papers, Box 91).

35. H. N. Hirsch, *The Enigma of Felix Frankfurter* (New York: Basic Books, 1981), p. 188.

36. Confidential interview, September 1982.

37. Justice Burton draft dissent of December 12, 1946, at 1 (available in Library of Congress, Burton Papers, Box 171).

38. Ibid. at 8.

39. Ibid. at 4.

40. Louisiana Code of Criminal Procedure—Act 2 of 1928—Article 569.

41. Justice Burton draft dissent of December 12, 1946; at 6 (available in Library of Congress, Burton Papers, Box 171).

42. Ibid.

43. Ibid. at 7; 329 U.S. at 474 (Burton, J., dissenting).

44. Justice Reed draft opinion of December 11, 1946, at 3, Box 100 (available at the University of Kentucky).

45. Justice Burton draft dissent of December 12, 1946, at 6 (available in Library of Congress, Burton Papers, Box 171).

46. Ibid.

47. Ibid.

48. Ibid. at 7–8.

49. *Trop* v. *Dulles*, 356 U.S. 86, 102 (1958), quoted in *Furman* v. *Georgia*, 408 U.S. 238, 289 (1972) (Brennan, J., concurring).

50. *Solesbee* v. *Balkcom*, 339 U.S. 9, 14 (1950) (Frankfurter, J., dissenting). In *Solesbee*, the Court upheld a state's policy that permitted a panel of doctors appointed by the governor to determine the sanity of those awaiting execution. The Court reasoned that this was a valid exercise of the executive power to grant reprieves. Ibid. at 13. Frankfurter dissented, maintaining that due process prevents execution of an insane person and that the defendant was entitled to a hearing on his claim of insanity. Ibid. at 24–25 (Frankfurter, J., dissenting).

51. James Boswell, *The Life of Samuel Johnson* (W. Croker edition, 1846), p. 309.

52. Justice Burton draft dissent of December 12, 1946, at 8 (available in Library of Congress, Burton Papers, Box 171).

53. Remarks of Attorney General McGrath at Memorial for Justice Murphy, 340 U.S. XIV (1951).

54. *Falbo* v. *United States*, 320 U.S. 549, 561 (1944) (Murphy, J., dissenting).

55. *Carter* v. *Illinois*, 329 U.S. 173, 183 (1946).

56. Justice Murphy draft dissent of December 13, 1946, at 1 (available at the University of Michigan, Murphy Papers, Box 72).

57. Ibid. By using the term "our consciences," Murphy anticipated Chief Justice Warren's valedictory: "in this Court . . . we have no constituency. We serve no majority. We serve no minority. We serve only the public interest as we see it, guided only by the Constitution and our own consciences." Retirement of Mr. Chief Justice Warren, 359 U.S. at xi (1969).

58. Justice Murphy draft dissent of December 13, 1946, at 2 (available at the University of Michigan, Murphy Papers, Box 72).

59. Ibid.

60. Ibid.

61. Ibid. at 2–3.

62. Ibid. at 3.

63. Ibid.

64. Justice Rutledge draft dissent of December 14, 1946, at 1–2 (available in Library of Congress, Rutledge Papers, Box 147). See also Fowler V. Harper, *Justice*

Rutledge and the Bright Constellation (Indianapolis: Bobbs-Merrill, 1965), pp. 353–356.

65. Justice Stevens later echoed Rutledge's beliefs in *Estelle* v. *Gamble*, 429 U.S. 97, 116 (1976) (Stevens, J., dissenting). Stevens maintained that the existence of a constitutional violation, rather than the intent of the individual causing it, was the proper focus of constitutional adjudication ("whether the conditions in Andersonville were the product of design, negligence, or mere poverty, they were cruel and inhuman").

66. Justice Rutledge draft dissent of December 14, 1946, at 1–2 (available in Library of Congress, Rutledge Papers, Box 147).

67. Ibid. at 2.

68. Ibid.

69. Ibid.

70. Ibid. at 3.

71. Murphy Papers, Box 72 (University of Michigan).

72. Rutledge-Burton Memorandum (December 31, 1946) (available in Library of Congress, Burton Papers, Box 171).

73. Burton Diary (entry of December 20, 1946) (available in Library of Congress, Burton Papers, Box 171).

74. Reed Papers, Box 100 (University of Kentucky).

75. Vinson Papers, Box 233 (University of Kentucky).

76. Justice Jackson's draft concurrence of December 20, 1946, at 1 (available in Library of Congress, Jackson Papers, Box 138).

77. Ibid.

78. Ibid.

79. Ibid. at 4.

80. Undated, unsigned memorandum (available in Library of Congress, Rutledge Papers, Box 147).

81. Justice Jackson's draft concurrence of December 20, 1946, at 1 (available in Library of Congress, Jackson Papers, Box 138).

82. Note 72, supra.

CHAPTER VII

1. Letter from Justice Frankfurter to Justice Burton (December 13, 1946) (available in Library of Congress, Burton Papers, Box 171).

2. Ibid. See also notes 13–14, Chapter 6, and accompanying text.

3. Ibid.

4. Ibid.

5. Ibid. at 1–2.

6. Ibid. at 2.

7. Ibid.

8. Ibid.

9. 329 U.S. at 472–473 (Burton, J., dissenting).

10. Letter from Justice Frankfurter to Justice Reed (December 14, 1946) (available at the University of Kentucky, Reed Papers, Box 100).

11. Letter from Justice Burton to Justice Frankfurter (December 26, 1946) (available in Library of Congress, Frankfurter Papers, Box 38).

12. Louisiana Code of Criminal Procedure—Act 2 of 1928—Article 569.

13. Letter from Justice Burton to Justice Frankfurter (December 26, 1946) (available in Library of Congress, Frankfurter Papers, Box 38).

14. Letter from Justice Frankfurter to Justice Burton (December 31, 1946) (available in Library of Congress, Burton Papers, Box 171).

15. Ibid.

16. Ibid.

17. Ibid.

18. Ibid.

19. Justice Burton's first diary entry for January 2, 1947, states: "conferred with Justice Frankfurter as to my dissent in (Francis). He has written an opinion concurring with majority." Burton Diary (entry of January 2, 1947) (available in Library of Congress, Burton Papers, Box 171).

20. Justice Frankfurter's draft concurrence of January 2, 1947, at 1 (available in Library of Congress, Burton Papers, Box 171).

21. Ibid.

22. Ibid. at 2.

23. Justice Jackson's draft concurrence of December 20, 1946, at 3 (available in Library of Congress, Jackson Papers, Box 138).

24. Ibid. at 2–3.

25. Justice Frankfurter's draft concurrence of January 2, 1947, at 2 (available in Library of Congress, Burton Papers, Box 171).

26. Ibid.

27. Ibid.

28. Ibid. at 3, quoting *Snyder* v. *Massachusetts*, 291 U.S. at 105.

29. Ibid. at 3–4.

30. Ibid. at 4.

31. Ibid.

32. Ibid.

33. Letter from Justice Frankfurter to Justice Reed (January 2, 1947) (available at the University of Kentucky, Reed Papers, Box 100).

34. Ibid.

35. Note from Justice Frankfurter to Chief Justice Vinson, undated (available in Library of Congress, Frankfurter Papers, Box 215).

36. Letter from Justice Frankfurter to Justice Reed (January 4, 1947) (available at the University of Kentucky, Reed Papers, Box 100).

37. Ibid.

38. Ibid.

39. Ibid.

40. Justice Black's draft concurrence of January 3, 1947, at 1 (available in Library of Congress, Black Papers, Box 287).

41. Ibid. at 3.

42. Ibid. at 2.

43. Ibid. at 1.

44. Ibid.

45. Ibid. at 4.

46. Ibid.

47. Ibid.

48. Ibid. at 5.

49. Ibid.

50. Alexander M. Bickel and Harry H. Wellington, "Legislative Purpose and the Judicial Process: The Lincoln Mills Case," *Harvard Law Review* 71 (1957): 1, 3.

51. See Lawrence Baum, *The Supreme Court* (Washington, D.C.: Congressional Quarterly Press, 1981), pp. 105–110.

52. See Merlo J. Pusey, *Charles Evans Hughes* (New York: Macmillan, 1951), pp. 286–287.

53. Note from Justice Jackson to Justice Reed, January 9, 1947 (available at the University of Kentucky, Reed Papers, Box 100).

54. Reed Papers, Box 100 (available at the University of Kentucky).

55. See Justice Reed draft opinions of December 11 and 12, 1946, and January 2 and 7, 1947, at 2 (available at the University of Kentucky, Reed Papers, Box 100).

56. Reed Papers, Box 100 (available at the University of Kentucky).

57. Ibid.

58. Ibid.

59. Justice Reed draft opinion of January 11, 1947, at 4 (available at the University of Kentucky, Reed Papers, Box 100).

60. Ibid. at 3.

61. Ibid. at back of page 7.

62. Justice Frankfurter Memorandum for Conference (January 11, 1947) (available in Library of Congress, Frankfurter Papers, Box 23).

63. Ibid.

64. Ibid.

65. 329 U.S. at 468, 470 (Frankfurter, J., concurring).

66. 329 U.S. at 469–470.

67. 329 U.S. at 471.

68. Ibid.

69. See Arthur S. Miller, "Toward a Definition of the Constitution," 8 *University of Dayton Law Review* (1983): 633–711.

CHAPTER VIII

1. 329 U.S. at 470 (Frankfurter, J., concurring).

2. *Griswold* v. *Connecticut*, 381 U.S. 479, 519 (1965) (Black, J., dissenting).

3. Ibid.

4. *New Orleans Times-Picayune*, May 12, 1946.

5. 329 U.S. at 464.

6. 291 U.S. 97 (1934).

7. 291 U.S. at 105.

8. Retirement of Mr. Chief Justice Warren, 395 U.S. at xi (1969).

9. Benjamin N. Cardozo, *The Nature of the Judicial Process* (New Haven Conn.: Yale University Press, 1921), p. 13.

10. 332 U.S. 46 (1947).

11. 332 U.S. at 89 (Black, J., dissenting).

12. 211 U.S. 78 (1908).

13. 332 U.S. at 67 (Frankfurter, J., concurring).

14. 332 U.S. at 65.

15. 332 U.S. at 68.

16. 332 U.S. at 90 (Black, J., dissenting).

17. 332 U.S. at 71–72.

18. 332 U.S. at 89.

19. 332 U.S. at 69.

20. George D. Braden, "The Search for Objectivity in Constitutional Law," *Yale Law Journal* 57 (1948): 571, 588–589.

21. 342 U.S. 165 (1952).

22. 342 U.S. at 170–172.

23. 342 U.S. at 172.

24. 342 U.S. at 176, 177 (Black, J., concurring).

25. Hugo L. Black, *A Constitutional Faith* (New York: Alfred A. Knopf, 1968), p. 30.

26. 332 U.S. 596 (1948).

27. 332 U.S. at 617 (Burton, H., dissenting).

28. Letter from Justice Frankfurter to Justice Burton (January 5, 1948) (available in Library of Congress, Frankfurter Papers, Box 38).

29. 332 U.S. at 603 (Frankfurter, J., concurring).

30. 332 U.S. at 602.

31. Ibid.

32. 332 U.S. at 603.

33. 332 U.S. at 604.

34. E. Barrett Prettyman, *Death and the Supreme Court* (New York: Avon Books, 1961), p. 120.

35. Max Freedman, William M. Beaney, and Eugene V. Rostow, *Perspectives on the Court* (Evanston, Ill.: Northwestern University Press, 1967), p. 15.

36. Ibid. at 16. Cf. Robert M. Cover, *Justice Accused* (New Haven, Yale University Press, 1975), pp. 235–236. ("The discomfort incidental to a difficult choice will be heightened insofar as the judge views himself as having had personal responsibility for a choice from among many alternatives before him. The discomfort will be reduced insofar as he can view himself as a mechanical instrument of the will of others.")

CHAPTER IX

1. W. Francis as told to S. Montgomery, "My Trip to the Electric Chair" (1947).

2. *The World's Messenger*, July 1946.

3. Ibid.

4. Ibid.

5. Ibid.

6. Ibid.

7. Ibid.

8. *The Defender*, Chicago, February 1, 1947.

9. *New York Times*, January 14, 1947.

10. *New York Daily News*, January 14, 1947.

11. *Philadelphia Record*, January 14, 1947.

12. Ibid. See also *Washington Evening Star*, January 14, 1947.

13. *The Washington Daily News*, January 14, 1947.

14. *New York Daily News*, January 14, 1947.

15. *Philadelphia Record*, January 14, 1947; *New York Daily News*, January 14, 1947.

16. W. Francis as told to S. Montgomery, "My Trip to the Electric Chair" (1947).

17. Willie's plight had even attracted international attention. See, for example, *London Times*, January 14 and May 10, 1947.

18. *New York Herald Tribune*, January 19, 1947.

19. Ibid.

20. Ibid.

21. Ibid.

22. Newspaper P.M. Inc., January 14, 1947.

23. Ibid.

24. *Pittsburgh Press*, January 14, 1947.

25. Ibid.

26. *The Norfolk News*, Norfolk, Va., January 25, 1947.

27. Ibid.

28. Ibid.

29. *New York Law Journal*, January 14, 1947.

30. *Washington Post*, February 24, 1947.

31. Ibid.

32. Ibid.

33. *The Greenville News*, January 15, 1947.

34. *The Age-Herald*, Birmingham, Ala., January 15, 1947.

35. Ibid.

36. *New York Times*, January 15, 1947.

37. *The Defender*, Chicago, March 8, 1947.

38. Ibid., January 25, 1947.

39. *New York Herald Tribune*, January 15, 1947.

CHAPTER X

1. Frankfurter Papers, Box 179 (available at the Harvard Law School Library).

2. Ibid.

3. Ibid.

4. Ibid.

5. Ibid.

6. Philip Elman, "The Solicitor General's Office, Justice Frankfurter, and Civil Rights Litigation, 1946–1960: An Oral History," *Harvard Law Review* 100 (1987): 817.

7. Frankfurter Papers, Box 179 (available at the Harvard Law School Library).

8. Felix Frankfurter, *Of Law and Men*, P. Elman, ed. (New York: Harcourt, Brace and World, 1956), p. 98. Frankfurter, in a self-serving statement, remarked that "there was no question about (Francis') guilt." Ibid. Frankfurter made this statement during the summer of 1953 while he was a witness before the British Royal Commission on Capital Punishment.

9. Letter from Justice Frankfurter to Monte Lemann (February 3, 1947) (available in Library of Congress, Frankfurter Papers, Box 38).

10. *New York Times*, September 23, 1959. See also Max Freedman, ed., *Roosevelt and Frankfurter: Their Correspondence 1928–1945* (Boston: Little, Brown and Co., 1967), p. 459.

11. *New York Times*, September 23, 1959.

12. Felix Frankfurter to Monte Lemann (January 22, 1931) (available in Library of Congress, Frankfurter Papers, Box 76).

13. Freedman, *Roosevelt and Frankfurter*, p. 457.

14. Ibid. at 458.

15. Burton Papers, Box 171 (available in Library of Congress). The papers of the other justices examined in the research for this book do not reveal a copy of this letter.

16. Ibid.

17. Ibid.

18. Ibid.

19. Ibid.

20. Letter from Monte Lemann to Judge Simon (April 19, 1947) (available in Library of Congress, Frankfurter Papers, Box 38).

21. Ibid.

22. Ibid.

23. Ibid.

24. Frankfurter, J., Memorandum to Supreme Court (April 23, 1947) (available in Library of Congress, Burton Papers, Box 171; Douglas Papers, Box 189).

25. Letter from Justice Frankfurter to Monte Lemann (April 22, 1947) (available in Library of Congress, Frankfurter Papers, Box 38).

26. Ibid.

27. Ibid.

28. 369 U.S. 186 (1962).

29. 369 U.S. at 266 (Frankfurter, J., dissenting). According to Frankfurter, the "appeal for relief . . . must be an informed, civically militant electorate. Relief must come through an aroused popular conscience that sears the conscience of the people's representatives." 369 U.S. at 270.

30. Bruce A. Murphy, *The Brandeis/Frankfurter Connection, The Secret Political Activities of Two Supreme Court Justices* (New York: Oxford University Press, 1982).

31. Nicholas Lemann, *Out of the Forties* (Austin: Texas Monthly Press, 1983), p. 85.

32. Gunnar Myrdal, *An American Dilemma: The Negro Problem and Modern Democracy* (New York: Harper, 1944), p. 24. See also *Primaries*: "White Supremacy," *Newsweek*, July 15, 1946, at 30.

33. 321 U.S. 649 (1944).

34. *Newsweek*, July 15, 1946.

35. William O. Douglas, *The Court Years, 1939–1975* (New York: Random House, 1980), p. 123.

36. Allan P. Sindler, *Huey Long's Louisiana* (Baltimore: Johns Hopkins University Press, 1956), p. 34. By 1961, a little over twenty years later, this figure had only marginally improved. According to the Federal Civil Rights Commission, there

were 1,067,651 whites registered to vote in Louisiana and only 153,166 blacks. Four parishes with large black populations had no blacks registered, and thirteen others had fewer than 100. In one parish, of 5,032 eligible blacks, only 30 were registered to vote, while 5,487 of the 6,415 whites were registered. *New York Times*, May 7, 1961. See also Thomas Clark, *The Emerging South* (New York: Oxford University Press, 1968), p. 215.

37. *The State Times*, Baton Rouge, La., May 27, 1946.

CHAPTER XI

1. *The Washington Daily News*, January 14, 1947.

2. 329 U.S. at 480–481 (Burton, J., dissenting).

3. Petition for Rehearing, *Louisiana ex rel. Francis v. Resweber*, 329 U.S. 459 (1947) (hereinafter cited as Petition for Rehearing).

4. Act of July 15, 1946, Louisiana Acts, No. 149, section 1 (1946) codified in La. Code Crim. L. and Proc., ch. 1. art. 570 (Dart. Supp. 1949).

5. *The State Times*, Baton Rouge, La., May 14, 1946. See also 1946 Senate Calender of the State of Louisiana, Thirteenth Regular Session of the Legislature 8 (1946).

6. Petition for Rehearing at 4.

7. Ibid. at 8.

8. Ibid. at 4.

9. Supreme Court Rule 51 (formerly Rule 58) (1980).

10. 330 U.S. 853 (1947).

11. *New York Times*, April 19, 1947.

12. Interview with Bertrand DeBlanc, Esq., Lafayette, La., September 25, 1982; Interview with Louie M. Cyr, Esq., New Iberia, La., February 23, 1988.

13. Habeas Corpus Petition (affidavit of Louie M. Cyr).

14. Ibid.

15. Ibid.

16. Ibid.

17. Habeas Corpus Petition (affidavit of Ignace Doucet).

18. Ibid.

19. *New York Times*, April 23, 1947.

20. *Washington Times Herald*, April 23, 1947.

21. Motion of a New Trial, State of Louisiana, Parish of Iberia, filed April 23, 1947.

22. Ibid.

23. Transcript of the Application of the Defendant for a New Trial and for an Arrest of Judgment at 2, May 5, 1947.

24. Ibid.

25. *State of Louisiana ex rel. Francis v. Resweber*, No. 14382 at 3.

26. Ibid. at 5.

27. 329 U.S. at 471 (Frankfurter, J., concurring) (emphasis added).

28. Habeas Corpus Petition at 4.

29. Ibid.

30. Ibid. at 5.

31. 331 U.S. at 786, 786–787 (1947).

32. 321 U.S. 114 (1944).

33. Habeas Corpus Petition at 10.

34. 331 U.S. at 786–787.

35. See E. Barrett Prettyman, *Death and the Supreme Court* (New York: Avon Books, 1961), p. 127.

36. Interview with Bertrand DeBlanc, Esq., Lafayette, La., September 25, 1982.

37. Ibid.

38. *Time*, May 19, 1947. See also *The Defender*, Chicago, May 17, 1947.

39. *Washington Daily News*, May 9, 1947.

40. *Washington Times Herald*, May 8, 1947.

41. Interview with Bertrand DeBlanc, Esq., Lafayette, La., September 25, 1982.

42. Ibid.

43. *Time*, May 19, 1947.

44. *Washington Star*, May 8, 1947.

45. Ibid.

46. *Washington Post*, May 10, 1947.

47. *Pittsburgh Courier*, May 17, 1947.

48. *The Washington Daily News*, May 9, 1947.

49. Interview with Sidney Dupois, St. Martinville, La., September 24, 1982.

50. *Washington Post*, May 10, 1947.

51. *The Defender*, Chicago, May 17, 1947.

52. *Pittsburgh Courier*, May 17, 1947.

53. Ibid.

EPILOGUE

1. "In its finality, the death penalty may cruelly frustrate justice. Death is the one punishment from which there can be no relief in light of later developments in the law or the evidence." *District Attorney for Suffolk District* v. *Watson*, 411 N.E. 2d 1274, 1282 (S. Ct. Mass. 1980).

2. Hugo Adam Bedau and Michael L. Radelet, "Miscarriages of Justice in Potentially Capital Cases," 40 *Stanford Law Review* (1987): 21.

3. 471 U.S. 1080 (1985) (Brennan, J., dissenting).

4. 471 U.S. at 1091 n.34 and 1094.

5. *Washington Post*, October 17, 1985.

6. *New York Times*, December 13, 1984.

7. *Washington Post*, October 14, 1983; *Newsweek*, October 17, 1983.

8. *Washington Post*, March 14, 1984. More recently, "confused" Texas officials strapped Robert Streetman to the Texas death table, took him off the table for an hour, and then returned him to the table where he was then executed. *Washington Post*, January 8, 1988.

9. *The Clarion Ledger*, Jackson, Miss., September 2, 1983.

10. Ibid.

11. *Washington Post*, April 24, 1983; *Mobile Register*, April 23, 1983; *Birmingham News*, April 24, 1983; and *Chicago Sun-Times*, May 1, 1983.

12. *Mobile Register*, April 25, 1983.

13. *Glass* v. *Louisiana*, 471 U.S. at 1081 (Brennan, J., dissenting).

14. A 1906 hanging in Minnesota which took nearly fifteen minutes led Minnesota to abolish the death penalty altogether in 1911. Sol Rubin, *The Law of Criminal Correction* (St. Paul: West Publishing, 1963), p. 324.

15. Testimony of Clinton T. Duffy, Hearings Before the Subcommittee on Criminal Law and Procedure of the Senate Committee on the Judiciary on S. 1760 to Abolish the Death Penalty, 90th Cong., 2d Sess. (1968) quoted in Michael Meltsner, *Cruel and Unusual Punishment* (New York: Random House, 1973), p. 62.

16. Michael V. DiSalle, *The Power of Life or Death* (New York: Random House, 1965), pp. 20–21.

17. 329 U.S. at 464.

18. See *Chaney* v. *Heckler*, 718 F.2d 1174, 1191 (1983), rev'd on other grounds, 470 U.S. 821 (1985). See also Royal Commission on Capital Punishment, 1949–1953 Report (1953) for earlier concerns regarding the lethal injection method; Gardner, "Executions and Indignities—An Eighth Amendment Assessment of Methods of Inflicting Capital Punishment," *Ohio State Law Journal* 39 (1978): 96, 126–127.

19. 718 F.2d at 1191.

20. A. Camus, *Resistance, Rebellion and Death* (New York: Alfred A. Knopf, 1961), p. 187.

21. 718 F.2d. at 1191.

22. *New York Times*, August 9, 1987.

23. *In re Kemmler*, 136 U.S. at 447.

24. *Trop* v. *Dulles*, 356 U.S. 86, 101 (1958).

Bibliography

BOOKS

Abraham, Henry J. *Justices and the Presidents*. New York: Penguin, 1975.

Alsop, Joseph, and Catledge, Turner. *The 168 Days*. Garden City, N.Y.: Doubleday, Doran & Co., 1938.

Baker, Leonard. *Back to Back: The Duel Between F.D.R. and the Supreme Court*. New York: Macmillan, 1967.

Baker, Liva. *Felix Frankfurter*. New York: Coward-McCann, 1969.

Baum, Lawrence. *The Supreme Court*. Washington, D.C.: Congressional Quarterly Press, 1981.

Bedau, Hugo A. *The Courts, The Constitution, and Capital Punishment*. Lexington, Mass.: Lexington Books, 1977.

_____. *Death Penalty in America*. Garden City, N.Y.: Anchor Books, 1967.

Berger, Raoul. *Death Penalties*. Cambridge, Mass.: Harvard University Press, 1982.

Berry, Mary F. *Stability, Security and Continuity*. Westport, Conn.: Greenwood Press, 1978.

Biddle, Francis. *In Brief Authority*. Garden City, N.Y.: Doubleday, 1962.

Bishop, George. *Executions*. Los Angeles: Sherbourne Press, 1965.

Black, Hugo L. *A Constitutional Faith*. New York: Alfred A. Knopf, 1968.

Black, Hugo L., Jr. *My Father, A Remembrance*. New York: Random House, 1975.

Brasseaux, Carl A.; Conrad, Glenn R.; and Robison, R. Warren. *Courthouses of Louisiana*. Lafayette, La.: Center for Louisiana Studies at the University of Southwestern Louisiana, 1977.

Byrnes, James F. *All in One Lifetime*. New York: Harper, 1958.

Cardozo, Benjamin N. *The Nature of the Judicial Process*. New Haven, Conn.: Yale University Press, 1921.

Cash, W. J. *The Mind of the South*. New York: Alfred A. Knopf, 1941.

Clark, Thomas. *The Emerging South*. New York: Oxford University Press, 1968.

Congressional Quarterly. *Guide to the U.S. Supreme Court*. Washington, D.C.: Congressional Quarterly, 1979.

Cover, Robert M. *Justice Accused*. New Haven: Yale University Press, 1975.

Cummins, Light, and Jeansonne, Glen. *A Guide to the History of Louisiana*. Westport, Conn.: Greenwood Press, 1982.

Curtis, Charles P. *Law as Large as Life*. New York: Simon and Schuster, 1959.

DiSalle, Michael V. *The Power of Life or Death*. New York: Random House, 1965.

Douglas, William O. *The Court Years, 1939-1975*. New York: Random House, 1980.

_____. *Go East, Young Man*. New York: Random House, 1980.

Dunne, Gerald T. *Hugo Black and the Judicial Revolution*. New York: Simon and Schuster, 1977.

Elliott, Robert G. *Agent of Death*. London: J. Long, 1941.

Fine, Sidney. *Frank Murphy, The Washington Years*. Ann Arbor: University of Michigan Press, 1984.

Francis, Willie, as told to Sam Montgomery. "My Trip to the Electric Chair." 1947. (Pamphlet.)

Frank, John P. *Marble Palace*. New York: Alfred A. Knopf, 1961.

Frankfurter, Felix. *Of Law and Men*. (P. Elman, ed.) New York: Harcourt, Brace and World, 1956.

Freedman, Max, ed. *Roosevelt and Frankfurter: Their Correspondence 1928-1945*. Boston: Little, Brown and Co., 1967.

_____; Beaney, William M.; and Rostow, Eugene V. *Perspectives on the Court*. Evanston, Ill.: Northwestern University Press, 1967.

Friedman, Leon, and Israel, Fred L., eds. *The Justices of the Supreme Court: Their Lives and Major Opinions*. New York: Chelsea House Publishing, 1969.

Friendly, Fred W., and Elliott, Martha J. H. *The Constitution, That Delicate Balance*. New York: Random House, 1984.

Gerhart, Eugene C. *America's Advocate: Robert H. Jackson*. New York: Bobbs-Merrill, 1958.

Harper, Fowler V. *Justice Rutledge and the Bright Constellation*. Indianapolis: Bobbs-Merrill, 1965.

Hirsch, H. N. *The Enigma of Felix Frankfurter*. New York: Basic Books, 1981.

Horwitz, Elinor. *Capital Punishment, USA*. Philadelphia: J. B. Lippincott Co., 1973.

Howard, J. Woodford, Jr. *Mr. Justice Murphy: A Political Biography*. Princeton, N.J.: Princeton University Press, 1968.

Hughes, Charles Evans. *The Supreme Court of the United States*. New York: Columbia University Press, 1928.

Kane, Harnett T. *The Bayous of Louisiana*. New York: W. Morrow and Co., 1943.

_____. *Louisiana Hayride: The American Rehearsal for Dictatorship, 1928-1940*. New York: W. Morrow and Co., 1941.

Kniffen, Fred B. *Louisiana: Its Land and People*. Baton Rouge: Louisiana State University Press, 1968.

Kurland, Philip B. *Mr. Justice Frankfurter and the Constitution*. Chicago: University of Chicago Press, 1971.

Lash, Joseph, ed. *From the Diaries of Felix Frankfurter*. New York: W. W. Norton and Co., 1975.

Lemann, Nicholas. *Out of the Forties*. Austin: Texas Monthly Press, 1983.

Long, Huey P. *Every Man a King*. New Orleans: National Book Co., 1933.

Mason, Alpheus T. *Harlan Fiske Stone: A Pillar of the Law*. New York: Viking Press, 1956.

Meltsner, Michael. *Cruel and Unusual Punishment*. New York: Random House, 1973.

Mendelson, Wallace J. *Justices Black and Frankfurter: Conflict in the Court*. Chicago: University of Chicago Press, 1966.

Miller, Arthur S. *A "Capacity for Outrage," The Judicial Odyssey of J. Skelly Wright*. Westport, Conn.: Greenwood Press, 1984.

_____. *Toward Increased Judicial Activism: The Political Role of the Supreme Court*. Westport, Conn.: Greenwood Press, 1982.

Murphy, Bruce A. *The Brandeis/Frankfurter Connection, The Secret Political Activities of Two Supreme Court Justices*. New York: Oxford University Press, 1982.

Murphy, Walter F. *Congress and the Court*. Chicago: University of Chicago Press, 1962.

_____. *Elements of Judicial Strategy*. Chicago: University of Chicago Press, 1964.

Myrdal, Gunnar. *An American Dilemma: The Negro Problem and Modern Democracy*. New York: Harper, 1944.

Opotowsky, Stan. *The Longs of Louisiana*. New York: E. P. Dutton and Co., 1960.

Pearson, Drew, and Allen, Robert S. *The Nine Old Men*. Garden City, N.Y.: Doubleday, 1936.

Peltason, Jack W. *Fifty-Eight Lonely Men—Southern Federal Judges and School Desegregation*. New York: Harcourt, Brace and World, 1961.

Prettyman, E. Barrett, Jr. *Death and the Supreme Court*. New York: Avon Books, 1961.

Pritchett, Herman C. *Civil Liberties and the Vinson Court*. Chicago: University of Chicago Press, 1954.

_____. *The Roosevelt Court*. New York: Macmillan, 1948.

Pusey, Merlo J. *Charles Evans Hughes*. New York: Macmillan, 1951.

Reeves, Miriam G. *The Governors of Louisiana*. New Orleans: Pelican, 1972.

The Report of the President's Committee on Civil Rights. Washington, D.C.: United States Government Printing Office, 1947.

Rodell, Fred. *Nine Men, A Political History of the Supreme Court of the United States from 1790 to 1955*. New York: Vintage Books, 1955.

Rubin, Sol. *The Law of Criminal Correction*. St. Paul: West Publishing, 1963.

Sheridan, Lee W. *I Killed for the Law*. New York: Stackpole Sons, 1938.

Simon, James F. *Independent Journey: The Life of William O. Douglas*. New York: Harper and Row, 1980.

Sindler, Allan P. *Huey Long's Louisiana*. Baltimore: Johns Hopkins University Press, 1956.

Stern, Robert L., and Gressman, Eugene. *Supreme Court Practice*. Washington, D.C.: BNA, Inc., 1978.

Westin, Alan F. *The Anatomy of a Constitutional Law Case*. New York: Macmillan, 1958.

_____. *An Autobiography of the Supreme Court*. New York: Macmillan, 1963.

_____, ed. *The Supreme Court: Views from Inside*. New York: W. W. Norton and Co., 1961.

Williams, T. Harry. *Huey Long*. New York: Alfred A. Knopf, 1969.
Works Project Administration in the State of Louisiana. *Louisiana*. New York: Hastings House, 1941.

ARTICLES

Bedau, Hugo Adam and Radelet, Michael L. "Miscarriages of Justice in Potentially Capital Cases," *Stanford Law Review* 40 (1987): 21.

Black, Hugo L., "The Bill of Rights." *New York University Law Review* 35 (1960): 865.

Braden, George D., "The Search for Objectivity in Constitutional Law," *Yale Law Journal* 57 (1948): 571.

Elman, Philip. "The Solicitor General's Office, Justice Frankfurter and Civil Rights Litigation, 1946–1960: An Oral History," *Harvard Law Review* 100 (1987): 817.

Fairman, Charles, "Does the Fourteenth Amendment Incorporate the Bill of Rights?: The Original Understanding." *Stanford Law Review* 2 (1949): 5.

Frankfurter, Felix, Memorandum on "Incorporation of the Bill of Rights into the Fourteenth Amendment." *Harvard Law Review* 78 (1965): 746.

Gardner, Martin R., "Executions and Indignities—An Eighth Amendment Assessment of Methods of Inflicting Capital Punishment." *Ohio State Law Journal* 39 (1978): 96.

Goldberg, Arthur J., and Dershowitz, Alan M. "Declaring the Death Penalty Unconstitutional." *Harvard Law Review* 83 (1970): 1773.

Grant, J. A. C., "Felix Frankfurter: A Dissenting Opinion." *U.C.L.A. Law Review* 12 (1965): 1013.

Greenberg, Jack, "Capital Punishment as a System." *Yale Law Journal* 91 (1982): 908.

Gressman, Eugene, "The Constitutional Image of Mr. Justice Murphy." *Georgetown Law Journal* 47 (1959): 631.

Grey, Thomas C., "Do We Have an Unwritten Constitution?" *Stanford Law Review* 27 (1975): 703.

Kadish, Sanford H., "Methodology and Criteria in Due Process Adjudication—A Survey and Criticism." *Yale Law Journal* 66 (1957): 319.

Leuchtenburg, William E., "The Origins of Franklin D. Roosevelt's 'Court-Packing Plan.'" *The Supreme Court Review* (1966): 347.

Miller, Arthur S. "Toward a Definition of the Constitution," *University of Dayton Law Review* 8 (1983).

Miller, Arthur S., and Bowman, Jeffrey H., "'Slow Dance on the Killing Ground'—The Willie Francis Case Revisited." *DePaul Law Review* 32 (1982): 1.

Miller, Arthur S., and Scheflin, Alan W. "The Power of the Supreme Court in the Age of the Positive State," *Duke Law Journal* (1967): 522.

Morrison, Stanley, "Does the Fourteenth Amendment Incorporate the Bill of Rights?: The Judicial Interpretation." *Stanford Law Review* 2 (1949): 140.

Note, "In Memoriam—Harold Hitz Burton." *Harvard Law Review* 78 (1965): 799.

———, "Recent Cases." *Loyola Law Review* 4 (1947): 84.

———, "Recent Decisions." *Marquette Law Review* 31 (1947): 108.

_____, "Recent Decisions." *St. John's Law Review* 22 (1948): 270.

_____, "Recent Cases." *Temple Law Quarterly* 20 (1946–1947): 584.

_____, "Criminal Law." *Tulane Law Review* 21 (1947): 480.

_____, "Recent Decisions." *Virginia Law Review* 33 (1947): 348.

_____, "Double Jeopardy." *National Bar Journal* 7 (1948): 259.

Schlesinger, Arthur M., Jr., "The Supreme Court: 1947." *Fortune* 35 (1947): 73.

Wright, J. Skelly, "No Matter How Small." *Massachusetts Law Quarterly* 58 (1973): 58.

_____, "Professor Bickel, The Scholarly Tradition and the Supreme Court." *Harvard Law Review* 84 (1971): 769.

_____. "The Role of the Supreme Court in a Democratic Society—Judicial Activism or Restraint?" *Cornell Law Review* 54 (1968): 1.

Index

About the Authors

ARTHUR S. MILLER was, most recently, Professor Emeritus of Law at George Washington University. His numerous works include *Democratic Dictatorship: The Emergent Constitution of Control* (Greenwood Press, 1981), *Toward Increased Judicial Activism: The Political Role of the Supreme Court* (Greenwood Press, 1982), *A "Capacity for Outrage": The Judicial Odyssey of J. Skelly Wright* (Greenwood Press, 1984), *Politics, Democracy, and the Supreme Court* (Greenwood Press, 1985), and *The Secret Constitution and the Need for Constitutional Change* (Greenwood Press, 1987). He was the editor of *On Courts and Democracy: Selected Nonjudicial Writings of J. Skelly Wright* (Greenwood Press, 1984) and coeditor of *Nuclear Weapons and Law* (with Martin Feinrider, Greenwood Press, 1984), and *Corporations and Society: Power and Responsibility* (with Warren J. Samuels, Greenwood Press, 1987). He was a frequent contributor to legal and political science periodicals.

JEFFREY H. BOWMAN is Assistant to the Chairman of the Federal Elections Commission.